KU-648-541

To my wife

A nation should be like an audience in some great theatre – 'In the theatre,' said Victor Hugo, 'the mob becomes a people' – watching the sacred drama of its own history; every spectator finding self and neighbour there, finding all the world there, as we find the sun in the bright spot under the burning glass.

W. B. Yeats, note to 'Three Songs to the Same Tune' in *The King of the Great Clock Tower*, 1934

THRESHOLD OF A NATION

THRESHOLD OF A NATION

A study in English and Irish drama

PHILIP EDWARDS

King Alfred Professor of English Literature
University of Liverpool

WITHDRAWN FROM STOCK

CAMBRIDGE UNIVERSITY PRESS

CAMBRIDGE

LONDON · NEW YORK · MELBOURNE

11990

Published by the Syndics of the Cambridge University Press
The Pitt Building, Trumpington Street, Cambridge CB2 1RP
Bentley House, 200 Euston Road, London NW1 2DB
32 East 57th Street, New York, NY 10022, U.S.A.
296 Beaconsfield Parade, Middle Park, Melbourne 3206, Australia

© Cambridge University Press 1979

First published 1979

Filmset in 10/12 point Baskerville
Printed litho and bound in Great Britain by
W & J Mackay Limited, Chatham

Library of Congress Cataloguing in Publication Data

Edwards, Philip.
Threshold of a nation.
Includes bibliographical references and index.
1. English drama – History and criticism.
2. Irish drama – History and criticism. I. Title.
PR625.E38   822'.009   78–72085
ISBN 0 521 22463 2

Coláiste
Mhuire Gan Smál
Luimneach
Class No. 822·009
Acc. No. 40,472

CONTENTS

PLATES

PREFACE

This book is a series of studies each of which deals with an aspect of the relation between theatre and nation, first (and chiefly) in the England of Shakespeare when the British Empire was in its very first stages, and secondly in the Ireland of Yeats at the time of the dissolution of that empire. The controlling ideas of the book are described in the introductory chapter. Here I want to say a word about its shape. From the first it was conceived as a group of more or less self-contained essays on English and Irish drama which would relate with each other and contribute to a single if panoramic view of the rôle of the dramatist and the province of the theatre in periods of expanding national consciousness. The narrative of the book as a whole is not continuous and the argument is not sequential. If the reader feels that the movement from one chapter to the next is sometimes abrupt, I can only hope that in the end an organic relationship between the chapters will compensate for their disjunctiveness. Even so, the book may seem like a fishing net, mostly holes surrounded by string. It is a study *in* English and Irish drama, not *of* it, and it has taken its own shape from the topics within the proposed subject which I was most eager to explore and to which I thought I might have something to contribute. It is perhaps the minimal gathering which can exhibit the cultural and historical arc which links Shakespeare in Elizabethan London with Yeats in post-Parnellite Dublin, but, skeletal though the structure is, the book is long enough.

I must distinguish, however, between deliberate omissions (however capricious) and those which were fortuitous. The balance between the English section (six essays, some of them very long) and the Irish section (three) looks like English arrogance. It was never my intention to include extensive critical studies of the major Irish dramatists, Yeats, Synge, and O'Casey. I wished rather to provide a context for plays which are well known and frequently discussed, whose relationship to the emergence of a nation is not in need of that kind of elucidation which I give to well-known plays by Marlowe or Shakespeare. Even so, as I explain in the Introduction, the Irish section suffered unexpected attrition and erosion; I hope that as a result my treatment of the corpus of twentieth-century Irish drama does not seem in its brevity altogether too tangential.

One of the following essays, 'The Royal Pretenders' (Chapter 7), was published in *Essays and Studies 1974*, edited by Kenneth Muir, and I am grateful to the English Association for permission to reproduce it here (in revised form). My inaugural lecture at Liverpool, delivered in December 1975 and published by the Liverpool University Press, was a preliminary sketch of material which I later developed in a number of the succeeding chapters. A great many sentences from the lecture have been salvaged and economically reused.

It is a pleasure to acknowledge the assistance I have had in writing this book, particularly from my colleagues Ann Thompson and Nicholas Grene, who read and commented on my typescript, from my former colleague at Trinity College, Dublin, David Greene (now at the Dublin Institute for Advanced Studies), who most kindly looked over the introductory chapter, from other friends and colleagues who helped to find answers to problems, and from Mrs Joan Welford, who prepared most of the typescript.

This book could not have been written at all if I had not had three months clear of teaching and administration at the Henry E. Huntington Library in California in the winter of 1977. I am deeply grateful to all who made this possible; to the University of Liverpool for granting me study leave, to the Huntington Library for awarding me a fellowship, to the British Academy for a grant, and to the United States–United Kingdom Educational Commission for very generous travel assistance. I could not have had a more congenial place to work in than the Huntington, and I owe much to the kindness and hospitality of the Director, James Thorpe, and his staff, and to the conversation of my fellow scholars, particularly William Ringler, E. S. Morgan, and Eugene Waith.

All quotations in the book have been given in modern spelling. In quoting Shakespeare I have acted as my own editor, though I owe much to Peter Alexander's complete Shakespeare (Collins), and to the New Arden and New Penguin editions of individual plays. I have brought the line-numbering into accord with that of the Riverside

Shakespeare. My great indebtedness to the Clarendon Press *Ben Jonson* will be apparent whenever I discuss or quote from Jonson's work.

I began thinking about this book in the early seventies, when I was chained and shackled to an edition of Massinger's plays. When at last I became free to think purposefully about the venture, both history and I had moved on. The United Kingdom, which in a way is what this book is about, was now under discussion only as to what particular form its dismemberment was to take, and I had taken up residence among the ruins of one of the most important centres of Britain's imperial trade and communications. Inevitably, the study more and more assumed a threnodic note. I felt myself haunted by the spirits of the departed nation, by the energy, imagination, idealism, ambition, greed, cruelty, and stupidity which had gone into both the creation of the British nation and empire and its undoing. I also thought sometimes that I could hear more clearly the voices of the dramatists of two nations which I have tried to transcribe in the book which follows.

Liverpool, November 1978

1

INTRODUCTION:
THE KING'S THRESHOLD

In 1888, when Yeats was twenty-three, he wrote: 'To the greater poets everything they see has its relation to the national life, and through that to the universal and divine life . . . You can no more have the greater poetry without a nation than religion without symbols. One can only reach out to the universe with a gloved hand – that glove is one's nation, the only thing one knows even a little of.'[1] Yeats at this time owed much of his thinking about the relation of literature and nation to John O'Leary, the old Fenian, and he acknowledged his debt to O'Leary in a famous remark of 1889: 'He, more clearly than any one, has seen that there is no fine nationality without literature, and seen the converse also, that there is no fine literature without nationality.'[2]

We no longer use the word 'nationality' in the sense in which Yeats is using it. We should probably say 'nationalism', but 'nationality' was a wider and more useful word including both an individual's devotion and commitment to his nation, and a spirit of national aspiration. I am not concerned with the general truth of Yeats's propositions, but they form the text for this book because the interactions between drama and 'nationality' in Shakespeare's England and Yeats's Ireland are so vital and intense. It is impossible to think of Shakespeare's work without its preoccupation with nation – England or Britain. It is not only in the 'Histories' proper, nearly a third of his entire life-work taken up with dramatising English history, but also in plays like *King Lear*, *Macbeth*, and *Cymbeline* that the idea of the English or British nation is of fundamental importance. Jonson's work, too, is meaningless except when seen as a relationship with nation. His plays became more and more rehearsals of a connection between himself and national authority which he then attempted to enact as masque-writer-in-chief at James's court. Of Yeats, Lady Gregory, and Synge, it is unnecessary to make the point; their art was of Ireland, deliberately and inalienably. As for the converse view, that there is no fine nationality without literature, the shape of English nationhood at the turn of the sixteenth century and Irish at the turn of the nineteenth, as it is received in our minds, is literary as well as political. 'England' means Spenser and Shakespeare as well as the Armada and Jamestown, as 'Ireland' means Yeats, Moore, and Synge as well as Parnell and Easter 1916.

Shakespeare's England and Yeats's Ireland have not been chosen for study just because the interaction between theatre and nation are there particularly strong and fruitful. It is a single subject that I propose, the beginning and the end of a single historical cycle. We have to look at the association of the theatre first with the beginnings of a nation and an empire, and then with the most important moment of its decline and disintegration. If there had been no inauguration of Great Britain, no conquest of Ireland, no institution of an overseas empire, all of which were seen in Shakespeare's lifetime, there would have been no separatist and nationalist movement needing its spiritual voice in Yeats's lifetime. With a strong cyclical view of history, Yeats saw the vigour of a renovated Irish culture, drawing strength from deep uncontaminated roots, superseding an effete, cosmopolitan, commercialised English culture, and creating a new beginning like the English Renaissance. It doesn't look like that now. The Irish literary renaissance was a golden sunset, not a golden dawn. Its originating cause was the policy of the late Tudors and early Stuarts in Ireland, and it provided the conclusion of that policy. Yeats, seeing himself as a new beginning more than an ending, paid the closest attention to the work of the writers of the English Renaissance as a model for the Irish renaissance, as we shall see in both this and a later chapter. This attention increases the unity of my subject: Shakespeare's plays are as alive and seminal in the later stages of the story as in the earlier. We shall see how Yeats built up Shakespeare in a Celtic image to authorise his own work, and then found this image directing him into radically new paths. Yeats and Shakespeare dominate this book. Shakespeare's influence on Yeats is clear enough and is written about often enough, but we also have to think in a way of Yeats's influence on Shakespeare. Yeats's perceptiveness about his Elizabethan cultural forbears is partly due to his so often seeing himself in their place, facing their very problems with relation to their society three hundred years after their time. Very often, therefore, I

find myself looking at the Elizabethans with Yeats's eyes, and inter-
preting their work by the light of his perceptions. I think this is
probably most clearly seen in the acceptance of the Yeatsian *schema* of
a tension between the values of an older way of life and of a new one
that is superseding it as a primary issue in Renaissance literature. The
Shakespeare in this book is heavily influenced by Yeats.

There is another way of seeing the study of the theatre of Shakespeare's England and Yeats's Ireland as a single study. The daimon of
this book is the Reformation. In the second chapter I deal with the
strange paradox of a proud, self-sufficient, national Protestantism
inspiring, nourishing, bullying, and in the end extinguishing the great
professional drama of the Elizabethans and early Stuarts. Without
the Reformation there is no new nation with a deified monarch at the
centre for the new drama to cluster around. Without the Reformation
there is no mercantile Protestantism to protest against the theatre as
an offence against God and hard work. Without the Reformation
there are no sovereign monarchs of the English kind to provide drama
with its chief themes and images. Without the Reformation there is no
growth of an anti-monarchical Puritanism which eventually destroys
both crown and stage. Without the Reformation there is no need to
secure new frontiers against Spain, no sense of Protestant destiny to
expand first to Ireland and then to Virginia. The Elizabethan conquest of Ireland and the Jacobean pacification bore a markedly
religious colour at the receiving end. Had the Irish been somehow
induced to accept the new religion as the bewildered Welsh did, Irish
intransigence would have eased and finally disappeared, for over the
centuries the great subliminal strength of Irish intractability was the
stubbornness of an outlawed religion which refused to be quenched
and which took on more and more the features not of belief but of
tribalism. The leaders of the new-fangled nationalist movements in
Ireland which came in with the American and French Revolutions
were high-minded Protestants – Grattan, Tone, Emmett, Davis,
Parnell – but in the end the Protestant leadership was dispensable.
George Moore and John Eglinton were early to warn the Anglo-Irish
enthusiasts of their insecurity. On the great rock of Irish Catholic
xenophobia, sometimes submerged but never much below the surface, the Irish national drama, created by the Protestants Yeats, Lady
Gregory, and Synge, foundered, changed shape, and disappeared. Thus
the whirligig of time brings in his revenges. Extreme Puritanism snuffed
out the great 'Elizabethan' drama in 1642; extreme Catholicism

constantly opposed Yeats's theatre until finally it rendered the Abbey harmless by taking it over.

Anything approaching a thorough history of the relations between theatre and nation in Elizabethan England and post-Parnellite Ireland would be a monumental work of many volumes. In any case, the Irish side of it (in its obvious features) has been done nearly to death. The present study is a series of essays, a few shafts dug in different parts of the ground to try to show the range and complexity of a rich and absorbing subject. The lack of all pretension to comprehensiveness might be seen in the English section in the silence about Middleton's *A Game at Chess* and in the Irish section in the absence of any formal discussion of Lady Gregory's work in historical drama. Two projected chapters in the Irish section never got written. The first was to be on Irish national and historical drama before the Literary Revival, but the subject was jejune. The second was to be the relation between Pearse the playwright of *The Singer* and Pearse the actor in the Post Office; that was before I had read W. I. Thompson's outstanding book, *The Imagination of an Insurrection* (1967), which made a further examination an impertinence.

This book is not a history of its subject and all I can hope is that the methods I have adopted for treating my selected authors and topics may make students wish to apply them to the many authors and topics not noticed. Chapter 2 examines the rise of the professional drama in Elizabethan times, and its decline in the next century, in the context of the growth of the English nation and the cross-currents in the spirit of that nation; I begin with a look at a play in which Marston had a hand, *Histriomastix*, which is a remarkable attack on professional drama as a corrupting element in national life. My third chapter deals with the monarch in sixteenth-century drama: why the monarch is the principal image in that drama, how the queen herself is the focus of drama and of the lives of the dramatists (this I illustrate chiefly from Lyly), and how Marlowe treats kingship in his plays. In the fourth chapter I am concerned with England's imperial expansion, chiefly in Ireland and America, as it is reflected in historical plays and others. My chief texts are *Henry V*, *Cymbeline*, *The Tempest*, and *Eastward Ho!* Chapter 5 is a study of Shakespeare's English histories, and Chapter 6 a study of Ben Jonson in which I have more to say about his earlier comical satires and his masques than about his best-known comedies. Shakespeare and Jonson are inevitably studied as contrasts in the way in which a dramatist engages with his nation in his life and in his art. Chapter 7 attempts to show, in a study of Ford's *Perkin Warbeck* and Massinger's *Believe As You List*, how in Charles I's reign the age-old myth of the national leader who did not die and will one day return came to have new dramatic power as fears about Charles's leadership increased. Part Two, on Ireland, has three essays. The first examines Yeats's attempts to create a national drama and his preoccupation with Shakespeare's histories in the context of European cultural nationalism, and suggests an identification which is the main justification for writing this book. The second essay examines George Moore's failure to integrate himself with the national and literary movement. The final essay looks at some well-known Irish plays from O'Casey to Behan, and tries to characterise their despair.

One major theme in this book I wish to introduce here. That is the effort of the dramatist to occupy a central position in the political community, believing that without art a nation is sterile or deformed. This effort to move to the centre of political life invites the most serious challenge to the integrity of the artist and the independence of his art. The artist risks being seduced into flattering the leaders, conniving at dishonesty, and writing propaganda instead of poetry. Yeats's concern to be a voice for Ireland without compromising his art with the stridency of propaganda or the corrosions of political strife is of course a main topic of his verse and his prose writings. As usual, he transferred his own concerns to the Renaissance when he wrote his essay on Spenser in 1902.[3] He saw the English dramatists as men who followed their imagination wherever it led them; Shakespeare was indifferent to the state. But Spenser, Yeats thought, allowed his instinctive leanings to be perverted towards state morality, a system of life which he felt it was his duty to support. This 'poet who gave his heart to the State' 'loved his Queen a little because she was the protectress of poets . . . but a great deal because she was the image of the State which had taken possession of his conscience'. Though Yeats is unfair to Spenser, and far too complacent about the dramatists, with his usual acumen he has located exactly the anguish of the Elizabethan writer at large, as we shall see it in Lyly and Jonson, with Shakespeare's *Timon of Athens* as the index of Shakespeare's own awareness of the ease with which a poet becomes an establishment hypocrite (see pp. 153–4).

Yeats's dramatic image of the relation between the poet and the political authority was *The King's Threshold*, which he wrote in 1903 with the collaboration of Lady Gregory. The action takes place on the steps before the palace of King Guaire at Gort. Seanchan the poet (pronounced Shanahan, Yeats tells us) is on a long-drawn-out hunger strike because the king has taken away the ancient right of the poets to sit by the king at his council table. That right was 'established at the establishment of the world', but this king claims that *he* is the source of all laws,

> And that it was the men who ruled the world,
> And not the men who sang to it, who should sit
> Where there was the most honour.   (ll. 48–50)

The dying poet gets his oldest pupil to repeat the lesson he has taught him, 'why poetry is honoured':

> The poets hung
> Images of the life that was in Eden
> About the child-bed of the world, that it,
> Looking upon those images, might bear
> Triumphant children . . .
>   If the Arts should perish,
> The world that lacked them would be like a woman
> That, looking on the cloven lips of a hare,
> Brings forth a hare-lipped child.   (ll. 128–32; 136–9)

The action of the play is very much like that of *Samson Agonistes*: person after person enters to appeal to Seanchan to capitulate and eat, but he rejects them all, including the king. Finally it is the king who capitulates. 'He has the greater power.' He surrenders his crown to Seanchan.

> It is but right if hands that made the crown
> In the old time should give it when they will.   (ll. 841 k–1)

This is the ending of the original version. But in 1922 Yeats changed it all: Seanchan died, with the ancient right of the poets still abrogated by an unmoved king. Yeats said, 'I had originally intended to end the play tragically.'[4] Whether or not this is true, it is certain (as Peter Ure has argued)[5] that there is greater artistic integrity in the revised version than in the original with the sudden reversal in the king's collapse. The reception of the poet back into the centre of power is strained and facile, and its false tone is to be explained not by an artistic misjudgement of Yeats (his own excuse) but by the sheer human improbability of the solution. All endeavours by poets to make their uncompromised art the moral force at the centre of an active political movement end in disillusion or self-deception, and Yeats knew this in his bones as early as 1903. In the revised ending, the oldest pupil directs them to bury Seanchan's body on the mountain-side:

> And there he can sleep on, not noticing,
> Although the world be changed from worse to worse,
> Amid the changeless clamour of the curlew.
> . . .   .
> Not what it leaves behind it in the light
> But what it carries with it to the dark
> Exalts the soul: nor song nor trumpet-blast
> Can call up races from the worsening world
> To mend the wrong and mar the solitude
> Of the great shade we follow to the tomb.
>
> (ll. 886–8; 889–904)

Yeats derived the concept of the rightful position of the poet by the side of the king at council from two main sources: the traditional status of the Irish poet, and the theorising of Renaissance humanist-poets. To take the latter first, a notable article published by Thomas McAlindon in 1967, 'Yeats and the English Renaissance',[6] showed how deeply Yeats was affected by the ideas of Spenser and Jonson about the ancient dignity of the poet's office and the proper rôle of poetry as the moral core of political power. (I analyse aspects of these ideas in Chapter 6). Yeats transferred the great humanist ideal of poetry as the civilising force in society to early twentieth-century Ireland to help him define his own situation as the leading artist in that troubled community. *The King's Threshold* becomes a companion play to those plays of Jonson which McAlindon points out were of special interest to Yeats, and which I pay particular attention to in the chapter on Jonson – those plays in which Jonson makes a dramatic projection of the intellectual's relation with the ruling power in the state, *Every Man Out of his Humour*, *Cynthia's Revels*, and *Poetaster*. McAlindon also quotes from an important letter of 1906 in which Yeats says, 'I am thinking of writing something on Ben Jonson, or more likely perhaps upon the ideal of life that flitted before the imagination of Jonson and the others when they thought of the Court.'[7] Yeats's phrasing is extremely interesting, and one would give much to hear more. For Seanchan and for Jonson and for Yeats an ideal of a court which acknowledges the poet and radiates its standards of thought and conduct to the populace 'flitted before the imagination'.[8] The real thing, as Yeats implies, is another matter.

What I have to say of Jonson later is largely a matter of the vexatious gap between what Jonson's mind suggested the court ought to have been and what in fact James's court was.

Knowledge about the status and traditions of the ancient Irish poets was available to Yeats from all sorts of sources, chiefly perhaps from P. W. Joyce, to whom Yeats often turned in his youth for information on Gaelic literature and whose two-volume *Social History of Ancient Ireland* was published in 1903 and was known to Yeats at the time of writing *The King's Threshold*.[9] Joyce's work shows the Gaelic *filidh* or poets in precisely that kinship with men of learning which Renaissance-humanist theory postulated, and strongly emphasises the respect in which they were held.

In Ireland the position of the poets constituted perhaps the most singular feature of society. It had its origin in the intense and universal veneration for learning . . .   (I, p. 449)

The 'ollave' (the highest ranking in the learned professions) 'spent many years of preparation: and once admitted to the coveted rank, the guerdon was splendid; for he was highly honoured, had many privileges, and received princely rewards and presents' (I, p. 444). 'On state occasions the chief poet of all Ireland wore a precious mantle elaborately ornamented' (p. 447). 'An ollave sat next the king at table . . . and they had the same joint at dinner' (p. 459).

The best account of the Irish *filidh* is in Osborn Bergin's famous lecture of 1912, 'Bardic Poetry'.[10] We must remember, he says, that the Irish *file* – or bard if we must so call him – 'was not necessarily an inspired poet'.

He was, in fact, a professor of literature and a man of letters, highly trained in the use of a polished literary medium, belonging to a hereditary caste in an aristocratic society, holding an official position therein by virtue of his training, his learning, his knowledge of the history and traditions of his country and his clan. He discharged . . . the functions of the modern journalist. He was not a song writer. He was often a public official, chronicler, a political essayist, a keen and satirical observer of his fellow-countrymen. At an earlier period he had been regarded as a dealer in magic, a weaver of spells and incantations, who could blast his enemies by the venom of his verse, and there are traces down to the most recent times of a lingering belief, which was not, of course, confined to Ireland, in the efficacy of a well-turned malediction.

In a more recent account, David Greene has noted that the lay order of poets, still a great force in Ireland in Elizabethan times, continued in association with the Church to exercise the ancient powers of the druids.[11] 'A poet's satire was as terrible a weapon as the Church's excommunication, as we can see from a treaty between Manus O'Donnell and O'Connor Sligo, in which both sanctions are treated as of equal weight.'

Much of the poetry of the *filidh* was in honour of their kingly patrons. Here are some extracts from a poem to Cathal Redhand, King of Connaught, by the thirteenth-century poet, Giolla Bride Mac Con Midhe. This rhapsody of the fertility of the land under her true king reminds us how deep and ancient was the tradition which consciously or unconsciously Shakespeare dipped into in writing the hymn of peace at the end of *Richard III* (see pp. 110–11).

> Croghan's Redhand has rendered fruitful the green woods of the warm land . . .
> His rule has put grain into the ground, it has made blossoms to sprout through the tips of the branches . . .
> Ireland has recognised her ruler; she has brought forth the increase of a quarter in one month, so that the forest which trembled with age has put forth fruit again under his rule.
> When comes the autumn, the fruit will reach Galway's prince of the swift steeds; ear upon ear, cluster upon cluster will there be from Kesh Corrin to Croagh.
> The arms of each apple-tree are weighed to the ground in the land of Cathal of Cruachan-Aoi.[12]

Irish scholars seem agreed that the duty of praising those who so lavishly rewarded them led the poets into a good deal of routine adulation. Bergin said that 'all court poetry is more or less tainted by the vice of insincerity and formalism'. David Greene, speaking in 1958, said, 'Their weakness was that they were, by the very nature of their calling, as much the paid propagandists of the existing order of things as any writer east of the Iron Curtain.'[13] Bergin quotes a wonderful poem in which a poet warns his fellows that hell lies ahead for both the flatterer and his patron:

> O ye who fashion lies in verse, when the judgement day comes ye shall repent it; if His anger arise, the Creator of the elements will take vengeance for the false witness that ye bear against Him.
> . . . .
> From every man from whom you win a reward, you have deserved hatred and anger; because of your praise, alas! his last end will be hell.[14]

Such awareness of the pitfalls dug for the poet on the steps of the palace is as redeeming for the Irish as Shakespeare's *Timon of Athens* is for the Elizabethans. When the bards were in the sixteenth century facing what they knew was the possibility of their extinction in the challenge of the English invader, one can't help respecting the fervour with which they urged on the Gaelic chiefs to defend their lands and their ancient way of life. Here are some lines praising a man who stood firm as against one who defected:

> A man who never loved English ways is Eóghan Bán, beloved of noble women. To English ways he never gave his heart: a harsh life he chose.
>
> . . .   .
>
> He has no longing for a soft bed, he had rather lie upon rushes. Pleasanter to Donnchadh's good son is a hut of rough poles than the battlements of a tower.
>
> A troop of horse at the brink of a gap, a fierce fight, a struggle with footsoldiers, these are some of the desires of Donnchadh's son – and seeking battle against the foreigners!
>
> How unlike are you to Eóghan Bán – they laugh at your foot on the stepping-stone. Pity that you have not seen your fault, O man who follow English ways.[15]

Here in Ireland in Elizabethan times was a breed of poets occupying precisely that position of respect and honour as counsellor and friend at a king's court so eagerly sought by the Elizabethans Lyly, Spenser, Jonson. What did they have to say about their fellows across the water? The Elizabethans had plenty of information about the Irish bards. Indeed there is no Irish source for our knowledge of the practices of the later poets so full and detailed as that provided by Thomas Smyth early in Elizabeth's reign,[16] backed up by the fascinating woodcut of a poet reciting before his patron in John Derricke's *Image of Irelande*, 1581 (see Plate 1 and jacket). But the universal attitude of the Elizabethans – poets, dramatists, and all – to the Irish poets was one of contempt and hatred. The English view of those who were attempting to preserve their lands and way of life being that they were rebels (as I describe more fully in Chapter 4), those who by their verses stirred them to fight, encouraged them in battle, and celebrated their successes came in for peculiar execration. There is no greater nor more saddening testimony of the inability of the Elizabethans to put themselves even for a moment in the place of those who opposed their ambitions on the other side of the Irish Sea than the refusal of the poets to recognise their fellows, and to see that the rich and over-rich vein in which their own loyalty to the Queen flowed explained and justified (if their own was justified) the plangent heroics which they so scorned in the Irish. (On these matters, see further in Chapters 3 (pp. 39–40) and 4 (pp. 78–80).) The

Elizabethan poets hated the Irish precisely because they were loyal, and energetic in their loyalty. Campion knew how skilled they were but in general the English intellectuals were too prejudiced by the conviction that the Irish bards were traitors and seditious agitators to be able to look with anything but contempt on poets who had actually created that firm link between poetry, learning, government, and action which they themselves strove for.

In an important note in 1968, Katherine Duncan Jones suggested that words at the end of Sidney's *Defence of Poesie* may have been misunderstood. 'I will not wish unto you . . . to be rhymed to death, as is said to be done in Ireland.'[17] We have been influenced in reading this by our recollection of Shakespeare and Jonson to suppose that Sidney is talking of rhyming *rats* to death. In *As You Like It*, Rosalind says, 'I was never so berhymed since Pythagoras' time, that I was an Irish rat' (III.ii.16) and Jonson, in the 'Apologetical Dialogue' appended to *Poetaster*, says:

> Rhyme them to death, as they do Irish rats
> In drumming tunes.

But it was well understood that fatal curses were put on people as well as on beasts. Katherine Duncan Jones quotes, from Thomas Church-yard's *A General Rehearsal of Wars*, 1579,[18] a proclamation by Sidney's father, Sir Henry, the Lord Deputy in Ireland, that 'whosoever could take a rhymer (which were a kind of superstitious prophesier of Ireland) should spoil him and have his goods, without danger of law'. A group of English gentlemen in the army at Kilkenny seized 'certain blind prophesiers called rhymers', whipped them, stripped them of their possessions, and banished them from the town. The despoiled poets 'swore to rhyme these gentlemen to death, but as yet, God be thanked, they have taken no hurt for punishing such disordered people'. It is clear that Sir Henry Sidney agreed with Thomas Smyth about the special danger of the poets in the matter of the enemy's morale and the necessity of putting them down. Smyth writes as follows:

The third sort is called the Aosdan, which is to say in English, the bards, or the rhyming septs. And these people be very hurtful to the commonweal, for they chiefly maintain the rebels; and further they do cause them that would be true to be rebellious thieves, extortioners, murderers, raveners, yea and worse if it were possible. Their first practice is, if they see any young man descended from the septs of O's and Mac's, who has half a dozen men about him, they will make him a rhyme wherein they will commend his fathers and his ancestors, numbering how many heads they have cut off, how many towns they have burned, and how many virgins they have deflowered, how many notable murders they have done, and in the end they will compare him to Hannibal or Scipio or Hercules, or some other famous person; wherewithal the poor fool runs mad and thinks indeed it is so.[19]

The special venom in Spenser's discussion of Irish poetry is partly dictated by the same feeling that these are the men who stir up the Irish to 'rebellion'; but there is something else, too.

There is amongst the Irish a certain kind of people called the bards, which are to them instead of poets, whose profession is to set forth the praises and dispraises of men in their poems and rhymes, the which are had in so high regard and estimation amongst them that none dare displease them.

Spenser's interlocutor asks – as we ask, recalling Spenser's own words in *The Shepherd's Calendar* and *Mother Hubberd's Tale* (see below, pp. 138–40) – Well, isn't this traditionally the high office of poetry, by celebrating great deeds to define and enshrine the qualities of greatness? Yes, but, says Spenser, it is because they *abuse* a great ideal that they are so vicious.

These Irish bards are for the most part of another mind, and so far from instructing young men in moral discipline, that they themselves do more deserve to be sharply discipled. For they seldom use to choose unto themselves the doings of good men for the ornaments of their poems, but whomsoever they find to be most licentious of life, most bold and lawless in his doings, most dangerous and desperate in all parts of disobedience and rebellious disposition, him they set up and glorify in their rhymes, him they praise to the people, and to young men make an example to follow.

All this wickedness is 'tending for the most part to the hurt of the English, or maintenance of their own lewd liberty'.

Evil things being decked and suborned with the gay attire of goodly words may easily deceive and carry away the affection of a young mind that is not well stayed, but desirous by some bold adventure to make proof of himself.[20]

There is further discussion of Spenser's *View of the Present State of Ireland* in Chapter 4, in the context of *Henry V* and the Elizabethan campaigns in Ireland. The point I want to make here is obvious. Patriotism is not enough. For a poet to flatter Tyrone who is fighting off an invader is apparently a corruption of the poetic office. Spenser does not consider that he may surrender his right to judge in such matters by condoning the actions of Lord Grey in the massacre of Smerwick Bay (see below, p. 80). Spenser's abuse of political poets who write for his country's enemies is a severe comment on the

extreme risks which poets take in seeking to identify themselves, with
the highest possible motives, with the centre of political authority.
Spenser, not being a dramatist, is not properly a subject of this book,
but in these matters Jonson is his heir – Jonson, who got further up the
steps of the palace than Spenser ever did, and over the king's
threshold into the Banqueting Hall at Whitehall; and Jonson is one of
my major subjects. In Chapter 4 (pp. 96–7) I describe how at the end
of his *Irish Masque* of 1613 he brings in an Irish bard to herald the
movement of the Irish from barbarism to civility under James. The
Bard sings to two harps, preaching obedience and prophesying a new
age. The absurdity of this is that when the Gaelic way of life went, the
bards went too. There was no possibility that with the social and
political system – of which they were so integral a part – in ruins, *they*
should survive and serve an English polity. The Jacobean policy of
peace was the enforcement of English law and custom (see pp.
84–6; 95–6), and that meant no more bards.

> Here is thy poet – all that is left after the slaughter . . .
> All men have hated the art of our fathers since the glory of the Gaels has
>   set, the end of our term has come, alas! while English increases.
> O thou of mild glance and kindly eye, every one is full of hatred of the
>   poets; it was foretold that they should be as they are, and that men
>   should care only for howling and strolling jesters.
> Since generosity and honour have departed, all men – a tale of misery
>   unmerited by us – have with hard hearts turned their backs upon
>   listening to true art.
> The passing of the Gaels of the land of Fódla has made poetry an outlaw:
>   alas for her helplessness today![21]

It is unlucky when an art becomes entirely identified with a political
power. The following chapter describes how the English professional
drama came more and more to depend upon an increasingly unpopular monarchy. When the monarchy went the drama went. In August
1642 Charles I raised his standard at Nottingham, and ten days later
Parliament issued its decree banning stage-plays. It is an irony –
perhaps it was the rhyming of the dispossessed bards – that the first
reason given by Parliament for putting the dramatists and actors out
of work was that the new and terrible rebellion in Ireland, coupled
with the prospect of civil war in England, was no time for 'lascivious
mirth and levity'. So 'nationality' laid low the English dramatists as it
laid low the Irish bards.

   'No fine nationality without literature . . . and . . . no fine literature
without nationality.' It is clearly the tensions which a burgeoning and

expanding nationalism sets up which lead to great art, rather than the identification of the artist with nationalism. For the greater Elizabethan dramatists – Marlowe and Shakespeare in particular, and also their successors Ford and Massinger – sacred kingship, which was the inappropriate banner under which the new English nation marched until it was sure of its footing, provided the great theme and symbol for dramatic explorations of the spiritual perils of a new age. In Ireland, the excitements of a new independence emerging from the wreck of an old empire set off one of the most famous movements in the history of the theatre: the conscious building of a national drama. But the greatness of that drama, like that of the Elizabethans, rests in its perturbation and anxieties about the human cost of nationality, this time explored under the symbols of Cuchulain killing his son, two blind tinkers, and tenement-dwellers.

> Whatever flames upon the night
> Man's own resinous heart has fed.

PART ONE: SHAKESPEARE'S ENGLAND

2

A SUPERFLUOUS SORT OF MEN: THE RISE AND FALL OF THE PROFESSIONAL THEATRE

Yeats saw the Renaissance as a great flare-up caused by intense friction as the undivided imagination of earlier times broke up into fragments. It was pure transition: a brief conflagration.[1] The reality which the world was left with was 'the great famine, the sinking down of popular imagination, the dying out of traditional fantasy, the ebbing out of the energy of race'.[2] The place of drama in this passing incandescence was expressed in a remarkable way by Yeats in 1899:

Blake has said that all art is a labour to bring again the Golden Age, and all culture is certainly a labour to bring again the simplicity of the first ages, with knowledge of good and evil added to it. *The drama has need of cities that it may find men in sufficient numbers, and cities destroy the emotions to which it appeals, and therefore the days of the drama are brief and come but seldom.*[3]

Yeats's historical generalisations often seem too grand, sentimental, and simplistic, but there is a disconcerting acuteness within them. The image of a new city providing a temporary platform for dramatists to disseminate values which fundamentally the city does not want is arrestingly appropriate for the London of 1570 to 1642.

Shakespeare wrote at a time when solitary great men were gathering to themselves the fire that had once flowed hither and thither among all men, when individualism in work and thought and emotion was breaking up the old rhythms of life, when the common people, sustained no longer by the myths of Christianity and of still older faiths, were sinking into the earth.

The people of Stratford-on-Avon have remembered little about him, and invented no legend to his glory . . . In his day the glory of a poet, like that of all other imaginative powers, had ceased, or almost ceased, outside a narrow class. The poor Gaelic rhymer leaves a nobler memory among his neighbours, who will talk of angels standing like flames about his death-bed, and of voices speaking out of bramble-bushes that he may have the wisdom of the world. *The Puritanism that drove the theatres into Surrey was but part of an inexplicable movement that was trampling out the minds of all but some few thousands born to cultivated ease.*[4]

The great drama of Shakespeare's age came into being in the England of the Reformation, during the establishment of England as an independent, Protestant state moving towards a position of unassailable strength and expanding every frontier: geographical, economic, and intellectual. The drama centred itself in and around the swiftly growing metropolis of London, which was also the region where monarch, court, and Parliament were centred, which was also where the centre of mercantile development was, and which was also where the Reformation was breeding its strongest anti-theatrical prejudices. If the spirit of the country in the later sixteenth century, concentrating itself in London, showed itself in the magnificent drama produced at the turn of the century, it was surely also the same spirit which eventually snuffed drama out with a decree from the House of Commons in Westminster in 1642. 'Consumed with that, which it was nourished by'.

This is how Sir Edmund Chambers put it in 1923 at the beginning of his chapter 'Humanism and Puritanism' in *The Elizabethan Stage*:

A period of general acceptance of the stage as an element in social life might have been anticipated, in which it stood greatly to gain by the more settled and less migratory habits of the royal household and the possibilities of building up a permanent headquarters for itself in London which resulted from the change. Unfortunately, however, events moved otherwise. A new factor emerged, which militated against anything like general acceptance; and the period of the greatest literary vitality in the development of the English drama proved to be also a period of embittered conflict with widespread ethical and religious tendencies, which in fact ranged over the whole of social life and was ultimately destined to shatter, not only the stage, but the Tudor scheme of things itself.[5]

The sense which Yeats had, and which very many of the Tudor and Stuart dramatists had (and which is to some extent implied in Chambers's words), that the drama maintains the old ways and is opposed by the new sober-sides materialism of the Protestant ethic, is not at all the sense of things given in what is probably the most powerful and interesting contemporary document on the place of theatre in England's national life at the end of Elizabeth's reign. This is the anonymous play *Histrio-Mastix, Or the Player Whipt*, published in 1610 without any indication of when it was acted.

It belongs to Elizabeth's reign; a marginal note towards the end points out that by Astraea on her throne is meant '*Q. Eliza*.' It is before 1599, because a passage (III.iv.21–30) in Jonson's *Every Man Out of his Humour*, of that year, parodies the language and refers to the title 'Plato's *Histriomastix*' – a good term for a play which ends with the expulsion of players from the community.[6] It is generally accepted that John Marston was at least part-author. Some of the language is very Marstonian, and the Jonson speech is in a context of parody of Marston's language. The former view was that Marston refurbished and added to a much older play. This unnecessary theory has been followed by a new orthodoxy that Marston wrote the whole play at one time.[7] The extreme differences in the style and quality of the writing make it impossible to believe that it was by one man, however, and it is almost certainly a collaboration. Probably it was acted at one of the Inns of Court.[8]

It is the professional stage that *Histriomastix* is attacking. One of the greatest causes of indignation against the Elizabethan theatre was that what had been a natural social activity, the recreation of the people, should have become a sordid money-making commercial concern. Playing was not one of the professions or trades of society, it was an activity anyone and everyone could share. To leave one's recognised trade and to take money for acting was behaving like a prostitute, who made a profession out of sexual intercourse.[9] By leaving their trades and not taking up new ones, these new professional actors made themselves non-beings, hence their inclusion with masterless and idle men in the statute against Rogues and Vagabonds of 1572:

All and every person and persons being whole and mighty in body and able to labour, having not land or master, nor using any lawful merchandise, craft or mystery whereby he or she might get his or her living . . . and all fencers, bearwards, common players in interludes, and minstrels, not belonging to any baron of this realm . . . shall be taken, adjudged, and deemed rogues, vagabonds, and sturdy beggars.   (*ES*, IV, p. 270)

Time and again in pamphlets and decrees we come up against the revulsion of men against a new cancer in society: the professional actor, or 'common player'. Demanding the total suppression of playing in 1580, the Lord Mayor of London wrote to the Lord Chancellor that 'the players of plays . . . are a very superfluous sort of men' (*ES*, IV, p. 279). In 1584, the Corporation of London wrote a long complaint rejecting the conception that in suppressing theatres they were putting men out of work:

It hath not been used nor thought meet heretofore that players have or should make their living on the art of playing; but men for their livings using other honest and lawful arts, or retained in honest services, have by companies learned some interludes for some increase to their profit by other men's pleasures in vacant time of recreation.   (*ES*, IV, p. 300)

Histriomastix is a six-act moral play about the various stages of a commonwealth's material and spiritual condition, from Peace to Plenty to Pride to Envy to War to Poverty to Peace. These states were traditionally conceived as an ineluctable cycle.[10] The play demonstrates that each stage of the material condition of society begets its own quality of personal relationships. Its particular concern is with the place of learning in society, and the nature of theatre is seen as the prominent index of intellectual and spiritual health.

In the initial state of Peace, there is the necessary leisure to cultivate learning and eloquence and 'tread on barbarism'. The sadly undereducated nobility enthusiastically promise to better themselves, and Chrisoganus, the central humanist figure of the play, initiates them into the joys of learning.[11] But Peace has another ominous offspring. A group of tradesmen, Incle, Belch, Gut and Posthaste, come in singing 'The Nut-Brown Ale' and decide to desert their callings and 'make up a company of players', with the self-taught Posthaste as their poet, and the unrequested patronage of the play-loving Sir Oliver Owlet.

> *Incle.* This peace breeds such plenty, trades serve no turns.
> *Belch.* The more fools we to follow them.
> *Posthaste.* Let's make up a company of players,
>   For we can all sing and say,
>   And so (with practice) soon may learn to play.
>
> . . .   .
>
> *Belch.* I pray sir, what titles have travelling players?
> *Posthaste.* Why, *proper fellows*, they play lords and kings. (p. 250)[12]

These mean and threadbare artisans, with their ignorant, impudent, fluent poet, are now in the way to wear the fine clothes of their betters and represent to the world the doings of the great.

In the second act, Plenty is queen of the land, and everyone except the poor scholar Chrisoganus is effortlessly prosperous. Nobility, merchants, and lawyers are easily seduced from their vows to study, and take to the hunting field and sports of all kinds. In an excellent town-market scene, the players burst in to announce their play, *The Lascivious Knight and Lady Nature*. Posthaste reads out bits of the new play, *The Prodigal Child*, which he is composing at his usual speed, until he is overcome by emotion at his own rhetoric.

> Read the rest, sirs, I cannot read for tears.
> Fill me the pot, I prithee, fellow Gulch. (p. 259)

'Is't not pity,' says one, 'this fellow's not employed in matters of state?' As the players' major concern is money, they quickly cancel the town play on getting an invitation to perform in Lord Mavortius's house. Here everything is revelry. The players feast in the kitchens: 'We have caroused like kings,' says Posthaste simply. Posthaste now has social pretensions. 'A gentleman's a gentleman that hath a clean shirt on, with some learning, and so have I' (p. 263). And the players call him their 'gentleman scholar'. Their play is a marvellous gallimaufry, beginning with Troilus and Cressida and veering off into something else entirely.

Enter a roaring Devil *with the* Vice *on his back*, Iniquity *in one hand, and* Juventus *in the other.*
> *Vice.* Passion of me, sir, puff, puff, how I sweat, sir;
> The dust out of your coat, sir, I intend for to beat, sir.
> *Juventus.* I am the prodigal child, ay, that I am;
> Who says I am not, I say he is to blame.

A visiting Italian lord makes the audience ashamed of this 'base trash' – 'base brown-paper stuff' – and tells them of the divine entertainments of the splendid theatres in his land. The English resolve to improve the sophistication of their theatre – a prelude to the next act, when Pride rules.

The reign of Pride sees lawyers fattening themselves on the fruits of discord and dissension (so sadly lacking in the time of Peace), breaking the rules limiting their attire and wealth. The most significant ominous aspect of this new age, however, is Lord Mavortius's attitude to his old feudal responsibilities. He, like the other lords, is dismissing all his old servants who 'have served his father in the field' (p. 270). One servant says,

> For service, this is savage recompense.
> Your fathers bought lands and maintained men!
> You sell your lands, and scarce keep rascal boys,
> Who ape-like jet in guarded coats. (p. 271)

Mavortius says firmly,

> I keep a tailor, coachman, and a cook.
> The rest for their board-wages may go look.
> A thousand pound a year will so be saved
> For revelling, and banquetting, and plays.

Plays now clearly are the mainstay of the new life of vain luxury. And at this point there is the fascinating entry of the poor scholar Chrisoganus *offering the actors a play*, and demanding £10 for it. The players are not prepared to pay that kind of money 'while goosequillian Posthaste holds his pen', and Gut bluntly asks, 'Will not our own stuff serve the multitude?' The embittered Chrisoganus curses them.

> Write on, cry on, yawl to the common sort
> Of thick-skinned auditors: such rotten stuff's
> More fit to fill the paunch of Esquiline
> Than feed the hearing of judicial ears.
> Ye shades, triumph, while foggy Ignorance
> Clouds bright Apollo's beauty: Time will clear
> The misty dulness of spectators' eyes –
> Then woeful hisses to your fopperies.
> O age when every scrivener's boy shall dip
> Profaning quills into Thessalia's spring,
> When every artist-prentice that hath read
> The Pleasant Pantry of Conceits shall dare
> To write as confident as Hercules;
> When every ballad-monger boldly writes,
> And windy froth of bottle-ale doth fill
> Their purest organ of invention.
> Yet all, applauded and puffed up with pride,
> Swell in conceit, and load the stage with stuff
> Raked from the rotten embers of stale jests,
> Which basest lines best please the vulgar sense,
> Make truest rapture lose pre-eminence.

Clout, for the players, repeats that they are not having any:

> Farewell the Muses! Poor poet, adieu!
> When we have need, 't may be we'll send for you. (pp. 273–4)

It would be a mistake to think that collaboration or revision is the cause of the startling change in Chrisoganus, though undoubtedly the hand of a different author (presumably Marston), enlivening the previous wooden character, accentuates the novelty of his new direction. Since the stage has become such a prominent feature in the commonwealth which the play describes, Chrisoganus, lacking advancement in an affluent society which is totally uninterested in continuing its earlier patronage of him, needs money and at the same time makes a bid to improve the literary and moral content of the omnipresent play. The situation is simple enough, and the force of his predicament and his aspiration will become abundantly clear in succeeding chapters. His only avenue for livelihood has become the public stage, and he can make virtue of necessity by using the stage to disseminate sweetness and light. But the stage won't have him.

It is curious, if Marston is the author or part-author of *Histriomastix*, that he should be parodied in the Cambridge *Parnassus* plays of 1598–1602, since they wholeheartedly support his point of view with their vivid and amusing presentation of the plight of the alienated scholar, unable to find a career that brings social respect, self-respect, and a reasonable living. Towards the end of the Second Part of *The Return from Parnassus* the desperate graduates Philomusus and Studioso are forced to seek employment from the common players – represented by Burbage and Kempe.[13] They are tried out as actors. Kempe scorns university writers – 'Few of the university men pen plays well' – and it is clear that *their* Posthaste is 'our fellow Shakespeare', who 'puts them all down' (l. 1769). Philomusus withdraws, ashamed at having to seek relief of 'the basest trade' (l. 1846).

> Better it is 'mongst fiddlers to be chief
> Than at a player's trencher beg relief.
> But is't not strange these mimic apes should prize
> Unhappy scholars at a hireling rate?
> Vile world, that lifts them up to high degree
> And treads us down in grovelling misery.
> England affords those glorious vagabonds,
> That carried erst their fardels on their backs,
> Coursers to ride on through the gazing streets,
> Sooping it in their glaring satin suits
> And pages to attend their masterships.
> With mouthing words that better wits have framed
> They purchase lands, and now Esquires are named.
>
> (ll. 1916–28)

The same indignation is in *Histriomastix* as the pampered players charge more and more for their services. The lord's Steward reflects on the change of the times that has brought such vanity and luxury to those who so recently had such a different status:

> Farewell, ye proud – I hope they hear me not –
> Proud Statute Rogues!
>
> (p. 275)

The bitterness of the reign of Envy in Act IV leads to the internecine War in Act V. Here the players overreach themselves. They continue to post their bills announcing plays as though nothing had changed. 'What, plays in time of wars?' expostulates a Press-captain. Gut self-confidently explains that players act wars, not fight them.

> Alas, sir, we players are privileged.
> 'Tis our audience must fight in the field for us,
> And we upon the stage for them.   (p. 286)

The effrontery of this – an insolence previously implicit in ragged men acting the part of kings – is rewarded when they are pressed into the army. The sergeant bawls at his disconsolate troupe:

> Come on, players! Now we are the sharers
> And you the hired men. Nay, you must take patience.
> 'Slid, how do you march!
> Sirrha, is this you would rend and tear the cat
> Upon a stage, and now march like a drowned rat?
> Look up and play the Tamburlaine, you rogue you!   (p. 291)

The scandal of making a profitable career out of acting is compounded by the offensiveness of men taking it upon themselves to image on a stage essential social activities which for the life of them they could not perform in reality. The idea that it is immoral to act on a stage what you cannot perform in life bewilders us; it seems a senseless point of view. It brings us into deep anti-theatre; a distrust and a dislike of acting as a falseness in human conduct are the fundamental elements in anti-theatrical prejudice. It is the more remarkable that we should meet this attitude *in a play*, even if it was performed by amateurs before their own peers.

There are scenes of wild conflict on stage, cries of 'Havoc! Havoc!', and Chrisoganus the scholar is left alone on stage. The reign of Poverty succeeds. The nobles are now beggars, and Chrisoganus recommends to them the stoicism which he has been forced to practise for a long time. Once again Chrisoganus has pupils; his lessons now are in very practical moral philosophy.

The players are living in squalor, and can't pay their rent, though the constable complains that, in spite of their professed poverty, 'each maintains his punk/And taverns it with drunken suppers still'. Naturally, the players begin to think of returning to their own trades, though Posthaste cries 'Fall to work after playing? Unpossible!' The constable gives them a choice: to be banished, or to take up honest trades, and if they play to give the proceeds to the poor (p. 229).

> *Posthaste.* Constable, do you know what you do?
> *Constable.* Ay, banish idle fellows out o' th' land.

While they are making up their minds, sailors enter. They carry off the players. The land is purged, and we are ready for the final reappearance of Peace. But Peace must surrender to a higher power. Astraea enters – and by Astraea, a marginal note tells us, is meant Queen Elizabeth – ushered by Fame, supported by Fortitude and Religion, followed by Virginity and Arts; she mounts the throne previously occupied in turn by Peace, Plenty, Pride, Poverty, and War.

> Mount, Empress, whose praise for Peace shall mount,
> Whose glory, which thy solid virtues won,
> Shall honour Europe whilst there shines a sun,
> Crowned with Heaven's inward beauties, world's applause,
> Throned and reposed within the loving fear
> Of thy adoring subjects. Live as long
> As Time hath life, and Fame a worthy tongue.
> Still breathe our glory, the world's empress,
> Religion's guardian, peace's patroness.
> Now flourish arts; the Queen of Peace doth reign.   (p. 301)

The final song is:

> Religion, Arts, and Merchandise
>   Triumph, triumph!
> Astraea rules, whose gracious eyes,
>   Triumph, triumph!   (p. 301)

Interestingly, Chrisoganus does not assist in this theophany (as his successor does in *Cynthia's Revels*), but he is there in spirit, for the moral is clearly that Queen Elizabeth breaks the remorseless cycle of Peace, Plenty, Poverty, and assures a continuing commonwealth based on the concord of religion, intellectual, and commercial life; a commonwealth innocent of professional theatre.

It is not this drama of *Histriomastix* which we see played out in the national life of England between 1570 and 1642, but an intense drama there was, in which the professional theatre fought for its life, secured itself, and was finally suppressed, and in which many people, on both sides, saw a vital connection between the continuance of theatre and the spiritual condition of the nation. Some of the dramatis personae are the same. The ending is significantly different in that the monarch is expelled soon after the professional theatre.

The script of the 'real' drama, or most of it, is available in the unsensational pages of E. K. Chambers's *Elizabethan Stage* and G. E. Bentley's *Jacobean and Caroline Stage*. There is an enormous cast, containing, for example, the Lord Mayor of London, with his attendants

Colaiste Mhuire
40,472
Luimneach

spirit the Plague, the Sovereign, the Privy Council, the Arch-bishop of Canterbury, the Enraptured and Unsubduable Audience, and of course the Players. There is a tremendous amount of doubling; with Philip Stubbes reappearing as William Prynne, the Earl of Leicester as Queen Henrietta Maria, Edmund Tilney as Henry Her-bert, and so on.

The growth of the English metropolitan theatre is dealt with so well in so many places that it is necessary here only to give the skeleton list of a few important dates.[14] During Elizabeth's reign all public performance was subject to licence. In 1572 any actors who were not in the service of a baron of the realm (or above) or else licensed by two Justices of the Peace were liable to be punished as rogues or vagabonds. In 1574, Leicester's men were licensed under the Great Seal by the Queen to perform their plays in any city in England, including London, provided that the Master of the Revels had approved of the plays. In 1576 and 1577 were built the first two permanent theatre-buildings, the Theatre and the Curtain, just north of the City of London boundary in order to avoid the continuous attempts of the City authorities to suppress playing. In 1581, the Lord Mayor of London forbade advertising *within* the city of plays to be performed *outside* the city. This was supplemented in 1582 by an injunction to the City Guilds demanding that all freemen refrain from visiting plays and prohibit their apprentices and servants from attending them. In 1583, the Queen formed her own company of players – or rather it was formed for her. In 1589, the first theatre outside the southern limits of the City, the Rose, across the Thames in Southwark, was opened (to be followed by the Swan in 1595 and the Globe in 1599). In 1597, the Privy Council appeared to surren-der to what Glynne Wickham calls 'fifty years of bludgeoning from the City' and agreed, because of 'very great disorders', to suppress playing completely and 'pluck down' all the theatres north and south of the City.[15] It is not on record why the decree was never carried out.

On the accession of James in 1603, all public acting companies came under the direct patronage and control of the monarch and his family. Shakespeare's company, the Lord Chamberlain's men, became the King's men; the Admiral's company became Prince Henry's men. In 1609 the King's men began playing at the indoor Blackfriars theatre (formerly used by children's companies) as well as the open-air Globe, and a second important indoor theatre, the

Phoenix or Cockpit in Drury Lane, was opened in 1617. In 1633, William Prynne had his ears cut off for appearing to condemn the royal family for their encouragement of and participation in plays in his book *Histriomastix*. In 1642, on the outbreak of the Civil War, Parliament took over from the Master of the Revels the control of the theatre and suspended playing because of the national crisis, and in 1647 banned theatre altogether as intolerable among professors of the Christian religion. There were no public plays (to speak of) between 1642 and the restoration of the monarchy in 1660.

The objections to the presence of a professional public theatre as a part of the life of the English nation, and in London in particular, range from the simplest matters of policing crowds to the most deeply held beliefs about the nature of man and the purpose of his existence. It is no good pretending that the new craze of theatre-going was not something of a public nuisance and that all statements about disorder were the inventions of the Malvolios of London town. The middle-class audience of today arriving in motor-cars to listen respectfully to a revival of an Elizabethan or Jacobean play is a different sort of gathering from that which trooped across the fields or made their way across the river to the original performance some afternoon in Elizabeth's or James's reign. There is plenty of evidence of the nuisance caused by the crowds, of violence and disorder in the theatres, of violent and disorderly lives among the players and poets. The world of the public theatre was rough, and the opponents of theatre had some justification for what they condemned. It is no service to the great plays which this theatre produced to see the audience as a well-mannered and attentive group improving their minds. Distortion and exaggeration of the nuisance are another thing. But basically the question is what sort of a threat to city and nation the new invasion of the players represented.

Two extracts from the Lord Mayor's complaints will express clearly the City's disquiet. In 1592 the Lord Mayor wrote to the Archbishop of Canterbury, trying to enlist his support by consulting with the Master of the Revels so that the City may be 'freed from these continual disorders'.

Whereby your Grace shall not only benefit and bind unto you the politic state and government of this city, which by no one thing is so greatly annoyed and disquieted as by players and plays, and the disorders which follow thereupon, but also take away a great offence from the church of God, and hindrance to His gospel, to the great contentment of all good Christians, specially the preachers and ministers of the word of God about this city, who have long time and yet do make their earnest continual complaint unto us for the redress hereof.   (*ES*, IV, p. 308)

The second extract is from the petition of the Lord Mayor and Aldermen to the Privy Council of 1597 which actually secured the never-implemented agreement to 'pluck down' the theatres.

We have signified to your highnesses many times heretofore the great inconvenience which we find to grow by the common exercise of stage plays. We presumed to do, as well in respect of the duty we bear towards her Highness for the good government of this city as for conscience sake, being persuaded (under correction of your highness's judgement) that neither in polity nor in religion they are to be suffered in a Christian commonwealth, specially being of that frame and matter as usually they are, containing nothing but profane fables, lascivious matters, cozening devices, and scurrilous behaviours which are so set forth as they move wholly to imitation and not to the avoiding of those faults and vices which they represent.   (*ES*, IV, p. 321)

They then give the usual complaint against the plays as magnets for 'the refuse sort of evil-disposed and ungodly people that are within and about this city', and then plead for 'the present stay and final suppressing of the said stage-plays, as well at the Theatre, Curtain, and Bankside as in all other places in and about the city'. In the attached memorandum, entitled 'The inconveniences that grow by stage-plays about the City of London', they repeat much of what has already been said but complain also of the innovation of continuous drama, as against drama for seasonal festivities, 'contrary to the rules and art prescribed for the making of comedies even among the heathen, who used them seldom and at certain set times, and not all the year long as our manner is'. Paragraph 3 is a notable statement of the offence given by playing to the Protestant ethic of industrious piety:

They maintain idleness in such persons as have no vocation and draw apprentices and other servants from their ordinary works, and all sorts of people from the resort unto sermons and other Christian exercises, to the great hindrance of trades and profanation of religion established by her highness within this realm.   (*ES*, IV, p. 322)

The deeper objections, implicit and explicit, to acting are:
First, that plays encourage sexual immorality
  (*a*) by the content of plays (plays being by definition exciting and persuasive);
  (*b*) by the freedom of behaviour generated in the gathering of spectators;

(c) by the example of the dissolute life of the players;

(d) by the practice of boys wearing women's clothes in love-scenes.
Secondly, that they discourage the proper and necessary work-habits
of the people

(a) by having performances during the working day;

(b) by actors themselves being men of no vocation;

(c) by introducing festive occasions as a regular element in city life.
Thirdly, that they are anti-religious

(a) in the use of transvestism;

(b) by drawing people away from divine service and sermons;

(c) by encouraging sexual licence, and incontinent revelry;

(d) because impersonation is itself basically evil.

It is in this third series of objections that we move into matters of
fundamental importance, since if there were no ideological objections, the main support for the other objections would disappear.[16] A
horror of revelry is the root of anti-theatre, revelry being seen as
self-abandonment in a double way: first, 'letting oneself go' in self-
indulgence and licence (chiefly sexual), secondly, assuming another
self in disguising and impersonating.[17] The basic distrust of impersonation took on in England a very strong anti-Catholic flavour. The
distrust was justified by a comparison of Catholic ceremony in which
a priest would have the effrontery to act as God, and pretend to
inhabit the Divine Being, with the simple Protestant preaching of the
Word.

For, whereas the profane and wicked toys of Passion-plays, plays setting forth
Christ's passion, procured by Popish priests, who, being corrupted from the
simplicity that is in Christ, as they have transformed the celebrating of the
sacrament of the Lord's Supper into a Mass-game, and all other parts of
ecclesiastical service into theatrical sights; so, instead of preaching the word,
they caused it to be played; a thing put in practice by their flowers, the Jesuits,
among the poor Indians.

This is an extract from John Rainolds's *Th'Overthrow of Stage-plays*,
1599 (p. 161), but it can be paralleled in many other anti-theatrical
writings, especially Prynne's *Histriomastix* of 1633. Rainolds's very
dull book keeps harping on the transvestism of boy-actors taking
women's rôles, and it is perfectly clear from his emphasis on the
sexual provocativeness of boys dressed as women (e.g. pp. 97–105)
that his objection is not a matter of religious dogma but a deep-seated
fear of the danger of altering the given self in impersonation.

It was inevitable that since the attempt by city authorities and puritan propagandists to extirpate professional playing was always breaking on the rock of the Privy Council's authority, the controversy over the continuance of the theatre should begin to assume lines of battle with the monarchy on one side, and puritans and city governors on the other. The demarcation is subliminal in the sixteenth century, but it exists, and it became more and more visible and irreconcilable during the reign of James, with the adoption of all theatre companies by the royal family, the increase in the number and the lavishness of the court masques, and the devotion of Charles's queen to acting.

To say that the players had an ally in Queen Elizabeth is to put things too simply. But revelry was an indispensable part of court life. It was desirable that competent actors should exist, though essential that playing, on a national scale, should be controlled. If anyone was to control the theatre, it should be the Queen in Council. For the only idea of control recognised by city authorities, and church authorities,[18] was extinction. The Christmastide festivities of the Tudor court had been in the charge of the Lord of Misrule. In 1545 the permanent office of the Master of the Revels was created; and from 1579 to 1610 it was held by Edmund Tilney, who greatly extended the scope and importance of the post.[19] John Lyly and Ben Jonson were both apparently offered the reversion of the post, but it never left the hands of courtiers, who paid good money for a post which brought handsome licensing fees from the professional theatre. Tilney gave way in 1610 to his nephew George Buc, who was followed by John Astley and Henry Herbert. Although the players were subject to a crossfire of limitation and control by municipal authorities, the church, and the state, it was primarily the Master of the Revels who had the responsibility for permitting and prohibiting plays and playing from the 1570s to the closing of the theatres in 1642.[20]

The Queen and her greater nobles were the patrons of players. The royal control of playing through the Privy Council secured the growing professional theatre against its enemies, allowed it to establish itself, and maintained it, while at the same time watching very carefully over its behaviour. The infant professional theatre was valuable only in so far as it strictly remained an obedient servant and property of the court, and did not stray into anarchy or disruption of state authority (as for example by impersonating politicians or writing plays which might seem critical of government policy).

The essential thing is that the Queen and her councillors recognised that acting was not an evil in itself, that recreation was desirable among the people and essential among the aristocracy. For the professional theatre to continue in the cities was an assurance that there would be a high standard of playing before her Majesty at Christmas. The fine language of the 1574 Patent for Leicester's men is repeated on many occasions. James Burbage and his fellows were given permission 'to use, exercise and occupy the art and faculty of playing comedies, tragedies, interludes, stage-plays . . . as well for the recreation of our loving subjects as for our solace and pleasure when we shall think good to see them' (ES, II, pp. 87–8). The Privy Council wrote imperatively to the Lord Mayor in 1581 on behalf of 'these poor men the players', telling him to allow them to act, because their 'readiness with convenient matters for her highness' solace this next Christmas . . . cannot be without their usual exercise therein'. In the same vein, in 1582, the Council reminded the Lord Mayor that it allowed certain companies of players 'for honest recreation sake, in respect that her Majesty sometimes taketh delight in those pastimes' (ES, IV, pp. 283, 287), and Walsingham in 1583 pointed out that 'without frequent exercise of such plays as are to be presented before her Majesty, her servants cannot conveniently satisfy her recreation and their own duties' (p. 296).

The City responded without the least enthusiasm to the argument that professional playing in London was necessary because it was a rehearsal for entertaining the Queen at court. 'It is not convenient that they present before her Majesty such plays as have been commonly played in open stages before all the basest assemblies in London and Middlesex' (ES, IV, p. 300). They request the Archbishop of Canterbury to consult with the Master of the Revels to find some other way than public performances whereby 'her Majesty may be served with these recreations as hath been accustomed (which in our opinions may easily be done by the private exercise of her Majesty's own players in convenient place)' (ES, IV, p. 308).

The strong determination of the crown both to allow and to supervise drama is excellently put in an order of the Privy Council of June 1600, which acknowledged the abuses of public playing and the necessity of controlling it.

It is considered that the use and exercise of such plays, not being evil in itself, may with a good order and moderation be suffered in a well-governed estate, and that her Majesty being pleased at some times to take delight and recreation in the sight and hearing of them, some order is fit to be taken for the allowance and maintenance of such persons as are thought meetest in that kind to yield her Majesty recreation and delight, and consequently of the houses that must serve for public playing to keep them in exercise.

(*ES*, IV, p. 330)

The identification of the players with the crown eventually caused their extinction, but at the start of James's reign it was clear that, for a time, they were safe in England, and that those who felt the nation would be a cleaner place without a professional theatre had lost. The patent by which the Chamberlain's men became in May 1603 the King's men is a moving document.

We ... do license and authorise these our servants Lawrence Fletcher, William Shakespeare, Richard Burbage, Augustine Phillips, John Heminges, Henry Condell, William Sly, Robert Armin, Richard Cowley, and the rest of their associates, freely to use and exercise the art and faculty of playing comedies, tragedies, histories, interludes, morals, pastorals, stage-plays· ... as well for the recreation of our loving subjects as for our solace and pleasure when we shall think good to see them, during our pleasure. And the said ... stage-plays and such-like to show and exercise publicly to their best commodity ... as well within their now usual house called the Globe ... as also within any town halls or moot halls or other convenient places within the liberties and freedom of any other city, university, town, or borough whatsoever within our said realms and dominions.   (*ES*, II, p. 208)

That the hated drama was being fostered by their own Queen was a problem that was recognised and met by the puritan polemicists. William Rankins (whose *Mirror of Monsters*, 1587, is heavily indebted to Stubbes's *Anatomy of Abuses*) agrees that it may seem out of order 'to speak against them that are privileged by a Prince, nay more, sworn servants to the Anointed, allowed by magistrates, and commended by many' (B2r). His margin retorts more succinctly than his text, 'The coat of a prince cannot alter the condition of the corrupted.' Anthony Munday in 1580 rebuked the nobility for supporting players, and saw the seamy side of noble patronage just as the author of *Histriomastix* did.

Alas, that private affection should so reign in the nobility that to pleasure, as they think, their servants, and to uphold them in their vanity, they should restrain the magistrates from executing their office! What credit can return to the noble, to countenance his men to exercise that quality which is not sufferable in any commonweal? whereas it was an ancient custom that no man of honour should retain any man but such as was excellent in some one good quality or other, whereby, if occasion so served, he might get his own living? Then was every nobleman's house a commonweal in itself; but since

the retaining of these caterpillars, the credit of noblemen hath decayed; they
are thought to be covetous by permitting their servants, which cannot live of
themselves, and whom for nearness they will not maintain, to live at the
devotion or alms of other men, passing from country to country, from one
gentleman's house to another, offering their service, which is a kind of
beggary.   (*ES*, IV, p. 210)

Munday strikes exactly the same note as the play *Histriomastix*. The
encouragement of the new drama by the nobility is *not* a continuance
of the best traditions of feudal England. It is precisely a dereliction of
those traditions, for the nobles are fostering a meaner sort of entertainment and a useless breed of man, and the bond between servant
and patron is not a proper feudal bond but a crude and cheeseparing
financial one.

A fine gesture affirming the value of stage-plays for the London
community and for the health of the nation as a whole is in the play
Three Lords and Three Ladies of London, possibly a decade earlier than
Histriomastix. (It was printed in 1590 and almost certainly was an
Armada play.) If the usual identification is correct, the author,
'R.W.', is Robert Wilson, a professional actor who had been with
Leicester's men in the seventies. The play is full of pride in London –
and one of the consequences of the victory over the Spaniards is that
Usury is laid by the heels and branded ⊗ to indicate a maximum
interest rate of ten per cent.

> And know that London's Pomp is not sustained by Usury
> But by well-ventured merchandise and honest industry.[21]

When the Spanish invasion is reported imminent it is decided to show
London's contempt for the Spaniards by carrying on as usual, and,
indeed, making something of a carnival. Instead of suppressing plays
as vain frivolities at a time of emergency, plays become the sign of
London's confidence in herself.

> Let nothing that's magnifical,
> Or that may tend to London's graceful state,
> Be unperformed; as shows, and solemn feasts,
> Watches in armour, triumphs, cresset-lights,
> Bonfires, bells, and peals of ordnance.
> And, Pleasure, see that plays be publishèd [*announced*],
> May-games and masques, with mirth and minstrelsy,
> Pageants and school-feasts, bears and puppet-plays.
> Myself will muster upon Mile-end Green,
> As though we saw, and feared not to be seen;

Which will their spies in such a wonder set,
To see us reck so little such a foe,
Whom all the world admires, save only we,
And we respect our sport more than his spite,
That John the Spaniard will in rage run mad,
To see us bend like oaks with his vain breath.[22]

When the Spaniards have been defeated, the victory is to be celebrated

With pageants, plays, and what delights may be
To entertain the time and company.[23]

This could not be more removed from the vindictive note of the
players being triumphantly driven off to fight in *Histriomastix*.

Thomas Nashe is one of the few to come back at the cant about the
theatre's encouragement of idleness, although his own lack of cant
about theatre audiences may not commend playing as strongly as it
ridicules the city fathers.

Whereas some petitioners of the Council against them object they corrupt the
youth of the city and withdraw prentices from their work, they heartily wish
they might be troubled with none of their youth nor their prentices; for some
of them – I mean the ruder handicrafts' servants – never come abroad but
they are in danger of undoing; and as for corrupting them when they come,
that's false; for no play they have encourageth any man to tumults or
rebellion, but lays before such the halter and the gallows; or praiseth or
approveth pride, lust, whoredom, prodigality, or drunkenness, but beats
them down utterly.

As for the hindrance of trades and traders of the city by them, that is an
article foisted in by the vintners, alewives, and victuallers, who surmise if
there were no plays they should have all the company that resort to them lie
boozing and beer-bathing in their houses every afternoon. Nor so, nor so,
good brother bottle-ale, for there are other places besides where money can
bestow itself. The sign of the smock will wipe your mouth clean; and yet I
have heard ye have made her a tenant to your tap-houses. But what shall he
do that hath spent himself? Where shall he haunt? Faith, when dice, lust, and
drunkenness and all have dealt upon him, if there be never a play for him to go
to for his penny he sits melancholy in his chamber devising upon felony or
treason, and how he may best exalt himself by mischief.[24]

The best 'answer' to *Histriomastix*, however, is the dramatist
Thomas Heywood's *Apology for Actors*, published in 1612, but possibly
written a few years earlier. Some of his important remarks are on the
value of the history play, and these will be looked at later. In the
dedication 'to my good friends and fellows, the city actors' he shows
his pride in the position which the English theatre has now reached.

'That our quality hath been esteemed by the best and greatest, to omit all the noble patrons of the former world, I need allege no more than the royal and princely services in which we now live.' It is Heywood's argument that a flourishing theatre is the sign of a flourishing commonwealth. 'The Romans, in the noon-tide of their glory and height of all their honour . . . edified theatres and amphitheatres; for in their flourishing commonweal, their public comedians and tragedians most flourished, insomuch that the tragic and comic poets were all generally admired of the people, and particularly every man of his private Maecenas' (C1r). 'I never yet could read of any history of any commonweal, which did not thrive and prosper whilst these public solemnities were held in adoration' (C2r). But 'I.G.', writing in 1615 his *Refutation* of Heywood, thought little of assertions like this. At Rome, he wrote, 'whiles plays were had in greatest honour, by the corruption of manners that proceeded from them was the Roman Commonwealth changed into a monarchy, and the monarchy afterwards into tyrannical government' (B4v).

I.G.'s words are ominous. For the particular form of national corruption associated with the theatre (in 1615) was a drift towards absolutism and tyranny. In the early years of James I's reign, the monarchy appropriated the theatre. All the major professional companies were reassigned to the patronage of members of the royal family. The players naturally identified themselves with those who adopted them and protected them, and in the opportunities for court performances provided them with a substantial revenue. Monarchy and court committed themselves to drama as a necessary part of their way of life in a manner not seen under Elizabeth. The annual masque was more than entertainment; it was a self-realisation and a preservative. The professional players were needed for the speaking parts in the iconic rituals and were thus even more fully drawn into the orbit of the court. In Charles I's reign, his wife's passion for theatricals turned courtiers into actors, actresses and dramatists, and at a time of growing national suspicion and unhappiness about the direction in which the monarchy was going helped to cement the association of drama with the monarchy. John Taylor, the great actor of the King's men, went daily to Whitehall to give acting lessons to the ladies-in-waiting who were rehearsing *The Shepherd's Paradise* in 1632.[25] It was a great misfortune for Prynne that his prolix diatribe *Histrio-Mastix, The Players' Scourge*, with its strong attack on actresses, should eventually appear in print just when it must seem to be a direct attack on the pastimes of the royal family. Yet the extreme severity of the sentence on Prynne, which took the nation by surprise, showed a recognition that this most formidable of all the condemnations of acting and playgoing as belonging to the devil was an attack upon an institution indissolubly connected with the monarchical way of life.

For the dramatist, the tensions set up by the continued drift of the drama into identification with an increasingly unpopular monarchy were much greater than for the largely non-political players. In *The Roman Actor* (1626), however, Massinger generously transferred to Paris the player the problems which he himself was experiencing in maintaining self-respect in a dependent theatre. How far Jonson was able to reconcile service to his royal patron with the need to speak his own mind is the subject of Chapter 6, while Chapter 7 suggests that it is not only plays like *A Game at Chess* which are critical of royal policies. Yet the dramatists themselves, writing more and more directly for the more exclusive audiences of the indoor 'private' theatres, helped to establish a drama more limited in its social appeal than its Elizabethan predecessor, belonging more to a section of society sympathetic in outlook to the court.

One of the most interesting signs that in the later part of James's reign and under Charles the professional theatre was not maintaining its hold as an accepted national institution lies in the records of performances in the provinces. Although organised research is at last getting under way in this strangely neglected field,[26] records are very scanty, and it is only the sketchiest picture that can be made out. In a pioneer effort to establish statistical trends, L. G. Salingar (with G. Harrison and B. Cochrane) found a peak in provincial playing in 1615–19 and thereafter a steady decline as municipal authorities increasingly tended to refuse companies permission to perform in their towns. The findings can be confirmed from other sources.[27] It is clear that the authorities in provincial towns and cities, who were always as apprehensive about the disorders and absenteeism associated with performances as the London authorities, were becoming increasingly bold in flouting the royal writs, countenancing performance in every shire and city, with which the professional companies came armed. That royal licence which in 1574 had been a triumphant liberation for the professional theatre was now under Charles a liability. The actors found their audiences and their livelihood disappearing before their eyes, and in 1641, the year following the meeting of the Long Parliament, one actor showed how very well he understood what was happening. This is how he put it in the anonymous *Stage-Player's Complaint*:

For monopolers are down, projectors are down, the High Commission Court is down, the Star Chamber is down, and (some think) bishops will down; and why should we then, that are far inferior to any of those, not justly fear lest we should be down too?[28]

The players were the puppets of the King and the municipalities of the country had given a lead in denying them. When war broke out in 1642 between King and Parliament, Parliament took over from the King the regulation of the theatre and made an order – by no means unusual in times of national crisis, as Salingar points out[29] – banning stage-plays. But the difference in this order is that the motivation behind it was undoubtedly puritan anti-theatre sentiment, and that it was never revoked. It was followed by several ordinances against playing; the third, of 1647, says quite clearly that stage-playing is not to be tolerated among professors of the Christian religion.

The suppression of the drama in 1642 was of course only a temporary victory for the anti-theatrical forces in England. But when drama returned with the monarchy eighteen years later it is evident that although for a long time they played the old plays a new epoch in the theatre was beginning. 1642 was a death.

3

ASTRAEA AND CHRISOGANUS

The development of the charismatic image of the monarch

With a religious Reformation which was supposed to sweep away superstition, sixteenth-century England began to create itself as a modern, secular, national state. The chief instrument of its advancement was the mystical and talismanic appeal of ancient kingship. 'The crown became, as never before, the focal point, the nerve center of the nation's religious, political and economic life.'[1] The development of royal authority and the cult of royalty which went with it were necessary for several reasons. A strong central authority was needed to unify the nation and protect it against both the internal threat which ideological antagonism could generate and the external threat from Catholic Europe. Strong alternative allegiances could not be tolerated. It was necessary not only to build up the authority but to inspire men's loyalty to it. It was also necessary to provide an object of emotional and spiritual allegiance to take the place of the Pope and the international church. And it was necessary to strengthen the legitimacy of the new authority by investing it with religious and traditional sanctions.

The country united itself round monarchs who were carefully sanctified with the unchallengeable status of divine authority. The Divine Right of Kings, said J. N. Figgis, was 'forged on the anvil of the Reformation': it was 'historically the form in which the civil state asserted its inherent right . . . and the independence of politics from merely ecclesiastical control'.[2] The theory of kingship which was created at the Reformation was far from being an out-and-out absolutist theory; the king was to share his rule with Parliament and be bound by the Law which was supreme in the state.[3] And although the king as Supreme Head of the Church of England had control over the appointment of bishops and the interpretation of doctrine, Henry VIII's Parliament stopped short of giving sacerdotal functions to the monarch,[4] and it was left to Charles I's theorists to express the belief that the king should also be High Priest. 'I think both offices, regal and sacerdotal, might well become the same person, as anciently they were under one name.'[5] Nevertheless, the doctrine of rigid obedience and non-resistance in the subject, which is such a feature of the strict Tudor régime, got its warrant from the divinity of a king, who was to human society as God was to the universe, a sole, imperial, and supreme being whom it was not given to man to question or challenge.

The sacredness of the Tudor monarchy, then, may be seen as a magic somewhat carefully contrived to promote the unity, obedience, and loyalty of the people, and allow the infant secular nation to survive and advance. The worship of the monarch grew to astonishing proportions under Elizabeth. Latimer had spoken of 'the God of England' but it was in Queen Elizabeth's time that the figure of Christ on the cross was removed from the rood-screen of country churches and replaced by the royal coat of arms.[6] The poets could blend the pagan world with Christianity.

> Of fair Elisa be your silver song,
>   That blessed wight:
> The flower of virgins, may she flourish long
>   In princely plight.
> For she is Syrinx daughter without spot,
> Which Pan, the shepherds' god, of her begot:
>   So sprung her grace
>   Of heavenly race,
> No mortal blemish may her blot.[7]

Joel Hurstfield writes that Elizabeth encouraged her own deification not because of any mystical political theory but as a technique:

Policies in the national interest would – along with her personality – pass out of the reach of human criticism ... It was a technique, rather than a philosophy, of government; and she would use it over and over again. As the reign proceeds we are witnessing, in the fields of politics as in literature, the apotheosis of a woman, a monarch transformed into a god.[8]

The richness of the symbolism used by writers to portray the Virgin Empress may be studied in E. C. Wilson's indispensable 'study of the idealization of Queen Elizabeth', *England's Eliza* (1939), and the blending of mythology with new political aspirations may be seen in Frances Yates's classic essay, 'Queen Elizabeth as Astraea', originally published in 1947, and republished in her *Astraea: The Imperial*

Theme in the Sixteenth Century (1975). The beautiful balance which the Queen herself achieved in describing the nature of her office is shown in the 'Golden Speech' delivered to Parliament in 1601.

> I know the title of a King is a glorious title: but assure yourself that the shining glory of princely authority hath not so dazzled the eyes of our understanding but that we well know and remember that we are also to yield an account of our actions before the great Judge. To be a King and wear a crown is a thing more glorious to them that see it, than it is pleasant to them that bear it. For myself, I was never so much enticed with the glorious name of a King or royal authority of a Queen, as delighted that God hath made me his instrument to maintain his truth and glory, and to defend this Kingdom (as I said) from peril, dishonour, tyranny and oppression.
>
> There will never Queen sit in my seat with more zeal to my country, care for my subjects, and that will sooner with willingness venture her life for your good and safety, than myself.[9]

While in England Queen Elizabeth, an immensely practical, courageous, statesmanlike, and successful ruler, happily received the unforced devotion of a loyal people without ever trying to theorise about it, James VI in Scotland, living in perpetual fear of yet another kidnapping, or worse, at the hands of his violent and unruly lords, was elaborating a theory of kingship that might perhaps achieve more relevance and propriety when he achieved what he so long lusted for: his departure from his anarchic and insolent kingdom to assume the throne of England. *Basilikon Doron* and *The True Law of Free Monarchies*, fruits of years of brooding, were written in 1598. Monarchy is the most perfect form of government because it most resembles the Divinity, and kings are called gods in the Psalms 'because they sit upon God his throne in the earth'. By 1609 James through long practice could phrase the dominant ideas about kingship, which he developed in his earlier works, with masterly succinctness.

> The state of MONARCHY is the supremest thing upon earth. For Kings are not only GOD's lieutenants upon earth, and sit upon GOD's throne, but even by GOD himself they are called Gods. There be three principal similitudes that illustrate the state of MONARCHY; one taken out of the word of GOD; and the two other out of the grounds of policy and philosophy. In the Scriptures, Kings are called Gods, and so their power after a certain relation compared to the divine power. Kings are also compared to fathers of families; for a King is truly *parens patriae*, the politic father of his people. And lastly, Kings are compared to the head of this microcosm of the body of man.[10]

In *The True Law of Free Monarchies*, he had claimed 'the King is above the law, as both the author, and giver of strength thereto', but he goes on, 'yet a good King will not only delight to rule his subjects by the law, but even will conform himself in his own actions thereunto' (edition of 1603, sig. D1v). For all the pretensions of his writings, and the bitter and almost continuous wrangling about the extent of his prerogative with the Commons, the judges, and divines, it has been argued that James did not in practice exceed a moderate and recognised constitutional position in regard to his powers.[11] The old Queen had been much more authoritarian and absolutist in her actions. Even Charles I, imperiously dissolving Parliament and engaging in the personal rule which led to his downfall and the temporary abolition of the monarchy, even he, feared by parliamentarians as an innovator bringing in a new absolutist monarchy, was not exceeding an acceptable interpretation of his constitutional rights.[12] Yet there is no doubt about it: the Stuarts had fallen into a trap dug for them by the Tudors. 'It was the Stuarts who had to pay the political bill for the exaltation of Elizabeth.'[13] That is to say, the mystical idea of the king-god, worshipped by the people he protects and guides, was accepted too complacently and with all too little recognition of the origin of the cult in the practical necessities of the young Protestant state. The Stuarts were clinging to an image of kingship which, if not backed up by hard work, political wisdom, and more than competent statecraft, could only work against the popularity of the monarch. Unless their control of the kingdom inspired loyalty, the image could seem vanity, arrogance, and pretence. If James had been more capable of understanding the real implications of his incessant asseveration that a king was to the people as a father was to the family, and that the man who strove to rule others must have complete command over himself, there might have been a less contemptuous attitude to the claims made for him in *God and the King*, an anonymous booklet published in both English and Latin in 1615, 'imprinted by his Majesty's special privilege and command' and ordered by James (unavailingly) to be studied by every child in the kingdom:[14]

From whence have they received their sovereignty to be here upon earth as gods over men? God himself answereth, 'I (and not any creature whatsoever) have said ye are gods; and as by my word the world was made, so are ye appointed by the same word to rule the world.' Who hath given unto them their kingdoms? The Most High, he ruleth in the kingdom of men, and giveth it to whomsoever he will. What power hath seated them in their thrones? The power of the Almighty . . . Their crown, their anointing, their sceptre and throne are God's, and their persons adorned with all these are so divine and sacred that they themselves are the angels of God and sons of the Most High.

(pp. 40, 41)

In the extreme adversity of his trial and death, Charles may have found the quality of conduct which gave meaning to the image which he inherited. Owen Felltham wrote,

> . . . 'twas a far more glorious thing,
> To die a MARTYR, than to live a KING.
> . . .   .
> When He had rose thus, Truth's great sacrifice,
> Here CHARLES the First, and CHRIST the Second lies.[15]

The causes of the rebellion of 1642 are extraordinarily complex and contradictory, and during the growing hostility to Charles I it is very perplexing to decide who is progressive and who is reactionary. (This is discussed in Chapter 7.) But it seems that Charles was caught in both ways. He inherited a mystical and sacramental concept of kingship, 'able to gain currency by appealing to some of the deepest instincts of human nature',[16] sanctioned by time and tradition, and it made him feared as a new absolutist breaking down the time-honoured constitutional rights of the English people. The idea of the sanctified monarchy as a necessary but transitory stage of the English nation is often stressed. G. R. Elton writes, 'England was not able to do without the visible embodiment of her nationhood until she had first passed through a condition where that visible embodiment was more obvious than the national foundation beneath.'[17] Charles was a victim of the image-making of the Tudors, which was prolonged and extended by the poets who wrote his court masques.

The Queen and the drama

The revels and pageantry associated with the Tudor and Stuart monarchs make a huge subject which I do not touch more than the fringes of in this chapter. At the various royal palaces, on royal progresses, in the cities and the universities the monarch was entertained with shows of all kinds – masques, disguisings, tilts, plays, pageants, and displays of every sort.[18] As the monarch was the centre of national life, theatre and pageantry associated with the court inevitably became to some extent political. Henry VII had used public ceremonies to affirm and consolidate his rule.[19] In the late 1530s, Sir Richard Moryson advocated a programme of drama to be used for anti-papal propaganda, 'and to declare and open to them th'obedience that your subjects by God's and man's laws owe unto your majesty. Into the common people, things sooner enter by the eyes, than by the ears.'[20] Thomas Cromwell actively encouraged John Bale and other Protestant playwrights, but after his downfall the idea of a direct political drama was positively avoided as altogether too dangerous. The strength of Elizabeth's objection to plays which reflected on contemporary affairs seems partly due to an extreme sensitivity and touchiness about personal allusions. In 1565 when a debate between Juno and Diana on the relative merits of chastity and marriage ended in a victory for marriage, the Queen turned to the Spanish ambassador and said 'This is all against me.'[21] The skill and deftness of Lyly in phrasing his beautiful dramatic comments on the Queen's love-life later in the reign are all the more impressive in the light of responses like this.

The Queen's delight in plays and entertainments which did not reflect on her person or her government is illustrated in the rich annals of the revels during her reign. There are excellent brief accounts of the theatrical life of the court in recent books by G. K. Hunter, M. C. Bradbrook, and D. M. Bevington.[22] One famous occasion was the presentation of the play *Palamon and Arcite* (not extant), by Richard Edwardes, before the Queen in Christ Church during her visit to Oxford in 1566. As the performance was due to begin, the press of people was so great that a wall collapsed, killing a student, a brewer, and a cook. The Queen was greatly concerned, and sent to help the injured, but the play was not cancelled. The Queen's interested and enthusiastic comments during the performance have been preserved. At the end, she sent for the author 'and gave him great thanks with promise of reward'.[23]

It may seem a minor and tangential matter that so very many plays and interludes of the earlier part of the sixteenth century conclude with a prayer for the monarch. E. C. Wilson's chapter 'Eliza in the Drama' in *England's Eliza* gives many examples of the convention, including an excellent one from the conclusion of Thomas Ingelend's *The Disobedient Child* (about 1560):

Here the rest of the players come in and kneel down all together, each of them saying one of these verses.

> And last of all to make an end,
> O God to thee we most humbly pray
> That to Queen Elizabeth thou do send
> Thy lively path and perfect way!
> Grant her in health to reign
> With us many years most prosperously,
> And after this life for to attain

> The eternal bliss, joy and felicity!
> ...   .
> And that we thy people, duly considering
> The power of our Queen and great authority,
> May please thee and serve her without fainting,
> Living in peace, rest, and tranquillity.
> God save the Queen!

Thirty years after *The Disobedient Child*, Robert Wilson ended his *Three Lords and Three Ladies of London* in very similar fashion:

> And we, my lords, that praise this happy day,
> Fall we on knees, and humbly let us pray.
>
> First that from heaven upon our gracious queen
> All manner blessings may be multiplied,
> That as her reign most prosperous hath been
> During world's length so may it abide,
> And after that with saints be glorified.
> Lord! grant her health, heart's ease, joy and mirth.
> And heaven at last, after long life on earth.

The importance of this convention is twofold. It is a common and expected thing in institutions and on public occasions to express loyalty; in England to express it to the monarch. That plays should include or terminate with such public devotion in the sixteenth century seems not a forced but a voluntary gesture, recognising the place of the play within the community and within the nation. The players unite with the audience in a gesture of formal devotion to the monarch. Whatever the Puritan thinks of playing, within the bounds of the playing-place there is no feeling of being a national outcast. Until very recently in England, well after the Second World War, it was standard convention to 'formalise' the proceedings both in theatre and cinema by terminating every evening's performance with the National Anthem. When this tie with the nation had been severed the reciprocal tie was severed – the control of contents of plays by the Lord Chamberlain (1968).

Secondly, the convention is important because it was a first movement towards bringing the Queen herself into the play. We have seen that the justification of public playing was that by means of it the actors polished their wares for presentation to the Queen. All public plays could become court plays. Some plays, like Lyly's, as we shall see shortly, are so dependent on the Queen's presence that they have only a tithe of their meaning outside the court. With other plays, it is not always clear how much an ending directed towards the Queen herself as a kind of terminal president *within* the play might have been altered in public performance. Jonson probably copied *Histriomastix* in his *Every Man Out of his Humour* in introducing a person or image representing the Queen at the culmination of the play; he got into trouble for it and altered it with a bad grace.[24] Dekker's *Old Fortunatus* (1599) has a very beautiful detachable envelope for court performance, in which two old men meet, one 'travelling to the temple of Eliza', and another of her own country.

Some call her Pandora, some Gloriana, some Cynthia, some Belphoebe, some Astraea: all by several names to express several loves. Yet all those names make but one celestial body, as all those loves meet to create but one soul.

They approach Elizabeth's throne at the centre of the audience, fall on their knees, and offer the play.

> O vouchsafe,
> Dread Queen of Fairies, with your gracious eyes
> T'accept theirs and our humble sacrifice.

But even within the ending of the play of *Old Fortunatus* itself, there is a rendering up to the person of the Queen as the final arbiter. Fortune, Vice, and Virtue have made their assignments of the dramatis personae, and they vie with each other for mastery. Fortune turns to the audience and suggests them as judges, but Virtue turns to the Queen:

> My judge shall be your sacred deity.

All the allegorical deities kneel. Fortune immediately admits that she is not the supreme power. Virtue, triumphant, surrenders to the Queen in a different way, and couples her submission with a plea for favour to the actors ('shadows').

> Virtue alone lives still, and lives in you;
> I am a counterfeit, you are the true;
> I am a shadow; at your feet I fall
> Begging for these, and these, myself and all.
> All these that thus do kneel before your eyes
> Are shadows like myself. Dread Nymph, it lies
> In you to make us substances.

A play declared its existence as part of the life of the nation by ending with a devotion to the Queen. It was also a part of the national life in that if it was fortunate it was acted before the Queen herself, as part of her entertainment. She is brought into the play as the final umpire and judge. The play thus claims her for itself: she becomes a part of the theatre. But equally the play by incorporating the Queen in its final stages is making even stronger claims to become part of the wider life of which the Queen is symbol and governor. In this most cunning movement in *Old Fortunatus*, the characters claim Elizabeth as a player, the ultimate authority in their play-world, and then they slide out of their rôles into their position as subjects of the Queen, acknowledging her as ultimate authority in the state.

The best-known example of including the senior person in the state and the senior member of the audience within the play world is George Peele's *The Arraignment of Paris*, presented before the Queen in 1584 by the Children of the Chapel Royal. The Children of the Chapel were one of the remarkable companies of boys who dominated playing at court and whose culminating achievements were to perform Lyly's plays. They were choirboys, sometimes forcibly recruited and trained not by kindness only to what must have been an extraordinary proficiency in acting. They performed elsewhere than at court, and their encouragement by Elizabeth is understood to be an aspect of her famous ability to economise. By using the boy professionals at court, she was sure of a high standard of acting without having to provide the entire subsistence of her actors from the royal purse. This financial realism, however, is precisely the kind of thing which infuriated Anthony Munday and the authors of *Histriomastix* as a sign of decline of feudal responsibility and the substitution of the cash-nexus for the old reciprocal ties of master and servant.

The Arraignment of Paris would have been an enchanting play to watch, though it is now a rather tedious play to read. The centre is of course the altercation on who deserves the golden apple, to be given to the fairest. Venus, Juno, Pallas ask the shepherd Paris to solve the problem, and he is taken off by Venus, to whom he awards it, away from his true love Oenone. At a session of the gods, Jupiter gives Diana the ball to settle the matter once and for all. Diana describes a place of perfect climate, Elizium, governed by Eliza.

> An ancient seat of kings, a second Troy,
> Ycompast round with a commodious sea.

Peele, ever the most patriotic of playwrights, makes Diana eulogise this queen for twenty-five lines or so. The warring goddesses all defer to her. The three Fates join them and they all approach the Queen, sitting in state. The Fates resign their powers to the Queen, and Diana delivers the ball of gold to the Queen's own hand.

John Lyly

For years John Lyly stood on the Queen's threshold, writing plays for her but not gaining admittance: the post he had hoped for was Master of the Revels.

Most gracious and dread sovereign, I dare not pester your Highness with many words, and want wit to wrap up much matter in few . . . I was entertained your Majesty's servant by your own gracious favour, strengthened with conditions that I should aim all my courses at the Revels . . . (I dare not tell with a promise, but a hopeful item of the reversion), for which these ten years I have attended with an unwearied patience . . . If your sacred Majesty think me unworthy, and that after ten years tempest I must at the court suffer shipwreck of my time, my hopes, my wits, vouchsafe in your never-erring judgment some plank or rafter to waft me into the country where in my sad and settled devotion, I may in every corner of a thatched cottage write prayers instead of plays – prayers for your long and prosperous life and a repentance that I have played the fool so long, and yet live.

G. K. Hunter (whose text I use) dates this petition as probably of 1598. The second probably belongs to 1601. Aspiration for the Revels had been abandoned: Lyly had then aimed at the Mastership of the Tents and Toils and that also had been refused.

Most gracious and dread sovereign: time cannot work my petitions, nor my petitions the time. After many years service it pleased your Majesty to except against Tents and Toils . . . Thirteen years your Highness' servant, and yet nothing . . . A thousand hopes, but all nothing; a hundred promises, but yet nothing . . . My last will is shorter than mine inventory – but three legacies: patience to my creditors, melancholy without measure to my friends, and beggary not without shame to my family.

Si placet hoc meruique, quid O tua fulmina cessant
Virgo, Parens, Princeps.[25]

G. K. Hunter's book on Lyly describes with great vividness the aspirations of the man of learning in the sixteenth century, no longer destined for the church, but a humanist believing that the fruits of learning were in action, seeking secular preferment as the sphere of his talents. For the humanist, learning was the spiritual centre of life, and since the court was the material centre, he sought the court.

The Humanist dream forced the learned into dependence on a court which did not really need them . . . The progressive and intellectual elements in the country were gradually squeezed into Puritan opposition . . . Yet the dream that the centre of power was the natural home of learning and eloquence was by now so ingrained that it was not to be denied; reluctance to enter the Church, together with inability to find any other niche for learning was the common lot of those Elizabethans who made the 'pilgrimage from Parnassus', John Lyly among them.[26]

After writing *Euphues* in 1578, Lyly entered the service of Edward de Vere, Earl of Oxford, hereditary Lord Great Chamberlain. He began presenting his plays to the Queen in 1583–4, *Campaspe* and *Sapho and Phao*, performed, like all his plays, by boys' companies. *Gallathea*, *Endimion*, and *Midas* were all performed at court before the end of the decade. (The brilliant *Mother Bombie* may be later, and Hunter thinks it probable it was never given before the Queen.) It is Hunter's contention that Lyly sought to please the Queen by dramatic entertainments in order to gain her favour, and that he thought little of the 'toys' which were to attract notice and bring him office. Of the petitions to the Queen, Hunter says they are 'a despairing comment on the Humanist dream of Eloquence to move princes' (p. 87). The learned man was forced into the rôle of fool to entertain princes. Throughout the whole great period of the professional Tudor and Stuart drama, there is audible a note of bitterness from the university-trained – or at least, learned (to include Jonson) – dramatist forced by need to write for an audience he disapproves of. The note is clearest in Greene, Jonson, and Massinger. The junction of humanist eloquence and the popular stage may have been awkward and uncomfortable, but it produced an outstanding drama.[27] Things were not all as Marston (?) portrayed them in *Histriomastix*. There Chrisoganus (the name means 'golden born'),[28] thwarted by neglect in an affluent society bent on superficial pleasure, tried to find money and an outlet for his wisdom by writing for the professional players. But his price was too high; they had their own writers, their Shakespeares, and Chrisoganus was thwarted again. Perhaps this was the experience of some university would-be dramatist who foundered on his inability to meet the public taste. But we generally reckon that the greatness of the Elizabethan drama came about from the collaboration between Chrisoganus and Posthaste, symbolised by the 'infinite riches in a little room' of Christopher Marlowe, down from Cambridge after refusing a career in the church, and Thomas Kyd, abandoning his father's calling of scrivener in order to write for the stage, both in the service of the same lord and patron of players, sharing lodgings in London in 1591. The services of university men – Lyly, Greene, Peele, Marlowe – were most certainly needed and were used by the professional companies (boys and men), and anyone who wishes to do it can try to work out in what ways the university group inspired and in turn learned from the grammar-school group – Kyd, Shakespeare, Dekker.

Gallathea, one of the most searching and interesting of Lyly's plays, starts from the improbable assumption that on the banks of the Humber an angry Neptune sends a monster to devour the fairest virgin and that two fathers independently decide to disguise a beautiful daughter as a boy to avoid being chosen for the sacrifice. Each of the girls falls in love with the other, thinking her a young man, and Lyly's teasing pursuit of the sexual and personality problems involved in transvestite disguise is remarkable, culminating in the ironic judgement of Venus that the two girls can be married but aren't to know until the very steps of the altar which of them is to undergo a sex-change. *Gallathea* is most certainly a court play: it opens with a prologue making a total committal of the subject's life to the prince: 'Your majesty's judgement and favour are our sun and shadow . . . We in all humility desire that, by the former receiving our first breath, we may in the latter take our last rest.' The divine machinery of the play involves a challenge between Diana's chastity and Venus's philoprogenitiveness. Cupid gets loose from Venus and creates havoc among Diana's nymphs until he is nabbed and (to some extent) chastened by Diana. All this is very suitable as compliment to the Virgin Queen and tantalising to curiosity about possible direct allusions to recent happenings,[29] but the play is not anything like so exclusively dependent, in significance and in effect, on its reference to the Queen as are *Endimion* and *Sapho and Phao*. The early *Campaspe* is not so interesting as a play of state as it ought to be and seeks to be. The doctrines which generate and explain it are, first, that the greatness of a king, moving from war to peace, is to encourage the arts and philosophy, and be tolerant of the unavoidable eccentricities of learned men; and secondly, that a great conqueror to become a great king must be able to conquer and subdue the passion of love. So Alexander forgoes Campaspe and allows her to pair off with the painter whom Alexander has patronised. This scheme of subduing love in order to reign is of course the basic theme of the mythological plays, but there is something thin in the dramatic image of the interplay of authority, learning, the arts, and sexual life in *Campaspe*.

It is the new-worked myth of *Sapho and Phao* which seems to me the most successful and important example in Lyly of a play, directed to the monarchy, which by its existence and continuance shows that Lyly, despite his personal losses and frustration, actually achieved the contribution to the life of his country that he hoped to provide by other means than plays. *Sapho and Phao* depends upon an understanding of its Prologue and Epilogue, and of its second scene, in which a courtier and a scholar debate the value of courts. In the Prologue Lyly says, 'We present no conceits nor wars, but deceits and loves, wherein the truth may excuse the plainness; the necessity, the length; the poetry, the bitterness.' So the play is a poetical 'deceit', about love, which is true, necessary, and bitter. Its 'truth' might be seen to be on three levels. First, it is a general image of Queen Elizabeth's relation with her subjects. Secondly, it has a special application to recent events in the Queen's life and at court. Thirdly, the play as a whole being an offering from a hopeful client, it reflects in Phao Lyly's own position: encouraged and then rejected. The middle, allegorical level, which fascinated Lyly's earlier commentators, rightly produces little excitement now. It is the first and third levels which are all important; the first having the necessity of utterance, the last the bitterness.

The Prologue ends by entreating the Queen to imagine herself 'to be in a deep dream, that staying the conclusion, in your rising your Majesty vouchsafe but to say, And so you *awaked*'. The play is to be the Queen's dream, and at the end she will wake into her real life. The Epilogue insists with a series of different images that the audience *ends where it began*. The journey of the play is only to bring one back, as on awaking from a dream, to the place one has been in all the time.

They that tread in a maze walk oftentimes in one path, and at the last come out where they entered in. We fear we have led you all this while in a labyrinth of conceits, divers times hearing one device, and have now brought you to an end, where we first began.

The sleeper awakes from the dream and carries on where she left off when she fell asleep. What has changed is that her life now includes the memory of a vision, a vision of herself as Sapho, symbolising her own state as woman and as ruler, affirming what she is and strengthening her in what she has to be, by its beauty and truth. The bitterness belongs to others, who also by treading this labyrinthine vision understand that the necessity of the state requires things to be for individual subjects what they lamentably are. The fanciful vision of *Sapho and Phao* might seem entertainment and flattery. It is entertaining but, as Lyly said, it is true, necessary, and bitter. It is a vision or dream for the monarch and the subject, defining symbolically a relationship which for the good of both cannot be other than it is, yet can hardly be endured.

The small scene (I.ii) between Trachimus and Pandion seems a quite conventional debate about the virtues of the contemplative and the active life. Trachimus, meeting the young university man, paints a glowing picture of both university *and* court, with the confident belief that universities consider theoretically what in court has actually to be carried out. 'In universities virtues and vices are but shadowed in colour, white and black, in courts showed to life, good and bad.' Courts are real life, where decisions have to be made – but, it is implied, decisions are to be made according to the precepts taught in universities. But Pandion knows that if he is to come to court he must learn to dissemble (l. 32). Trachimus blusters a little; even if it were true of courts in general, 'this is the court of Sapho' (l. 38), an exception to every rule. But he cannot deny Pandion's charge. He excuses Sapho of responsibility for corruption at court; it is 'the easterly wind, which is thought commonly to bring cankers and rottenness'.

This scene includes a good deal of repartee about flattery, and it is a scene like this which shows Lyly's wish that we should all be aware of his own awareness of the delicacy of his position. He is bound to flatter. Tradition and convention demand it. He knows he is flattering and so does the Queen. And he knows that the court is a corrupting place. These admissions indicate the spirit in which Lyly wishes his myth to be accepted. His fancies are to be seen neither as the uncritical offerings of the devotee nor as the mercenary flattery of the cynic. Lyly authorises his vision by indicating his knowledge that both flattery and corruption are inevitably to be found in the court. Taken by a true understanding, his fancies become an imaginative perception of the truth latent within a court which is neither angelic nor damned.

The legend of Sapho and Phao as Lyly tells it is that Phao, a ferryman, is made by Venus the most beautiful man alive. Venus's purpose is the grim one of showing that her domination of mankind is absolute. No person is to be free of sexual desire and its pains. She speaks to Cupid: 'But come, we will to Syracusa, where thy deity shall be shown, and my disdain. I will yoke the neck that yet never bowed . . . Sapho shall know, be she never so fair, that there is a Venus, which can conquer, were she never so fortunate' (I.i.31–5). The great princess and Phao see each other, and they fall uncontrollably in love. Sapho dare not admit her affection to others nor countenance it to herself. She becomes desperately ill, and for several scenes she is on stage 'in her bed'. Is it possible, she asks, that a great lady like herself can love any but a great lord?

When Phao cometh, what then? wilt thou open thy love? Yea, No, Sapho! but staring in his face till thine eyes dazzle, and thy spirits faint, die before his face: then this shall be written on thy tomb, that though thy love were greater than wisdom could endure, yet thine honour was such as love could not violate.   (III.iii.108–13)

Venus, she who governs all and causes everyone to love, now herself falls a victim to her own decoy, the beautiful young man Phao. She gets Vulcan to make her a set of arrows for Cupid to shoot in order to make Sapho cease loving and to make Phao love herself, the goddess. Cupid strikes Sapho with the arrow of disdain, so that she overcomes her desire for the ferryman. But the insubordinate Cupid reveals the rest of the plot to Sapho, with whom he elects to stay. So Phao is struck with the arrow of hate for Venus, and remains irremediably in love with Sapho who, though she cannot now return his love, wishes him fortunate (V.iii.98). But Sapho now has Cupid, so that she becomes the 'goddess of affection' upon earth for all mankind in place of the cruel and indiscriminate goddess Venus. The play ends with Phao swearing constancy and loyalty.

This shall be my resolution; wherever I wander to be as I were ever kneeling before Sapho, my loyalty unspotted, though unrewarded . . . My life shall be spent in sighing and wishing, the one for my bad fortune, the other for Sapho's good.

This play may have its topical touches, but it does not work by close identification. Queen Elizabeth tossing in bed for love of a strong-thighed bargeman? Sapho of course must 'stand for' Queen Elizabeth, and Sapho's love for the common man Phao represents in a very pleasant way the Queen's mortal womanliness. She has affections and they are stirred by simple manliness. But her anguish in her illness makes us glad as well as sorry when she overcomes her infatuation: it was not a queen we saw in that bed. Venus, subjugating all, showed her weakness by being subjugated herself. Sapho, subjugated, shows her strength by overcoming passion. And by that mastery she earns the right to become 'the goddess of affections'. The Queen is not, as a woman, to give herself to any. Her sad and lonely rôle is to inspire love in others, but never to return it to any single other. Not really because all are beneath her – but because she is the Queen, and an amatory liaison is a political act. She is not to give herself to any if she is to preserve herself as untrammelled Queen to all her subjects. She must always suffer because she is human enough to love and princely enough to conquer love.

The later *Endimion* presents a much less interesting view of the Queen. Lyly reverses the myth. The youth falls in love with the Moon and she never knows of his passion until the end. He grows old in her service. When Cynthia knows of his devotion she admires his constancy, but has no intention of returning his love. She makes him young and that's it. This is much simpler and less rich, and has none of that movement from the private woman to the public monarch which makes *Sapho and Phao* reach Shakespearian levels of concern. *Sapho and Phao*, a charming and delicate tribute to the Queen's virgin state, is also a highly political play. Phao keeps his loyalty unspotted, though he is unrewarded. If Queen Elizabeth did *not* inspire love in ordinary people and great courtiers, the country would collapse. She is the centre, a queen: the prosperity and serenity of the nation depend upon service and obedience to her. If, because she is a woman, that service is expressed in terms of love, no harm is done. But if she literally or figuratively commits herself to any single person, her freedom and her power are at an end, and again the state collapses. It is impossible to read *Sapho and Phao* and not to think of what in a year or two was to happen to Ralegh and Essex, either of whom was great enough to shape the whole course of the country. Both these men accepted their servant relationship with the Queen in terms of love. Ralegh was never given the power which many would think he deserved. Always kept at a distance, disgraced and never fully back in favour, his star waned in the nineties as that of Essex rose.

In the period of disgrace after his marriage (probably), Ralegh wrote one of the strangest and most powerful of Elizabethan poems, the long incoherent *Ocean to Cynthia*, telling of love and bitterness, adoring the Queen and hating her. Its broken conclusion sees the end of the good times of her favour, now bringing 'new joys and new-born days' to his successors.

> So could she not, if she were not the sun,
> Which sees the birth and burial of all else
> And holds that power with which she first begun
>
> Leaving each withered body to be torn
> By fortune, and by times tempestuous,
> Which by her virtue once fair fruit have borne,
>
> Knowing she can renew, and can create
> Green from the ground, and flowers even out of stone,
> By virtue lasting over time and date,

> Leaving us only woe, which like the moss,
> Having compassion of unburied bones,
> Cleaves to mischance, and unrepaired loss

> For tender stalks

Here is the bitterness of the ferryman who was rejected, in real life, and here is the acknowledgement that though Elizabeth behaves like a fickle and cruel woman, the devotion which she inspires, and the transference of her trust from one to another as time and circumstances demand, are quite beyond mere womanhood: the devotion belongs to her as she *is* the continuing spirit of the nation. She draws men to her and casts them off; men grow and die in serving her: she is the sun. Essex, however, denied the system. She was only a woman on the throne. He simply disobeyed her in Ireland, returned flatly against her wishes, and rudely confronted her in her bedroom. Then he rose in armed rebellion against her and was defeated and executed.

Kingship in Marlowe's plays

It is not surprising that in the drama which grew up under the late Tudor monarchy the king became the central figure, and the crown the most potent symbol. Kingship, the mysterious state which transfigures and confuses all who achieve it or are born to it, and alters the lives of everyone within its magnetic field, is the focal point of the greatest English tragedies, *Hamlet*, *King Lear*, *Macbeth*. It is the inspiring force of hundreds of other plays of Shakespeare's time. I try in Chapter 5 to say something about the idea of kingship in Shakespeare's history plays; I discuss Jonson's use of the monarch figure in Chapter 6, and Massinger and Ford in Chapter 7. To conclude the present chapter, I want to show how Christopher Marlowe, the first man to make full dramatic use of the image of kingship, anticipated in *Tamburlaine* and *Edward II* the main lines of its development by his successors.

In Chapter 7 of *The Shakespearean Moment* (1954), Patrick Cruttwell wrote excellently about the profound division in the age, and in particular about the extraordinary way in which drama foresaw the political conflict of the seventeenth century and the execution of Charles. 'The imaginations of the Elizabethans anticipated the reality of civil war which their grandchildren suffered.' By 1649, the recurring *personae* of the drama of the age had received their incarnation in Cromwell and King Charles. The two *personae* were 'the military hero, the self-made conquering usurper' and 'the legitimate anointed monarch, the King by the Grace of God'. The one figure stands for 'the age's craving for individualist self-expression', and the other for 'its deep reverence for order and tradition'. We shall see in studying Massinger and Ford that before the Civil War Charles was by no means an unambiguous priest of the past, but the simplification is helpful. Both figures, it must be said, are king-figures. In Shakespeare, the sacrificial victims like Henry VI or Richard II or Duncan are balanced by the more energetic, practical, and (for a time) successful figures like Richard III or Henry IV or Claudius.

It is astonishing that Marlowe should have crystallised so much of all this in two such early plays as *Tamburlaine* (1587–8) and *Edward II* (1591–3). But Marlowe was himself a Janus figure, at once the most deeply religious of all Elizabethan dramatists and the most enthusiastic for the rich possibilities of the newly emancipated individual. No one else rendered so well the visions of the mind liberated from traditional sanctions, and no one else rendered so well the horror of the man whose own intellectual temerity has taken him outside the protecting hands of God. He knew in himself the contradictions which his age found in the figure of the king, incorporated them as two warring and irreconcilable foes within. Though Sir Thomas Browne declared that man was 'that great and true Amphibium, whose nature is disposed to live, not only like other creatures in divers elements, but in divided and distinguished worlds', he also said that the forces contending for government in man might with 'a moderate and peaceable discretion . . . be all kings and yet make but one monarchy, every one exercising his sovereignty and prerogative in a due time and place'. Marlowe did not seem to find it so.

In *Tamburlaine* kingship has a sacredness of a curiously non-religious kind. At least, the many associations between supernatural forces and Tamburlaine's ambition to be king over all do not amount to a view of kingship as a divine appointment; it is a very special state of life available to men of quite exceptional personality and ability.

> For fates and oracles of heaven have sworn
> To royalise the deeds of Tamburlaine.   (Pt 1:II.iii.8–9)[30]

The Oxford Dictionary gives this as the first use of the word 'royalise', but glosses it incorrectly as 'to render famous' rather than 'to render royal'. It means that the deeds are to be given their proper status, that of royalty. At the beginning of the play, when the Persian court is debating what to do about Tamburlaine, who is trying to 'make himself the monarch of the East', the effete king Mycetes asks for assurance about his plan.

> How like you this, my honourable lords?
> Is it not a kingly resolution?

To this, his brother Cosroe contemptuously replies,

> It cannot choose, because it comes from you.   (Pt 1:I.i.54–6)

Kingship is only a husk when a man as feeble as Mycetes wears the crown, a man whose resolutions are 'kingly' only because he has the title of king. Tamburlaine's deeds will be 'royal' because their quality will justify the title. To become royal, he will have to defeat and depose Mycetes, and this will be a revitalising of the office of king.

Kingship in *Tamburlaine* is mystical. It involves reaches of the human spirit which words find difficulty in describing, and it therefore tends to announce itself in ritual and in symbol. In the very first scene there is the solemn coronation of Cosroe as Emperor and 'monarch of the East'. This is the first time the crown comes on stage as a physical symbol – '*Enter Ortygius and Ceneus bearing a crown . . .*'. This is an attempt *by the people* to provide for themselves a better ruler than Mycetes. The investment is solemn, but it is a democratic recognition of human worth. The co-existence of solemn ritual and popular recognition of desert helps to define the specially elevated but not religious area which kingship occupies in this play. Above all, this coronation of Cosroe helps the all-important idea of 'detur dignissimo', the sense that it is not inheritance but ability which should win a crown. But it is not enough to talk about 'ability' as though monarchs were chosen on merit by some grave electoral college. Tamburlaine obtains his crown because he is ambitious for it, and is able to win his way to it by the force of his personality, by trickery, and by military skill. And he is ambitious for it because kingship is for him the highest fulfilment of the human spirit. The magic of kingship fires him as he hears the promise that Cosroe will 'ride in triumph through Persepolis'.

> 'And ride in triumph through Persepolis!'
> Is it not brave to be a king, Techelles,
> Usumcasane, and Theridamas?
> Is it not passing brave to be a king,
> And ride in triumph through Persepolis?   (II.v.49–53)

Theridamas replies:

> A god is not so glorious as a king.
> I think the pleasure they enjoy in heaven
> Cannot compare with kingly joys in earth.
> To wear a crown enchased with pearl and gold,
> Whose virtues carry with it life and death;
> To ask and have, command and be obeyed;
> When looks breed love, with looks to gain the prize,
> Such power attractive shines in prince's eyes.   (II.v.57–64)

The image of the jewelled crown is a figurative way of talking about the richness of kingship, but kingship itself (the power and the perquisites) is still only a metonymy for a human exaltation – the high pitch of all the powers of man – which is otherwise hardly to be described. So Tamburlaine breaks his pact with Cosroe, defeats him and dethrones him, and justifies himself, in the best-known speech in the play, on the grounds that life is competition, and that the aspiring mind of man

> Wills us to wear ourselves and never rest
> Until we reach the ripest fruit of all,
> That perfect bliss and sole felicity,
> The sweet fruition of an earthly crown.   (II.vii.26–9)

It is hard to understand how so sensitive a critic as Una Ellis-Fermor could possibly support Havelock Ellis's description of the climax of this speech as 'Scythian bathos', believing that Marlowe was unable to find an objective correlative for his own intellectual and spiritual aspirations and ambitions (which inform the body of the speech), and soiled them by concluding in a material satisfaction.[31] If by this stage in the play Marlowe and Tamburlaine have not managed to convey the magic and the excitement which make kingship more than a matter of material power and privileges, they have failed very sadly. The play is quite inexplicable unless we take these two lines as seriously as the rest of the speech, and, in particular, as these lines:

> Our souls, whose faculties can comprehend
> The wondrous architecture of the world
> And measure every wandering planet's course,
> Still climbing after knowledge infinite . . .

Tamburlaine may turn out to be terribly mistaken in his placing of 'sole felicity' in an earthly crown, but it is his considered opinion here that the state of kingship is the most satisfying haven for the most intellectually adventurous as well as the bravest and most martial of men.

So at the end of this scene, the end of the second act of the play, Tamburlaine solemnly crowns himself. But he does so only with the consent of his associates. His entitlement is in the quality of the man he is, which includes the ability to get the crown, as it is perceived and approved by his friends. With that consent, he says, he will reign. Within the poetry of the shepherd Tamburlaine's vision are included friendship and of course love. To be accompanied by Zenocrate's beauty and to know the richness of their love are indispensable to his dream of absolute power. Once he is crowned king of Persia he has to demonstrate the spiritual nobility of the man in power, the vision of which has sustained him on the way up. For the rest of Part 1, Marlowe puts to the audience the question whether Tamburlaine's idea of kingship works.

The difficulties assert themselves first over the implacable severity of his treatment of Bajazeth. In one long speech (IV.ii.85–110) Marlowe draws a sharp contrast between the cruelty of the triumphant man in caging the conquered emperor, and the old poetry of foreseeing luxury and riches yet in store, as Tamburlaine's mind dwells on winning the lofty towers of Damascus. The critical point is of course the siege of that city, where our reluctant admiration for the iron will of the man, and the strange splendour with which he clothes it (in the sequence of the colours of his tents as the possibility of mercy for the garrison ebbs away), is challenged by the barbaric cruelty of the slaughter of the virgins. Zenocrate has pleaded for pity for her own people within the city, and Tamburlaine has refused because he will not go back on what he has sworn. It is when he has ordered the death of the virgins that Tamburlaine has his long debate with himself on the claims of beauty on the warrior's soul (V.i.135–91). The beautiful woman whose presence sanctifies conquest and helps to make it beautiful is persuading him to softness and tenderness in the treatment of his enemies.

> What is beauty, saith my sufferings, then?

Most wonderfully, Tamburlaine images beauty as that one thing which would escape definition 'if all the pens that ever poets held' tried to create one poem to celebrate beauty. So far from its being effeminacy for the martial man to respect beauty,

> . . . every warrior that is rapt with love
> Of fame, of valour, and of victory,
> Must needs have beauty beat on his conceits.

It is here, while we wait for Tamburlaine to achieve his resolution of the claims of Mars and Venus, that the syntax of the speech crumbles, and we are left with the lameness of his defiant cry that 'virtue solely is the sum of glory'. But how (for heaven's sake!) does beauty and its tenderness have a place within the concept of *virtu*, or manly virtue? We have got nowhere. Some suspect that the text is corrupt, but it seems more likely that the obscurity of the conclusion of the speech reflects Tamburlaine's inability to reconcile within any programme of action the demands of both beauty and conquest.

At the end of Part 1, Tamburlaine, as prelude to marrying Zenocrate, solemnly crowns her Queen of Persia. This is the ceremonial and symbolic resolution of the conflict which could not be solved in debate. Beauty is married to him within the orbit of kingship:

> So looks my love, shadowing in her brows
> Triumphs and trophies for my victories.   (V.i.510–11)

Tamburlaine's achievements within the play have been magnificent, but everyone would feel, if there were no second part to follow, that Marlowe had left a big question mark on the finality of the spiritual victory of Tamburlaine in proving not merely that he who deserves a crown and is able to gain a crown should wear the crown, but also that kingship was a perfect fulfilment of the whole man.

Part 2 makes its point very heavily. There is a great coarsening of Tamburlaine as his brutalities increase, especially after the death of Zenocrate. That poetry in him which gave a splendour even to his cruelty disappears, and by the side of the cynicism of his son Calyphas he appears heavy, unimaginative, and inflexible. The stabbing of Calyphas shows how far he has gone. All that made him attractive to the audience and to his associates has gone and only a strident megalomania and thirst for conquest remain, reaching insanity at times in his rant against death. That which in the first part fulfilled his spirit is now seen to be killing it. Marlowe intelligently refuses an ending of disaster and retribution which might falsely indicate ways of divine punishment which do not exist. The metamorphosis of Tamburlaine's character in Part 2 is Marlowe's comment on the moral quality of his life. He is not a failure at all; he is a great political success, dying undefeated. But he has betrayed the best in himself in order to keep going. He has also proved his own early visions to be illusions. He has been unable to sustain a magical condition of human life where conquest and power were spiritualised by beauty and knowledge, providing a secure haven for all the energies of man. This condition of life was called kingship, or 'the sweet fruition of an earthly crown'. The mirage vanished, and all that was left for the professional conqueror was the emptiness of perpetual conquest.

If *Tamburlaine* shows the inability of the new masterful men, in their energetic pursuit of power, to make any sense out of the idea of kingship as something of great sacredness and spiritual nobility, one would expect Marlowe, if he wished to portray the other side of the medal, to choose something very different from the reign of Edward II. One would expect someone like Henry VI or Richard II – some saintly medieval figure preoccupied with his hieratic rôle as king, unfit to rule, pushed out of the way by some minor bustling Tamburlaine. I think Shakespeare was of this mind, and wrote *Richard II* to show the dead shepherd how he should have done it. But Marlowe had some kinds of cleverness which Shakespeare did not have, and it is a bolder stroke to choose as his hereditary monarch a figure like Edward II – and then, as Alfred Hart points out, never to mention the divine right of kings throughout the play.[32] It is enough that Edward is king by right according to the laws of the land, and not by conquest. He spends little time in the early part of the play reflecting on the nature of the position he occupies. He is a king and that means that he ought to be able to do exactly as he likes, and that everyone ought to obey him. In particular, if he wishes to lavish time, money, and honours on Gaveston, that is his own business. The attempts of the barons to restrict his authority simply infuriate him. The private world of pleasure and luxury which he thinks his position as king entitles him to is made the more extravagant by being homosexual, thus alienating him from his wife as well as from his barons. The childishness of his absolutism (the expectation, *jure oficii*, without any effort on his own part, of complete obedience) is seen in the dangerous advice of the Spencers and Baldock in III.ii. Young Spencer speaks:

> Were I King Edward, England's sovereign,
> . . .　　. . .　　. . .　　. . .　　. . .
> 　　　　　　　　　would I bear
> These braves, this rage, and suffer uncontrolled
> These barons thus to beard me in my land,
> In mine own realm?　. . .
> Did you regard the honour of your name,
> You would not suffer thus your majesty

> Be counterbuffed of your nobility.
> Strike off their heads, and let them preach on poles;
> No doubt such lessons they will teach the rest
> As by their preachments they will profit much,
> And learn obedience to their lawful king. (ll. 10–23)

Edward eagerly agrees that his trouble is that he has been too mild, and swears to be very tough. Baldock commends him:

> This haught resolve becomes your majesty –
> Not to be tied to their affection,
> As though your highness were a schoolboy still
> And must be awed and governed like a child. (ll. 28–31)

Edward is, like Charles I, a very silly king to rest so much on the privileges of his position, losing the affection of his people thereby, and doing nothing practical in the political or military field to justify the exaggerated awe he expects. The national situation however is nothing like the simple one in *Woodstock*, in which young Richard II is ruining his kingdom to the despair of his good uncle Woodstock, who works tirelessly for the good of the realm. Mortimer's protestations that he is working in the public interest are suspect. He and the barons are proud men, indignant that the King should advance a lowly born upstart to the highest offices in the realm. Mortimer emphatically says that it is not the moral aspect of Edward's relationship with Gaveston that worries him (I.iv.401) but we doubt the sincerity of the patriotic motives he professes. (And of course it later appears that Mortimer is only too keen to take Edward's place – in his bed as well as on his throne.) It is a contest in wounded pride: an indignant king against indignant barons. Yet it becomes clear that Edward, besides the unforgivable political folly of not binding his great lords to him, is seriously neglecting the claims of his kingdom (II.ii), so much so that his loyal brother Edmund temporarily deserts him for the rebels. Edward has an ideal of great luxury as the prerogative of a king, which is a debased version of Tamburlaine's ecstatic dream, and he has absolutely nothing of Tamburlaine's political and military energy and ability, which alone (in Tamburlaine's eyes) could justify the luxury.

So, like Richard II or Lear, by his own foolishness and shortsightedness he creates the situation for his enemies, and they defeat him. And now at last he begins to reflect on the nature of kingship. Gaveston's ''Tis something to be pitied of a king' (I.iv.130) is one of the very few moments in the first four acts of the play when an idea of

kingship, and its consequent ironies, are momentarily glimpsed. As
with Richard II, it is only by being deprived of kingship that Edward
learns what being a king means.

> But what are kings when regiment is gone
> But perfect shadows in a sunshine day?   (V.i.26–7)

This takes in the idea which is in *Tamburlaine* that kingship is defined
by activity, the activity of ruling. But unlike *Tamburlaine*, in which
titular kings could be tossed aside like empty shells, this play concen-
trates on the titular king as a person. The image of 'shadow' is a fine
one for that which has the shape only and not the substance (like Lear
when he has got rid of his land) and it is Edward's first realisation that
royalty is a matter of doing, not being. The physical attributes of
kingship now assume an arresting symbolic power.

> But stay awhile, let me be king till night,
> That I may gaze upon this glittering crown.
> So shall my eyes receive their last content.   (V.i.59–61)

He is asked to resign the kingship. He recognises, however, as
Shakespeare's Richard was to do, that for the hereditary king his
whole identity, his very being and the meaning of his life, are co-
extensive with kingship. To end kingship is to end personality.

> Here, receive my crown.
> Receive it? No, these innocent hands of mine
> Shall not be guilty of so foul a crime.
> He of you all that most desires my blood,
> And will be called the murderer of a king,
> Take it.   (V.i.97–102)

But, like Richard again, he eventually surrenders the crown, seeing
this as the end of his existence.

    The most important part of the play is still to come. At the height of
Edward's and Gaveston's cheerful irresponsibility at the beginning of
the play, they arrested the Bishop of Coventry, who had been responsible for Gaveston's exile. The King showed his malice thus:

> Throw off his golden mitre, rend his stole,
> And in the channel christen him anew.   (I.i.186–7)

(The channel being the open sewer.) He was imprisoned in the
Tower, and in the next scene the Bishop of Canterbury described the
violence against him.

> First were his sacred garments rent and torn,
> Then laid they violent hands upon him, next
> Himself imprisoned and his goods asseized.   (I.ii.35–7)

Edward is now to be the victim of the same delight in degradation which he showed in his sacrilegious violence to the bishop, only to a much fouler degree. Clifford Leech remarked that 'No other tragic figure in Elizabethan or Jacobean literature is treated in the degrading way that Mortimer permits for Edward.'[33] Yet Leech's fine essay concentrated on *Edward II* very much as a non-ideological and non-didactic play, emphasising the sufferings of Edward as an individual human being. It was left to Douglas Cole in *Suffering and Evil in the Plays of Christopher Marlowe* (1962) to remark that

Suffering as it is treated in *Edward II* is a problem caused not only by weakness of character and the cruelty of vicious persons, but by the nature of the sufferer's inherent status and role. The tragic element in Edward's suffering is due less to his humanity than to his kingship.   (p. 184)

Why should Mortimer so much want to grind Edward beneath his heel? His treatment of Edward is another of this play's terrifying anticipations, this time of the methods of the secret police of the twentieth century surely, slowly, unpityingly to destroy a man or woman's dignity, self-respect, and very identity. Marlowe found it all in Holinshed and Stow (except for the actual murderer, Lightborn) but his putting together of Edward's slow progress to the grave is a triumph of art. Edward is not to be allowed to sleep properly: he is to be continually moved at night to another place; he is to receive no kind word or comfort (V.ii.57–65). He is kept in a dungeon without food (V.iii.19–20); he is forcibly washed and his beard shaved off in foul water from a ditch. Then at Berkeley Castle he is kept in a vault up to the knees in sewage for days on end, and so towards the horrible conclusion. In all this, the emphasis is on the *degradation* of the king: that is what it is all about.

> This dungeon where they keep me is the sink
> Wherein the filth of all the castle falls . . .
> And there in mire and puddle have I stood
> This ten days' space. And lest that I should sleep,
> One plays continually upon a drum.
> They give me bread and water, being a king!
> So that for want of sleep and sustenance
> My mind's distempered and my body's numbed:
> And whether I have limbs or no, I know not,

> O would my blood dropped out from every vein
> As doth this water from my tattered robes!
> Tell Isabel the queen I looked not thus
> When for her sake I ran at tilt in France
> And there unhorsed the Duke of Cleremont.   (V.v.55–69)

His emphasis to the end is that he is a king in spite of the loss of everything, and in spite of his appalling experiences.

> Know that I am a king: O, at that name
> I feel a hell of grief! Where is my crown?
> Gone, gone – and do I remain alive?   (V.v.88–90)

And, as he knows he is to be murdered,

> Assist me, sweet God, and receive my soul.   (V.v.108)

The manner of the king's death was known to every member of the audience. It involved a table and a feather-bed, and a red-hot spit was forced up the king's fundament, so that his screams were heard all over the town of Berkeley. All the chronicles gave the details in full. It is a particularly terrible death and the mind can't help dwelling on it. All the implements are called for in the play. Was the death actually mimed on stage, as it is in modern productions? It is a vilely insulting and humiliating death, and as the culmination of a coldly plotted campaign of mental and physical torture against an epicene dilettante of a king it has a revolting aptness.

Why does Mortimer do it? It is not gratuitous, because Mortimer has his reasons for the reduction and later the killing of the King, but the cruelty is out of all proportion to any rational motive. It is the instinctive pollution of the holy office of kingship. Marlowe was cleverer than to make his king a saintly man. He was a bad king whose only thought about his office was the amount of pleasure it ought to afford him, and the amount of obedience he had a right to expect. As Edward himself does not realise what kingship is until it slips away from him, so we realise that we have been in the presence of sacredness only by our comprehending that what we see in the man in tattered robes soaked in ordure is the very image of desecration. *We*, also, don't realise what we have until we have lost it.

Unless Marlowe felt a kind of sacredness in kingship both *Tamburlaine* and *Edward II* are meaningless, and yet neither play talks about it much. The sacredness he drew in from the Tudor air about him, and the ironies he found out for himself. In *Tamburlaine*, in a superbly sympathetic study of the glowing mind of the ambitious shepherd he showed how impossible it was for the self-made Renaissance man of power to make valid by the quality of his life a new sort of secular sacredness in the office of kingship. And in *Edward II* we have a study which seems brilliantly contemptuous of almost everything – of feud-alism, of Stuart absolutism still to come,[34] of Renaissance ambition, of ancient loyalty – but is intensely serious about an idea of desecration and pollution. The fitness of Edward to rule does not seem the whole question, or even a very relevant question, as we watch those last terrible scenes. Mortimer's lust to bring down the man he wants to replace suddenly reveals in the most unlikely figure of the unlovable King Edward the lineaments of an ancient and sacred relic, perceived the moment before it is viciously destroyed.

4

NATION AND EMPIRE

The historical drama as a national literature

The English drama never shows its closeness to the nation more strikingly than in the large body of plays written in the last fifteen years of Elizabeth's reign with English and British history as their subject. If Shakespeare had not engaged himself in the genre, the achievement would be slight, and even taking into account Shakespeare's great contribution there is a coarse ruggedness about this whole area of drama that makes its status as a great national literary movement rather strange. The love of history and the aspiration to glorify one's country with a vernacular epic enshrining its origin, history, and destiny as the *Aeneid* enshrined Rome's were of course standard in the Renaissance, and in 1572 Camoens, in *Os Lusiadas*, had provided for Portugal just such a poem, weaving the history of his country around the unifying theme of Vasco da Gama's discovery of the sea-route to India in 1498.[1] That England's national epic was actually being written without the formality of a poet's design, in the discoveries of its industrious historians and the reports of its sea-adventurers and explorers, was suggested by both William Webbe and Gabriel Harvey, the first just before the Armada, the second after it. In his *Discourse of English Poetry* (1586), Webbe writes:

Now will I speak somewhat of that princely part of poetry, wherein are displayed the noble acts and valiant exploits of puissant captains, expert soldiers, wise men, with the famous reports of ancient times, such as are the heroical works of Homer in Greek and the heavenly verse of Virgil's *Aeneidos* in Latin; which works, comprehending as it were the sum and ground of all poetry, are verily and incomparably the best of all other. To these, though we have no English work answerable in respect of the glorious ornaments of gallant handling, yet our ancient chroniclers and reporters of our country affairs come most near them.[2]

Harvey, writing against Nashe in *Pierce's Supererogation* (1593), is attacking frivolous and wanton literature:

England, since it was England, never bred more honorable minds, more adventurous hearts, more valorous hands, or more excellent wits than of late . . . The date of idle vanities is expired: away with these scribbling paltries . . . The wind is changed, and there is a busier pageant upon the stage . . . But read the report of the worthy western discoveries, by the said Sir Humphrey Gilbert; the report of the brave West Indian voyage by the conduction of Sir Francis Drake . . . the report of the politic discovery of Virginia by the colony of Sir Walter Ralegh; the report of sundry other famous discoveries and adventures, published by M. Richard Hakluyt in one volume, a work of importance; the report of the hot welcome of the terrible Spanish Armada to the coast of England, that came in glory and went in dishonour . . . And when you have observed the course of industry, examined the antecedents and consequents of travail, compared English and Spanish valour . . . who of reckoning can spare any lewd or vain time for corrupt pamphlets . . . ?[3]

Spenser's *The Faerie Queene*, the first three books of which were published in 1590, was certainly a national epic dedicated to the greatness of Britain, with Prince Arthur and Gloriana-Elizabeth at its centre, celebrating the triumph of the Reformation and Elizabethan policy in Ireland; but chivalric and pastoral romance is a restricted means of recording recent history and heroism. Harvey was most discerning in suggesting that the sixteenth-century epic of England is indeed in Hakluyt and other prose accounts. Webbe was slightly off the mark. No one now reads Hall or Holinshed who isn't forced to. The Tudor chroniclers and antiquaries had worked hard and enthusiastically to satisfy the patriotic curiosity of their middle-class readers. 'They recognised that the most brilliant discovery of a brilliant age was the discovery of their own country.'[4] But it is the popular dramatists, pillaging their works, and refashioning their unsound history into plays for the public theatre, who gave England's past its fullest and broadest life in its own day, and made the Elizabethans' consciousness of their history available to all succeeding generations.

The origins of the English historical drama are obscure. F. P. Wilson's famous suggestion that Shakespeare invented and created the genre has not won wide acceptance.[5] D. M. Bevington and Wilbur Sanders, both writing in 1968, thought that the spirit of the earlier history plays was the unpleasant jingoistic xenophobia of the war-fever of Armada days.[6] There is certainly a cheap and unsavoury patriotism in many history plays, with crude and obscene attacks on everything to do with Catholicism, derision of the martial ability of foreigners, and strutting complacency about the justice of the English cause and the invincibility of her soldiers. There is plenty of this sort of fervour in Shakespeare as well, and not only in the Henry VI plays: it lingers into *Henry V*. A definition of Shakespeare's 'patriotism' is the subject of part of this chapter and most of the following one. The most interesting feature of this patriotism may well be the range of the national emotion in his plays; yet the co-existence in his work of patriotic hysteria, genuine pride in his country, and consciousness of error and evil, is not unique. While the English history plays vary as enormously in their attitude to the nation as in their dramatic and literary value, they all have something of that rather bewildering complexity of response to England's history which is so marked a feature of Shakespeare's histories. It would be interesting if we could see anticipated that division of philosophy about a national literature which so troubled the renaissance of Irish literature, between those who wanted a patriotic literature to feed Ireland's pride, and those who wanted to create a great literature for the nation avoiding cheap appeals to crowd-emotion, and the moral and artistic dishonesty which such appeals demand. But it is not that way. There is nothing unmixed in the English history plays.

It is possible to accept that those who created the English history plays had pretty low standards, that they were on the look-out for ready-made plots, that they knew the appeal of the sexual peccadilloes of rulers and great men, that they sought the easy rewards of appealing to the cruder patriotic sentiments and exploiting mass hatred, that in the versions of history they put out they were the mouthpieces of official propaganda, that they were either incompetent or indifferent dramatists. At the same time, amidst all the rant and crudity, something important was being built up. The history plays which Shakespeare and his fellow-dramatists of the professional theatre wrote in the ten years following the Armada must have done a great deal to create a sense of national identity among Londoners and the city-dwellers of England. It is not an exaggeration to say that the English history play provided a 'myth of origin' for the emerging nation. Those who stood or sat within the 'wooden O' of the first London theatres watching *The Troublesome Reign of King John* or *The Famous Victories of Henry V*, or *Edmond Ironside*, or *Richard III*, saw themselves developing as a people, and learned to know who they were by seeing what they had been. We have plenty of witnesses to show how powerful an element these plays were in the nation's life.

The most illustrious are the Earl of Essex and Queen Elizabeth herself. Essex, whom Shakespeare paralleled with Henry V,[7] made his own parallel with the usurper Henry IV when his followers got Shakespeare's company to act *Richard II* at the Globe on 7 February 1601, the day before his abortive rising. That summer, when the Queen was turning over archives with William Lambard, 'her Majesty fell upon the reign of King Richard II, saying, "I am Richard II, know ye not that?" '[8]

Nashe and Heywood we have already looked at as defenders of plays in general, and they are to some extent interested witnesses, but what they have to say, one at the beginning of the period and the other at the end, about the immediacy and vitality of the English history play is remarkable. Nashe, in 1592, talks of 'what a glorious thing it is to have Henry the Fifth represented on the stage leading the French King prisoner and forcing both him and the Dauphin to swear fealty'. Of the subject of the plays of that time he says:

For the most part it is borrowed out of our English chronicles, wherein our forefathers' valiant acts, that have lien long buried in rusty brass and worm-eaten books, are revived and they themselves raised from the grave of oblivion and brought to plead their aged honours in open presence, than which what can be a sharper reproof to these degenerate effeminate days of ours? How would it have joyed brave Talbot, the terror of the French, to think that after he had lien two hundred years in his tomb he should triumph again on the stage, and have his bones new-embalmed with the tears of ten thousand spectators at least, at several times, who in the tragedian that represents his person imagine they behold him fresh bleeding![9]

In Heywood's *Apology for Actors*, published in 1612 but probably written some years earlier, we find the following:

To turn to our domestic histories, what English blood seeing the person of any bold Englishman presented and doth not hug his fame and honey at his valour, pursuing him in his enterprise with his best wishes, and, as being rapt in contemplation, offers to him in his heart all prosperous performance, as if the personater were the man personated? So bewitching a thing is lively and well-spirited action that it hath power to new mould the hearts of the spectators and fashion them to the shape of any noble and notable attempt. What coward to see his countryman valiant would not be ashamed of his own cowardice? What English prince, should he behold the true portraiture of that famous King Edward the Third, foraging France, taking so great a king captive in his own country, quartering the English lions with the French flower-delyce, and would not be suddenly inflamed with so royal a spectacle, being made apt and fit for the like achievement? So of Henry the Fifth.[10]

Heywood touches on the sheer educational value of the history plays:

Plays have made the ignorant more apprehensive, taught the unlearned the knowledge of many famous histories, instructed such as cannot read in the discovery of all our English chronicles. And what man have you now of that weak capacity that cannot discourse of any notable thing recorded, even from William the Conqueror, nay, from the landing of Brute, until this day?[11]

The history in the history plays is totally uncritical about fact and fiction. There is no interest in sifting legendary tales from actual events, and there are astounding manipulations of the existing record in the interests of theatrical convenience, personal prejudice or state propaganda. Nevertheless, a devotion to history, even if it strikes us as a funny sort of history, is a paramount driving force. *The True Tragedy of Richard III*, acted by the Queen's men, possibly about 1591, begins with a meeting of Poetry and Truth.

> *Poetry*. Truth, well met.
> *Truth*. Thanks, Poetry; what makes thou upon a stage?
> *Poetry*. Shadows.
> *Truth*. Then I will add bodies to the shadows . . .

Truth then solemnly recites a history lesson, describes Richard of Gloucester, and then makes way for 'Truth's pageant'. At the end of the play, after Richmond's victory, a messenger gives a short life of Henry VII and Henry VIII – with a little on Mary – and the new queen breaks in to praise Queen Elizabeth herself, the players' patron:

> Then happy England 'mongst thy neighbour isles,
> For peace and plenty still attends on thee,
> And all the favourable planets smiles
> To see thee live in such prosperity.[12]

The first play in Shakespeare's Henry VI series has many rather clumsy history lessons, like this given by the dying Mortimer to Richard Plantagenet, future Duke of York.

> The reason moved these warlike lords to this
> Was, for that – young Richard thus removed,
> Leaving no heir begotten of his body –
> I was the next by birth and parentage;
> For by my mother I derivèd am
> From Lionel Duke of Clarence, third son
> To King Edward the Third; whereas he [Henry IV]
> From John of Gaunt doth bring his pedigree,
> Being but fourth of that heroic line.   (II.v.70–8)

Crude though this may seem, it has an important part in a play devoted to the pulse of history, showing the unceasing flow of deeds and consequences which eventually create the conditions of existence for the actors who impersonate the original historical figures and the audience who watch. They know it all comes home to *them*, because the plays keep rubbing it in.

The range of the English history plays is very wide, as Heywood's comments indicate, from the legendary British period (e.g. *Locrine* and *King Leir*) and the Anglo-Saxons (e.g. *Edmond Ironside*), right up to Heywood's own plays on the life of Queen Elizabeth herself (*If You Know Not Me You Know Nobody*, ?1604). The favourite themes are conquest, as in Peele's *Edward I*, the anonymous *Edward III* and Shakespeare's *Henry V*; resisting invasion, as in *Locrine*, *The Troublesome Reign of King John*; civil war, as in Marlowe's *Edward II* and Shakespeare's Henry IV plays. The deeper political concerns of the best plays – questions of the extent of the monarch's prerogative, the limits of a subject's obedience, the legitimacy of deposing a king – are not the subjects of this chapter, in which I am concerned to show, mainly from Shakespeare, how the drama reflected the growth and expansion of England as it began to develop into Great Britain and the British Empire. It will be clear that in some sense nearly all the history plays touch on this: they are concerned with problems and activities in the national past which reflect, or are made to reflect, contemporary matters. So *The Troublesome Reign of King John* has to do with national independence from international Catholicism up to the point of resisting invasion. The Henry IV plays and *Edmond Ironside* are concerned with the enemy within the gates who threatens national unity. Even a play which deals so severely with royal misrule and so sympathetically with the subjects' resistance to it as the anonymous Richard II play, *Woodstock*, is inspired by the same love of country and anxiety for the preservation of the nation which inspires those plays which deal with civil war as the ultimate evil. Plays which are about the need to maintain the unity and honour of the beloved country against invasion from without, against fragmentation from within, or destruction by tyranny from above, are the obverse side or negative version of those plays which are more obviously concerned with expansion. Not to be divided, not to be destroyed, to stand fast as a proud and integrated England, is the precondition and concomitant of expansion.

In the political sphere it is possible to see a similar complementarity between self-defence and aggrandisement. Between the Reformation and 1642 England incorporated Wales and effected a partial union with Scotland. It fought fierce wars to subdue, assimilate, and colonise Ireland, with the major successes marked by Tyrone's surrender to Mountjoy at Mellifont Abbey in 1603 and the plantation of Ulster. On the eastern coast of the American continent it sought out sites from Newfoundland to the Orinoco to develop and exploit, with the first permanent colony being established in Virginia in 1607, followed by settlements in the Bermudas, the West Indies, and Massachusetts.

A great deal of all this activity could be seen as the necessary consequences of England's statement of its doctrinal position in the 1530s. By setting up a Protestant state you acquire Catholic enemies. So were engendered the years of hostility with Spain, the chief energy of the counter-Reformation and of course the 'owner' of the New World and its riches. It was as necessary for the infant state to secure its naural frontiers against invasion from the sea as to suppress sources of disaffection within the realm, if it were to survive. The idea, therefore, of a single political unit for the great island of England, Wales, and Scotland, was one of great strategic appeal. Ireland, as a Catholic country restive about English control, was a danger from the very beginning of the Reformation, a centre of disaffection and a jumping-off ground for a Spanish invasion. Again, self-preservation made the subduing of Ireland a strategic necessity. As for America, the increasing sea war with Spain made a military and naval base in America very attractive, and much of the early philosophy of colonising had a military tinge.

But securing your frontiers is not done in a vacuum. England was fortunate in its speedy union with Wales, and eventually in its long-drawn out amalgamation with Scotland. But in Ireland every move provoked counter-move. Lives and property were interfered with, and resistance increased. So inevitably the grip was tightened, to retain at least what England started with. Authority was more strongly asserted, 'rebellion' more cruelly suppressed. There was no going back, and the only way forward came to be total conquest and union, depopulation of whole areas and resettlement with non-native loyal peoples.

The protection of the newly declared state may therefore lead inevitably to what looks like expansion. In any case there can be no passiveness, no 'steady state', in the situation. The mission of Protestantism demanded not only common cause with those fighting for their religion and independence from Spain in the Low Countries, but the active extension of the true faith by conversion, particularly in Ireland. And besides the local pugnacity and greed of those engaged in harrying the Spanish treasure fleets at sea, there is, finally and fundamentally, the in-built drive to rival and outgo Spain in wealth and territorial possessions, the sheer momentum of the thing which leads to the idea that it was the destiny of England not to stay still but to grow, to increase her might and power by acquiring more territory, at a time when every voyage brought news of further exploitable lands which others might appropriate if England didn't.

So self-defence, which is also defence of the true faith, merges easily with self-assertion, which is also the spread of the new faith, and with competitive reaching out for new territories. In 1582, Hakluyt wrote in his Preface,

I conceive great hope that the time approacheth and now is that we of England may share and part stakes (if we will ourselves) both with the Spaniard and the Portingale in part of America and other regions as yet undiscovered . . . And surely if there were in us that desire to advance the honour of our country which ought to be in every good man, we would not all this while have forslown the possessing of those lands which of equity and right appertain unto us.

Seventeen years later his exhortations were continuing. 'If . . . it shall please the Almighty to stir up her Majesty's heart to continue with her favourable countenance [renewed efforts in Virginia] . . . she shall by God's assistance, in short space, work many great and unlooked-for effects, increase her dominions, enrich her coffers, and reduce many pagans to the faith of Christ.'[13] And it was not the English only who could feel that there was a kind of general moral necessity for England to expand. In her important book on the Elizabethan attitude to imperialism, *Astraea* (1975), Frances Yates quotes the rhapsodic view of a foreigner, Giordano Bruno.

Of Elizabeth I speak, who by her title and royal dignity is inferior to no other monarch in the world . . . If her earthly territory were a true reflection of the width and grandeur of her spirit this great Amphitrite would bring far horizons within her girdle and enlarge the circumference of her dominion to include not only Britain and Ireland but some new world, as vast as the universal frame, which her all-powerful hand should have full scope to raise a united monarchy.   (p. 85)

In the early growth of the English nation, religious and moral idealism was blended with hard-headed strategies to secure the state, with a lust for a fair share and more of the growing globe, with the ferocity

Colaiste Mhuire Gan Smal
Luimneach

needed to implement an expansionist policy. This mixture produced paradoxes and ironies that take one's breath away. The history plays share these ironies, and it will be necessary to keep in view this continuum between dreams of imperial peace and the realities of brutal massacres.

'Henry V'

Shakespeare's *Henry V*, written in 1599, touches the expansion question at four points. First, the idea that the national unit was not England but the greater geographical unit of England, Wales, and Scotland, that is, Great Britain, to which Ireland is added. Second, the idea of the justice of invasion where there is an ancient right to a territory. Third, the Elizabethan conquest of Ireland. Fourth, the idea of union and peace through conquest.

The idea of 'Britain' was one of the major enthusiasms of Englishmen, and some Welshmen and some Scotsmen, in Tudor and Stuart times. However much they may have shared Polydore Vergil's scepticism about the legend that Britain had been founded by Brut, arriving fresh from Troy via Italy, they accepted as an emotional truth that Britain was the primary unit of the great island, and that the formation of independent nations within Britain was a disintegration which the Tudors and then the Stuarts were doing their best to repair. The idea of the island-unity was of great emotional power, as we shall see, but the confusion created in an Englishman's mind by oscillation between pride in his country, *England*, and the sense that he belonged properly to a larger region, *Britain*, is well illustrated by John of Gaunt's curious reference in *Richard II* to 'this sceptred isle . . . this England'.

Besides confusion, there is some conviction here of the dominance of England. *Henry V* is an English epic. Quite unhistorically, Shakespeare introduced his quartet of the Welsh Fluellen, the Irish Captain Macmorris, the Scottish Captain Jamy, and the English Gower as a tribute to the Tudor idea of Britain as a union of peoples setting out to conquer foreigners, or, as Richard Simpson put it in 1874, 'as if to symbolise the union of the four nations under one crown, and their co-operation in enterprises of honour, no longer hindered by the touchiness of a separatist nationalism'.[14] But the tribute is condescending. Fluellen and Macmorris are in their different ways fine, hard-working, devoted soldiers, but, being Welsh and Irish, they are inevitably made comic. English superiority in this matter is invincible, and the condescension may unfortunately diminish the importance for the play that the happy few, the band of brothers at Agincourt, contains English, Scots, Welsh, and Irish.

The most important moment in this discordant harmony seems generally misunderstood. Captain Macmorris, 'an Irishman, a very valiant gentleman', is right-hand man to the Duke of Gloucester in the siege of Harfleur. Fluellen objects to the lack of a theoretical basis in Macmorris's military work and proposes to him 'a few disputations . . . as partly touching or concerning the disciplines of war'. Macmorris, an impetuous, practical man, eager for action, impatiently rejects the idea: ''tis shame to stand still . . . and there is throats to be cut, and works to be done'. But Fluellen presses forward.

Fluellen. Captain Macmorris, I think, look you, under your correction, there is
    not many of your nation–
Macmorris. Of my nation! What ish my nation? Ish a villain, and a bastard,
    and a knave, and a rascal. What ish my nation? Who talks of my nation?
                                     (III.ii.120–4)

The 'national' edge to this whole interchange is sharpened in the Folio where the speakers' names are given simply as 'Welch.', 'Irish.' The usual interpretation of the exchange is that of W. J. Craig, printed in the old Arden edition of the play, and carried over into the new.

Macmorris, I think, spoiling for a fight, invites them to say one opprobrious word against his country or character or honour; – What are you going to say agin my country now? I suppose you'll be after calling me a villain and a bastard?

The typical Saxon indifference to the realities of Ireland, revealed in the ignorance shown in this paraphrase that the construction 'to be after' doing something refers to the past and not to the future, reflects the insensitivity of the note as a whole. But certainly Shakespeare's own rendering of the comic way he thinks the Irish speak has obscured the quite simple and direct question which Macmorris so explosively asks. 'What is my nation? Who talks of my nation?' Whatever it was that Fluellen was going to ask Macmorris, Macmorris flies off the handle at the sense of discrimination shown by Fluellen's phrase 'your nation'. The paraphrase should run something like this. 'What is this separate race you're implying by using the phrase "your nation"? Who are you, a Welshman, to talk of the Irish as though they were a separate nation from you? I belong in this family as much as you do.' This is the essence of it – indignation that a Welshman should think of Ireland as a separate nation from the great (British) nation which the Welshman apparently thought he belonged to.[15]

In an interesting survey of the Elizabethan use of the Irish in their forces in Ireland, written as background to the Fluellen/Macmorris dispute, Paul A. Jorgensen cleverly called attention to an important anecdote of 1599 recorded in Arthur Collins's *Letters and Memorials of State*, 1746 (ii. 137–8).[16] The author did not follow up the implications of the anecdote, however, and they show that the story is even more important, for the understanding of Macmorris's outburst, and the topical placing of *Henry V*, than he realised.

The anecdote is about an Irish Captain St Lawrence, being examined by Robert Cecil for using 'undecent speeches'. He claimed it was a special irritant to him to be told that 'he was an Irishman':

He said, I am sorry that when I am in England, I should be esteemed an Irishman, and in Ireland, an Englishman. I have spent my blood, engaged and endangered my life, often to do her Majesty service, and do beseech to have it so regarded.

All this he spoke 'with very great reverence to the place, but passionate as a soldier'. Here then is a Macmorris in real life who had apparently lost his temper and defends himself in that he, a loyal servant of the Queen, has been discriminated against as belonging to a separate nation. But how clearly and sadly this little anecdote enshrines the situation of the 'Anglo-Irish' from the sixteenth to the twentieth centuries! Aliens in Ireland and aliens in England – in neither country wholly accepted as of the people. That question, 'What is my nation?', which starts in Shakespeare's play as a furious repudiation of difference, continues down the centuries as an unanswerable problem for generation after generation of Irish people of English and Scottish descent. There was a strange book published in 1925 by an Anglo-Irishman, W. F. P. Stockley, M.A. 'Trinity College, Dublin. One of the Professors of English in the National University of Ireland'. It is called *King Henry the Fifth's Poet Historical*, and it is a rambling, fanatical, and fiercely anti-British book by one who has given a positive answer to the question of his nation. It nevertheless contains perhaps the best discussion of the Macmorris problem. 'Is the Irishman half-ashamed of himself?' he asks (p. 73). 'He has gained contempt from the English, or their complete indifference to him and his, except when called up for use.' Yet Macmorris denies his Irish birthright. 'Whatever were the complex workings in poor Macmorris's pate, his 'nation' was not to be his first thought, if his thought at all; not his boast, if possibly his pain: he himself being bought, or bribed, or promise-crammed, or crammed with bread' (p. 88).

Who was St Lawrence, and what was the incident which caused the 'undecent speeches'? The story occurs in a letter from Rowland Whyte to Sir Robert Sidney, dated 31 October 1599 – a month or two after the presumed date of the writing of *Henry V*. St Lawrence was Sir Christopher St Lawrence, son of Lord Howth. He was clearly a firebrand. But he had fought well in Ireland, and was devoted to Essex.[17] He was in England now because he had accompanied Essex on the latter's impulsive, unauthorised, and fatal return from his Irish campaign to see the Queen. Only a few months before, Essex's appointment to take command in Ireland had been greeted with acclamation in England and in April 1599 he had sailed with the biggest army the Queen had ever sent out of England. It was an appointment which in spite of its great popularity the Queen had made only after much delay and uncertainty. When Essex was in Ireland she bombarded him with letters full of reproaches and complaints, urging him to get on more quickly with his task of destroying the Irish forces under Tyrone. She specifically forbade him to return without her permission. Essex simply did not have the power to destroy Tyrone in battle, and both Essex and Tyrone knew it. Finally the two men met at their famous lone parley on horseback at a ford of the river Lagon, and less than three weeks later Essex was in London, bursting travel-stained into the Queen's bedroom before she was fully dressed, to vindicate himself and remonstrate with her. It was the last time he saw the Queen, and that night he was in custody.[18]

St Lawrence, a fortnight later, was at an ordinary, when he 'took a cup, and drank to the health of my lord of Essex, and to the confusion of his enemies'.[19] For this he was reprimanded by the Lord Treasurer 'but nothing else was done unto him'. Four days later (20 October) he and other close associates of Essex who had come with him from Ireland presented themselves before the Queen. 'She used them very graciously, but told them they had made a scornful journey.'[20] Meanwhile the fuss about St Lawrence's outburst at the ordinary continued, and at the end of the month he made his appearance before Cecil and gave the extenuation already recounted – that he was provoked by being called an Irishman.

Henry V was clearly written in the short time when England was excited at the prospect that the young hero would soon have the Irish licked. The prologue to Act V talks of Henry's triumphant return to England after the great victory of Agincourt – 'Behold . . . how London doth pour out her citizens' –

> As, by a lower but loving likelihood,
> Were now the general of our gracious empress,
> As in good time he may, from Ireland coming,
> Bringing rebellion broachèd on his sword,
> How many would the peaceful city quit
> To welcome him!

Dover Wilson thought that *Henry V* was written as a direct encouragement to Essex 'to become that kind of man, to perform that kind of work for England'.[21] And indeed it seems very likely that this play, so shallow as an exploration of men and power by comparison with contiguous plays like *Henry IV* and *Julius Caesar*, took its life from the exhilaration of battle in prospect, with the curious result that its history in England has been one of strong favour in times of war and general dislike in times of peace.[22]

The line 'Bringing rebellion broachèd on his sword' is very powerful. The abstract idea of rebellion is quickly transmuted to the very concrete image of the body of the rebel spitted on the sword like a chicken, brought back in triumph. 'So perish all traitors!' It is a line full of implications, emphatically placing the Irish as rebels and acknowledging military conquest as the solution of the Irish problem. W. F. P. Stockley wrote as follows:

This Irish question – the English question, rather, of how to rule Ireland, against professed English principles of justice, and support of right, and the good of the governed – had to be staring at Shakespeare, writing of his country's former prowess in the Hundred Years' War, and hearing, daily, of hoped-for triumphs over the Irish of his own day . . . And it is indeed impossible to think that, in *Henry V*, the author had no thoughts of England's settled domination in a 'British Isles', expressed by Irish, Scotch, Welsh captains, serving faithfully under English generals and princes.[23]

One of the most surprising things about the writings of Elizabethan intellectuals about Ireland is their inability to contemplate, even as a thesis to be disproved, that the Irish might have a case for resistance, an inability, even as a dialectical exercise, to put themselves in the Irishman's position and look at the conflict from his point of view. Had he written directly about an Irish 'rebel', as he wrote about a Jew, a black, a savage, Shakespeare would no doubt have shown his sympathies to be superior to those of his time as he did with Shylock, Othello, and Caliban. Or would he be like Ralegh, whose capacity for sympathy and tolerance, so notable when he spoke about the native inhabitants of the Orinoco or Virginia, dried up very rapidly at the edge of the Pale? E. P. Cheyney wrote: 'While Elizabeth and her councillors insisted on addressing the native Irish as "rebels" and "traitors", O'Neill appealed to a wavering fellow-countryman on the ground that "it is lawful to die in the quarrel and defence of the native soil", and that "we Irishmen are exiled and made bond-slaves and servitors to a strange and foreign prince".'[24] No Elizabethan I know has any conception of an Irishman thinking like this. They seem to entertain no doubt of their invincible right to kill those who resist their sway in Ireland. The reason why Spenser's *View of the Present State of Ireland* is such painful reading is not so much his enthusiasm for a quick and ruthless military suppression, including the starvation of the civilian population, as his complete indifference to any view of the Irish except that they were barbarians and rebels. Towards the old English like the Fitzgeralds who had been in Ireland for centuries and grown more Irish than the Irish he shows nothing but shocked indignation, especially in their preference for speaking Irish. 'It is unnatural that any people should love another's language more than their own.'[25] Eudoxus asks, 'Are not they that were once English abiding English still?' When Irenaeus tells him that they have 'degenerated and grown almost mere Irish', he replies, 'Is it possible that an Englishman brought up naturally in such sweet civility as England affords could find such liking in that barbarous rudeness that he should forget his own nature and forgo his own nation?' And later, 'Could they ever conceive any such devilish dislike of their own natural country, as that they would be ashamed of her name, and bite off her dug from which they sucked life?'[26]

For the Gaelic Irish themselves, the 'mere Irish', Spenser had nothing but contempt. He had a very strong dislike of different ways of pasturing cattle, wearing clothes, or cutting hair. Like most Englishmen, he was ignorant of the realities of the Brehon law, which he ridiculed. Their religion he called 'trash'. The right of England in Ireland, Spenser maintained, was that of conquest, not law. They had been conquered in the past, and they must continue to accept English dominance. Resistance had to be crushed completely and Irish ways of life obliterated. The island would have to be colonised when it was defeated. 'All the lands I will give unto Englishmen whom I will have drawn thither . . . Under every of those Englishmen will I place some of those Irish to be tenants.' He would prevent resurgence 'by translating of them, and scattering of them in small numbers amongst the English'.[27]

Part of Spenser's work is a defence of the Deputy, Lord Grey, who was prevented by softer counsels from finishing the job he was doing so well. He was 'blotted with the name of a bloody man, whom who that well knew, knew him to be most gentle, affable, loving, and temperate: but that the necessity of that present state of things enforced him to that violence, and almost changed his very natural disposition'. In particular, Spenser defends Grey for the infamous massacre of the garrison of the Fort del Oro in Smerwick Bay in 1580, after they had surrendered. Spenser is not concerned with the massacre itself, which he does not consider to need a defence, but with the prevalent belief that Grey had broken his word, that he had promised clemency but not granted it. Quarter was never offered, Spenser says. Grey refused the normal rights of prisoners of war because the Spanish soldiers were not licensed and commissioned, and because the people they had come to aid were not lawful enemies but rebels and traitors. He agrees that the garrison craved mercy, which it was 'not thought good to show them, both for danger of themselves [the English], if, being saved, they should afterwards join with the Irish, and also for terror to the Irish, who were much emboldened by those foreign succours'. 'There was no other way,' concludes Spenser, 'but to make that short end of them that was made.'[28] That 'short end' was the hanging and hacking to death of six hundred Spaniards, Italians, and Irish by English troops led by Ralegh and another captain.

The list of atrocities and cruelties committed by the English in Ireland during the Elizabethan war is very long. One is related, with approval, by Thomas Churchyard in his *A General Rehearsal of Wars, called Churchyard's Choice* (1579).[29] It is about Sir Humphrey Gilbert in Munster. It was his practice, says Churchyard,

that the heads of all those . . . which were killed in the day should be cut off from their bodies and brought to the place where he encamped at night, and should be laid on the ground by each side of the way leading into his own tent so that none could come into his tent for any cause but commonly he must pass through a lane of heads, which he used *ad terrorem*, the dead feeling nothing the more pains thereby; and yet did it bring great terror to the people when they saw the heads of their dead fathers, brothers, children, kinsfolk, and friends lie on the ground before their faces, as they came to speak with the said colonel.

The author of the rebellion Shakespeare referred to in *Henry V* was Hugh O'Neill, Earl of Tyrone, who had been brought up in England and who, after his surrender to Mountjoy in 1603, was honourably treated by both Mountjoy and James, who received him at court (though he had to be protected from the angry crowd). Tyrone had so far accepted the idea of English rights in Ireland that he had served in person against the Munster rebels. But he had foolishly imagined that England would allow the great Irish stronghold of Ulster to remain Gaelic under his authority. Eventually, in 1595, he appeared openly in arms to join the great northern chiefs in their rising, and, after his crushing defeat of the English in 1598, he found himself at the head of a national movement threatening to drive the English out of Ireland. It was at this juncture that Elizabeth put her new army in the field, with Essex at its head, to broach rebellion on the sword.

With Essex's failure and disgrace, the lines about him were removed from Shakespeare's play – they do not appear in the Quarto of 1600. The Quarto is a corrupt text but here at least it must reflect the play as it was staged. The scene of the Irish, Welsh, Scottish, and English captains was also omitted, possibly because 'Captain Jamy' seemed an insult to James VI of Scotland.

Having talked about brutality and insensitivity, I shall now try to show some of the ideology which accompanied it. Strategic considerations, which for Elizabeth herself were perhaps dominant, I have already mentioned. The best introduction to the higher view of the English presence in Ireland and elsewhere is in the closing scene of *Henry V*.

Our sense of the justice of the war in France has to survive the tortuousness of the arguments about the Salic law in Act I, and the movingly presented uncertainty of Michael Williams in Act IV – 'But if the cause be not good . . .' But God approves the English cause. It appears to the little, wasted, exhausted English army that their victory at Agincourt over the mighty French is miraculous. There is valour and skill, certainly, but praise is to God alone – 'God fought for us' (IV.viii.116–28). France is ruined. Burgundy (in V.ii) presents a moving picture of the dereliction of the whole country, from agriculture to education. If you want peace, says King Henry,

> you must buy that peace
> With full accord to all our just demands.   (V.ii.70–1)

They accept Henry's terms in full, including his marriage with the French princess, Katharine. These are the concluding speeches of the French King and Queen:

> *French King.* Take her, fair son, and from her blood raise up
> Issue to me, that the contending kingdoms
> Of France and England, whose very shores look pale
> With envy of each other's happiness,
> May cease their hatred, and this dear conjunction
> Plant neighbourhood and Christianlike accord
> In their sweet bosoms, that never war advance
> His bleeding sword 'twixt England and fair France!
> . . . .
> *French Queen.* God, the best maker of all marriages,
> Combine your hearts in one, your realms in one!
> As man and wife, being two, are one in love,
> So be there 'twixt your kingdoms such a spousal
> That never may ill office, or fell jealousy,
> Which troubles oft the bed of blessed marriage,
> Thrust in between the paction of these kingdoms
> To make divorce of their incorporate league –
> That English may as French, French Englishmen,
> Receive each other. God speak this Amen! (V.ii.348–55; 359–68)

The marriage of royal persons is a political cement between kingdoms, and marriage is also a symbol of the union of communities.[30] The defeated French accept their fate, and they see their defeat as the opportunity for the end of hatred and the beginning of love in a real unity symbolised by a marriage. This vision of international concord after conquest is given us by Shakespeare as a moment of rare value, given us indeed as a vision, something which the coarse facts of history will dispel. Immediately after this scene of concord, the Chorus enters to speak the Epilogue, reminding the audience that the issue of the marriage was Henry VI, whose bad advisers

> lost France and made his England bleed –
> Which oft our stage hath shown.

The Epilogue is a curious codicil and it has profound implications in a consideration of Shakespeare's views of history, as I shall argue in the next chapter. Up to that point, Shakespeare's story of what happened in France would be universally accepted as what was to happen in their own times, especially in Ireland. Richard Simpson wrote in 1874 that *Henry V* was 'a glorification of war, not as an agony of brutal passions, but as an agent of civilisation . . . In the camp, the rival nationalities of the Islands are symbolically brought together in friendly co-operation . . . The play ends with the union of the two belligerent countries, a symbol of the coming union with Scotland.'[31]. He might have added Ireland.

The rhapsodies about union which abound in the early seventeenth century very easily incorporate the idea of conquest because of the example of the Roman Empire. The basic notion was that the Britons in the days of their primitive barbarity had the good sense to be conquered and subjugated by the Romans, and so entered that great civilising community of nations, the Roman Empire. Camden, in his *Britannia*, told how the Romans 'reduced the natural inhabitants of the island unto the society of civil life'.

The brightness of that most glorious empire chased away all savage barbarism from the Britons' minds, like as from other nations whom it had subdued. For Rome, as saith Rutilius,

> – *Legiferis mundum complexa triumphis*
> *Foedere communi vivere cuncta facit*
> Compassed the world with triumphs bringing laws;
> And all to live in common cause doth cause.[32]

Philip Brockbank (in an article on *The Tempest*) notes Purchas's marginal comments to Strachey's account of Virginia:

Were not we ourselves made and not born civil in our progenitors' days? And were not Caesar's Britons as brutish as Virginians? The Roman swords were best teachers of civility to this and other countries near us.[33]

The romantic attraction of the Renaissance to the Roman Empire, for its achievement of uniting barbarous and warring peoples into a world-wide civilised community, living at peace under the Roman law, has been described for us by Frances Yates in her book *Astraea*. She shows how some Elizabethans began to see themselves as the new Romans, spreading 'an empire of purified religion'. 'Tudor imperialism is a blend of nascent nationalism and surviving medieval universalism.'[34] There is no doubt at all of the powerful appeal of the idea of nations forgetting their idiosyncracies and their hatred, and combining into an empire with a single language, religion, and way of life. There is no doubt either that the example of the Romans made conquest seem a reasonable means to an end in the eyes of those who were not at all narrowly nationalist nor aggressively imperialist (in the modern sense of the word). The excitement over union increased greatly when James I acceded to the throne. His accession brought about a union (to some extent) of Scotland and England, and he had the great good luck to inherit the final triumph of Elizabeth's army in Ireland. He was himself one of the rhapsodists, and a most articulate advocate of the principle of union.

In his speech to Parliament in the first year of his reign he spoke of the union of Scotland and England as 'that union which is made in my blood'.

Yea, hath He not made us all in one island, compassed with one sea? . . . These two countries . . . now in the end and fulness of time united, the right and title of both in my person . . . whereby it is now become like a little world within itself. . . What God hath conjoined then, let no man separate. I am the husband, and all the whole isle is my lawful wife; I am the head, and it is my body; I am the shepherd, and it is my flock.

He leaves us in no doubt that, as implied in the phrase 'fulness of time' above, he sees larger communities as in the nature of things.

Many of these little Kingdoms are now in process of time, by the ordinance of God, joined into great monarchies, whereby they are become powerful . . . Even as little brooks lose their names by their running and fall into great Rivers, and the very name and memory of the great rivers swallowed up in the ocean; so by the conjunction of divers little kingdoms in one are all these private differences and questions swallowed up.[35]

When the man who spoke this was born, his mother, Mary Queen of Scots, said to Sir William Stanley, 'This is the son whom I hope shall first unite the two kingdoms of Scotland and England.'[36] The lyricism about the import of his accession and his policies of union and peace is well charted and we shall come to it again in discussing Jonson, but, to give something of the spirit of the time, Camden spoke of James 'in whose person the two mighty kingdoms of England and Scotland, hitherto severed, are now conjoined, and begin to close together into one, in their most antient name of Britain'.[37] And Daniel, in a 'Panegyric Congratulatory' of 1603, said that England could never be 'entire in her full orb till now'.

> Now thou art all great Britain, and no more,
> No Scot, no English now, nor no debate.

To return, then, to Ireland; she had refused for over half a century to accept the benefits of belonging to a larger community and accepting common laws and a common language. Why *would* they not see the beauty and the truth of it? It was clear from their strangely different customs and archaic ways of doing things that they were uncivilised, and the religion which, unlike the mystified Welsh, they refused to surrender, was clearly false. The analogy of the Romans conquering, assimilating, and civilising the ancient Britons was constantly in the minds of the English, and the contrast between the compliance of the Britons in surrendering their primitive ways and the obstinacy of the Irish was infuriating. Sir John Davies, the poet, became Attorney-General for Ireland and was concerned both with the banishing of Catholic priests and the plantation of Ulster. In 1612 he published his fascinating book, *A Discovery of the True Causes why Ireland was never entirely subdued, nor brought under obedience of the Crown of England until the beginning of his Majesty's happy reign*. He most curiously uses the terms 'conquest' and 'subjection' to indicate the state of a nation which has become civilised within an empire. If in the past, he says, Ireland had been brought under English law, 'there had been a perfect union betwixt the nations, and consequently, a perfect conquest of Ireland' (p. 112). He describes how the Romans made the ancient British as Roman as they could, 'and so being come to the height of civility, they were thereby brought to an absolute subjection (p. 126). Now, in James's reign, a genuinely common culture based on common law was being established – the guarantee of true union.

Moreover, these civil assemblies at Assizes and Sessions have reclaimed the Irish from their wildness, caused them to cut off their glibs and long hair; to convert their mantles into cloaks; to conform themselves to the manner of England in all their behaviour and outward forms . . . So as we may conceive and hope, that the next generation will in tongue and heart and every way else become English; so as there will be no difference or distinction but the Irish Sea betwixt us.
(pp. 271–2)

The idea that getting rid of cultural differences, especially languages, was a goal to be striven for is now so strange to us that it is worth recalling that only a generation ago it was the ideal of the United States, *e pluribus unum*. That part of the Bible most ignored used to be the Sermon on the Mount and is now the story in Genesis II of the Tower of Babel: 'The whole earth was of one language and of one speech.' And men built a tower to reach unto heaven, so that God said 'now nothing will be restrained from them which they have imagined to do'. So He confounded their language, that they might not understand one another's speech and scattered them abroad upon the face of the earth. The trouble with the ideal of taking off the curse of Babel is that imposing a common culture by edict backed up by force is indistinguishable from brutal suppression. The union of Wales with

England was ardently desired by many Welshmen who were unfailingly loyal to the Welsh Tudors, and indeed some of them petitioned Henry VIII to be allowed 'the same laws and privileges which your other subjects enjoy'. They believed the difference of the languages of the two countries was no bar. 'Your highness will have but the more tongues to serve you.' They did not reckon on Elizabethan ideas of order. The 1536 Act of Union was completed in 1542 when Welshmen received full rights of citizenship, but all the work in all courts was to be in the English tongue, and no Welsh-speaker was to have any office 'unless he or they use and exercise the English speech and language'. The immediate result of this was that the people, almost entirely Welsh-speakers of course, felt that instead of joining a larger privileged community they had been put under alien rule.[38]

Every Englishman who wrote on the subject of union stressed the need for a totality of shared culture. Spenser wrote:

It hath been ever the use of the conqueror to despise the language of the conquered, and to force him by all means to learn his. So did the Romans always use.

. . .   .

I think it best by an union of manners and conformity of minds to bring them to be one people, and to put away the dislikeful concept both of the one and the other.[39]

The idea that the differences between united nations should become indistinguishable is strong in all King James's writings. In *Basilikon Doron* he spoke of 'so mixing through alliance and daily conversation the inhabitants of every kingdom with other as may with time make them to grow and weld all in one' (1603 edn, p. 149). In 1607, urging union with Scotland before a stony Parliament, he said, 'I desire a perfect union of laws and persons, and such a naturalizing as may make one body of both kingdoms under me your king.'[40]

Bacon's *Brief Discourse* of 1603, *Touching the Happy Union of the Kingdoms of England and Scotland*, describes the movement towards union as a law of nature by which new and inseparable substances are made. He cites Machiavelli's theory that the main cause of the growth of the Roman Empire was 'that the state did so easily compound and incorporate with strangers'. States that have not had this facility have 'kept alive the seed and roots of revolts and rebellions, for many ages'. The secret is the totality of the union – 'union in name, union in language, union in laws, and union in employments'.

'*Cymbeline*'

The vision of the complete loss of individual national identity in perfect union between nations lived awkwardly with a prevalent image of the separateness of Britain; and Shakespeare makes a strong point of the incompatibility of the two in *Cymbeline*. The national and imperial dimensions of this curious play of Shakespeare's later years have been very fully discussed in recent times.[41] In particular, it has been pointed out that one of the few important things about the reign of Cymbeline, King of Britain, was that it coincided with the birth of Christ, Prince of Peace, at a time when the whole world was at peace under the Emperor Augustus – the *pax romana*; thus, with its concluding mood of a victorious Britain at peace with the world, the play was particularly appropriate for the King's own players to put on as a tribute to their royal master, the peacemaker. I do not want to open all these matters again, but wish to show how the play's well-known political gestures take a rather different emphasis when they are seen in the light of the concerns of this chapter on nation, union, and empire.

The image I spoke of is of Britain as a world divided from the world. It was a favourite with Jonson, who in the *King's Entertainment* for James's coronation showed Monarchia Britannica as a woman with a globe in her lap inscribed '*Orbis Britannicus*. And beneath, the word *Divisus ab Orbe*. To show that this empire is a world divided from the world'.[42] Jonson used the idea in several of his masques, most notably in *Love Freed from Ignorance and Folly* (1611) where it is central, as the subject of the Sphinx's riddle:

> you must cast about
> To find a world the world without.

This Love does quite easily:

> 'Tis done, 'tis done. I have found it out,
> Britain's the world the world without. (*HS*, VII, pp. 364, 368)

The origin and wide extent of the idea are discussed by J. W. Bennett in an essay, 'Britain Among the Fortunate Isles' (*Studies in Philology*, vol. 53, 1956), and by Edgar Wind in *Pagan Mysteries of the Renaissance* (revised edn, 1967, pp. 222–30). The origin of the saying, it was said, was in the surprise of the Romans when they reached the sea at the northern edge of the continent and found that there was another world beyond. Virgil in his first Eclogue gave the first literary expression, *et penitus toto divisos orbe Britannos* (line 66: the Britons quite cut off from all the world). The many examples and versions of the saying in the sixteenth and seventeenth centuries collected by J. W. Bennett and Edgar Wind are supplemented by Bernard Harris in his essay on *Cymbeline* (see note 39). Everyone used the idea approvingly; it ministered to a pride in self-sufficiency and in an isolation considered to be redeeming. The only disparaging version I know is Imogen's in *Cymbeline* (III.iv).

Pisanio has just told Imogen – they are near Milford Haven – of his letter from Posthumus accusing her of adultery and ordering him to kill her. Pisanio suggests that he tell Posthumus that he has carried out his orders. But what then will Imogen do? 'Where bide? How live?' she asks. She refuses to go back to the court.

> Pisanio.   If not at court,
> Then not in Britain must you bide.
> Imogen.   Where then?
> Hath Britain all the sun that shines? Day? Night?
> Are they not but in Britain? I' th' world's volume
> Our Britain seems as of it, but not in't:
> In a great pool, a swan's nest. Prithee think
> There's livers out of Britain.
> Pisanio.   I am most glad
> You think of other place . . .

And he suggests that in disguise she should tag on to the Roman envoy and get to Rome, where Posthumus is.

I take it that at this point Imogen is plucking up her courage and putting the best face possible on things. She has just been disowned by her husband, and her life has no centre. The British court is a hateful place, where live her father who has banished her husband, and her would-be lover, the loutish Cloten. She defiantly says, 'Well, Britain's not the only place in the world – though to listen to them, you'd think it was.' The slighting reference to this rickety isolation of the swan's nest seems a direct comment on Cloten's patriotic defiance of Caius Lucius, the Roman envoy, in III.i:

Britain's a world by itself, and we will nothing pay for wearing our own noses.

Imogen's little piece has its own circumstantial explanation and she might have spoken differently about Britain at another time. But in the play as a whole her sharp little comment on British insularity has a most important place.

Shakespeare made up the political picture of *Cymbeline* with great clarity, cutting pieces out of Holinshed and joining them up to suit himself. We are given the several successive stages of the relationship between a subject nation and an imperial power. There was the time when as a free country Britain valiantly fought the Romans. This was the time of Posthumus's father, who 'served with glory' the British kings in the defence of their country. Posthumus's two elder brothers 'died with their swords in hand' in the same wars (I.i.28–36). But the Romans won, and the British agreed to pay annual tribute to the conquerors. The Romans (with the obvious exception of Iachimo) are presented throughout as urbane, civilised, courteous and honourable people. Subjects and conquerors mixed to the extent that Cymbeline spent much of his youth under Caesar (who knighted him) and learned honour from him (III.i.69–70). With curious forgetfulness, Shakespeare makes Posthumus's father (who was supposed to have died with grief at the death of his sons) go on to fight in the Roman army. (Philario in Rome says, 'his father and I were soldiers together' (I.iv.26).) In I.iv, the nations are all represented as living at their ease in the imperial capital. Philario and Iachimo are with 'a Frenchman, a Dutchman, and a Spaniard', and they are joined by the Briton, Posthumus.

But in spite of the sense of a harmonious international community, ominous cracks are beginning to appear in the Roman Empire. Shakespeare had read in his Holinshed how Augustus had more than once been diverted from his purpose to visit England to see about neglected tribute because of risings elsewhere within the empire.

But here receiving advertisements that the Pannonians, which inhabited the country now called Hungary, and the Dalmatians, whom now we call Slavons, had rebelled, he thought it best first to subdue those rebels near home, rather than to seek new countries, and leave such in hazard whereof he had present possession, and so, turning his power against the Pannonians and Dalmatians, he left off for a time the wars of Britain. (1587 edn, vol. 1, p. 32)

And a second time, 'the Sallasians (a people inhabiting about Italy and Switzerland), the Cantabrians and Asturians, by such rebellious stirs as they raised withdrew him from his purposed journey'. Holinshed gives a strong impression of the heavy responsibility laid upon Augustus to maintain continuous control of an empire which would otherwise fall apart. Shakespeare seized upon these Pannonians and Dalmatians and used them economically and brilliantly to suggest what is not in Holinshed at all, a sense of an empire restive with militant nationalist movements, a brief but uncanny anticipatory glimpse of the situation in the Iberian and British empires centuries later. Cymbeline tells Caius Lucius

> I am perfect
> That the Pannonians and Dalmatians for
> Their liberties are now in arms: a precedent
> Which not to read would show the Britons cold.   (III.i.72–5)

It was Caesar's ambition, says Cymbeline, that moved him, and 'against all colour' – without even a pretext – he

> Did put the yoke upon's; which to shake off
> Becomes a warlike people, whom we reckon
> Ourselves to be.   (III.i.51–3)

Cymbeline justifies his defiance as an attempt to restore the old British laws under which they used to live: this is the precise rejection of the ideal of common culture which was the spirit of the English imperialism.

> Say then to Caesar
> Our ancestor was that Mulmutius which
> Ordained our laws, whose use the sword of Caesar
> Hath too much mangled; whose repair, and franchise,
> Shall (by the power we hold) be our good deed,
> Though Rome be therefore angry.   (III.i.53–8)

So Cymbeline. Posthumus also, in Rome, has spoken with confidence of Britain's being able to stand up to Rome. The Britons were always courageous, but now they have added order and discipline:

> – they are people such
> That mend upon the world.   (II.iv.25–6)

But it is notorious that the two characters to whom Shakespeare gives the task of uttering the strongest nationalist defiance are the two villains of the play, the Queen and her son Cloten.

> *Queen.*   Remember, sir, my liege,
> The kings your ancestors, together with
> The natural bravery of your isle, which stands
> As Neptune's park, ribbed and paled in
> With rocks unscaleable and roaring waters,
> With sands that will not bear your enemies' boats,
> But suck them up to th' topmast. A kind of conquest
> Caesar made here, but made not here his brag
> Of 'came, and saw, and overcame'. With shame

(The first that ever touched him) he was carried
From off our coast, twice beaten: and his shipping
(Poor ignorant baubles!) on our terrible seas,
Like egg-shells moved upon their surges, cracked
As easily 'gainst our rocks. For joy whereof
The famed Cassibelan, who was once at point
(O giglot fortune!) to master Caesar's sword,
Made Lud's town with rejoicing-fires bright,
And Britons strut with courage.

Cloten. Come, there's no more tribute to be paid: our kingdom is stronger than
it was at that time: and (as I said) there is no more such Caesars, other of
them may have crook'd noses, but to owe such straight arms, none.

Cymbeline. Son, let your mother end.

Cloten. We have yet many among us can gripe as hard as Cassibelan. I do not
say I am one, but I have a hand. Why tribute? Why should we pay
tribute? If Caesar can hide the sun from us with a blanket, or put the
moon in his pocket, we will pay him tribute for light; else, sir, no more
tribute, pray you now.   (III.i.16–45)

Perhaps it is no offence to say, of a drama in which he plays so many
games, that Shakespeare is here playing a double game. He is reaping
the harvest of an appeal to the cruder emotions of national pride and
self-assertion, but he is insuring himself so that he can reap the
harvest of an appeal to the nobler emotions of international co-
operation and national self-denial. At this point we should remind
ourselves of the extraordinary ending of the play. The Romans bring
an army against the recalcitrant Britons, but they are defeated,
largely because of the sudden intervention of the missing sons of
the King, assisted by Posthumus. After the breathtaking poly-
anagnorisis of the final scene, the soothsayer interprets the riddle as
meaning that the reunion of the royal family 'promises Britain peace
and plenty'.

> *Cymbeline.*   Well,
> My peace we will begin: and, Caius Lucius,
> Although the victor, we submit to Caesar,
> And to the Roman empire; promising
> To pay our wonted tribute, from the which
> We were dissuaded by our wicked queen,
> Whom heavens in justice both on her and hers
> Have laid most heavy hand.
>   . . .   .
>
>   Laud we the gods
> And let our crooked smokes climb to their nostrils
> From their blest altars. Publish we this peace
> To all our subjects. Set we forward: let

A Roman and a British ensign wave
Friendly together. So through Lud's town march,
And in the temple of great Jupiter
Our peace we'll ratify, seal it with feasts.
Set on there! Never was a war did cease
(Ere bloody hands were washed) with such a peace.

(V.v.458–65; 476–85)

This submission to an enemy whom you have just defeated, including
the grant of the tribute whose refusal caused the war to be fought, is
certainly weird. In his very interesting study of *Cymbeline* in *The Crown
of Life* (1947), Wilson Knight argued that Cymbeline has to learn to
reject the Queen's and Cloten's ideas of national integrity.

> Britain's integrity is to be no hot-headed self-assertion; it must learn to reject
> such influences as the Queen and Cloten; and to recognise, but freely, its
> Roman inheritance and obligation.   (p. 139)

Knight also makes the excellent point that the 'massive union' of
Rome and England proposed by Cymbeline is 'not unlike the union of
lovers in a happy-ending romance'; it is 'a kind of majestic marriage,
where we are to imagine that the partners "lived happily ever afterwards"'. So Knight sees the movement from national defiance as a
progress, and the ending as a free, as opposed to enforced, acceptance
of the Roman inheritance, by one who is now partner more than
subject. But he goes further. The presentation of Iachimo as a corrupt
Renaissance Italian indicates, he feels, Shakespeare's conception of
the degeneracy of Rome. He argues that the contrary depiction of
Posthumus, with the symbolism of the Roman eagle winging its way
to the west and vanishing in the sunbeams, twice referred to
(IV.ii.346; V.v.471), indicates that Britain is taking over from Rome.
'The heritage of ancient Rome falls on Britain' – Jupiter's blessing
and the Soothsayer's vision 'symbolize a certain transference of virtue
from Rome to Britain'.

I think Knight's reading essentially right, and my interpretation of
the 'swan's nest' passage supports his view, but I think he averts his
eyes from the thin ice Shakespeare skates on so expertly. It is at least a
lucky escape. There is a bridge in the play when a defiance which
struts, to use Cloten's word, with a blustering insularity becomes a
display of vital national adulthood and virtue. This is the moment
when the King's lost sons join the battle and turn certain defeat into
amazing victory. Shakespeare has used his audience's patriotism to

approve the defiance of the Romans; but he has left the more discerning among them uncomfortable because of the rôle of the brutish clown Cloten as nationalist spokesman. The British defiance is a blend of truculent jingoism in the Queen and Cloten, and a much more sensitive but wrong-headed emotional attachment to ideas of freedom and national independence in Cymbeline. At this time, Britain is not herself. The Queen is working to make Cloten the King (III.v.65). The true princes are in Wales, and when, having killed Cloten, the false heir, they return to their father bringing all the strength which their primitive upbringing symbolises, that war which was the necessary consequence of arrogance and shortsightedness becomes the assertion of Britain's right to be accepted as an equal partner with Rome. The audience has no need to jettison its patriotic responses, and most of them, having no qualms about them, would probably not have realised what a drastic gear-change has occurred. Britain was in earlier years defeated by the Romans; she has, as Posthumus has said, and no doubt largely because of the Roman experience, grown in order and discipline, and when her missing princes return we have to accept that a war which should never have happened is transmuted into a sort of courtly trial of strength, a rerun of the earlier battle with an entirely different result. Britain now has the moral strength conferred on her by her display of physical strength. Having won the battle, she is free to abandon the nationalist intransigence which caused it, surrender the separatist claim and as an adult partner enter into a free union with Rome. It was necessary for Britain to prove that her acceptance of the tutelage of Rome was an unconstrained act, and not the result of conquest. So in a sense it was a good thing that Cymbeline was so misguided as to defy Rome.

I find it difficult to accept Knight's idea of Britain taking over from Rome. Iachimo is a corrupt Roman and he repents. Cloten is a villainous Briton and he is killed. Although there can be no doubt that some in the Jacobean audience would indeed see themselves as the successors of Rome, the play is not talking about the succession of empires but about the only true form of empire, which is when vassalage is removed, and union is a contract freely entered into. The marriage between states after a war is very similar at the close of both *Cymbeline* and *Henry V*. In the latter play, the marriage, however desirable, was forced upon the conquered by the conqueror. In *Cymbeline*, the war was fought to secure a divorce, and when the war was won, the marriage was renegotiated on different terms. So far as I understand it, *Cymbeline* implies a total rejection of the prevalent idea of civilising Ireland by conquest, and a rejection of the Roman analogy which was used to justify the idea. Those critics who maintain that *Cymbeline* was written by Shakespeare as a tribute to the pacific policies of James and his belief in world peace may wish to reflect on how diametrically opposed to the spirit of the ending of *Cymbeline* were the policies being actively and personally pursued by James in Ireland at the very time when Shakespeare was writing his play. These policies are briefly discussed in the section which follows.

Ben Jonson

We have no contribution of Jonson's to the English historical drama. Henslowe paid him in 1599 for part of a tragedy he was writing in collaboration with Dekker, Chettle, and others on 'Robert II, King of Scots', but it is not extant. Nor is 'Richard Crookback', in earnest of which, together with 'new additions for *Jeronimo*', Henslowe paid him £10 in 1602 (*HS*, XI, p. 308). There is no evidence that either of these plays was finished. A scheme for a play on the reign of Edward III called 'Mortimer His Fall' exists, with a rather novel use of a chorus, together with fragments of the opening scenes. These relate Mortimer's self-congratulation on his advancement and the amorous speech of the besotted Queen Mother (*HS*, VII, pp. 55–62). Jonson told Drummond of Hawthornden that he was going to write an epic poem called 'Heroologia' of the worthies of England, 'and was to dedicate it to his country' (*HS*, I, p. 132). A history of Henry V's reign, 'eight of his nine year', went up in smoke when his lodgings caught fire in 1623 (*HS*, VIII, p. 207). Of course, with *Catiline* before us, some might say that it is just as well Jonson didn't write English history plays, to which one has to ask whether in fact the superb power of *Sejanus* does not contain currents of feeling about government which given a local habitation in English history would have exploded all allowed limits of literary freedom (see below, Chapter 6, pp. 172–3). What Jonson has to say about nation, union, and empire he says in his masques and entertainments and is therefore solely the official story. The absurdly complacent survey of the achievements of the kings of England in *Prince Henry's Barriers* (1609), for example, might be compared with the acidulous review of the same subject being written at the same time, by James's prisoner in the Tower, Ralegh, in the Preface to his *History of the World*.

In 1606, he used the marriage of Lady Frances Howard to the Earl of Essex as a vehicle for exploring the mystical beauty of the political union which James's accession had brought about. D. J. Gordon's essay of 1945 exhaustively investigated the subtleties of Jonson's 'masque of union' and his use of the symbol of marriage to illuminate political union and to refer both to divine truth. But it has to be said that the disastrous failure of the actual marriage and the ugliness of its consequences (see pp. 167–70) are a dreadful warning of the gulf between ideals and reality in politics as in human relations. The beauty of union and the peacefulness of James were not so apparent either in Ulster or the highlands of Scotland as they were in Whitehall.[43] James's welcome to Tyrone in London was not followed by a live-and-let-live policy. The civilising of barbarous Ireland meant the extinction of everything that was Irish. In 1605 James committed himself to the absurdity of making Ireland Protestant, and refusing to tolerate Catholicism. This he hoped to do without persecution but he could not do it without force; he was therefore less than thorough and succeeded only in arousing hatred everywhere. In the north, the Deputy, Sir Arthur Chichester, was working hard to curtail the power of the great Gaelic chieftains, to anglicise the administration and introduce English and Scottish settlers. Increasing suspicion of James's policies led to the dramatic 'flight of the Earls' in 1607. Tyrone and Tyrconnel suddenly and secretly left their native land. They intended to recruit help from abroad, but none was to be had and they never returned. After his initial alarm at the prospect of a Spanish invasion, Chichester prepared to take advantage of the tremendous boon to England of the flight of the great landowners, and advanced a scheme for dividing the greater part of the land among the native Irish, and colonising the rest with English and Scots. But a short-lived insurrection by Cahir O'Doherty put paid to such a generous settlement. James accepted the plan for a thoroughgoing plantation of Ulster by 'undertakers', which left very little of the forfeited lands to the inhabitants. In addition very many Scots were brought under different arrangements to counties Antrim and Down. On the question before James, whether to put into operation Chichester's scheme or the more extreme one, S. R. Gardiner said way back in 1863, 'It is not too much to say that upon this apparently simple question the whole of the future fate of Ireland depended.' And of the immediate consequence of the tragic choice which James made, he wrote that the Irish who continued to live in Ulster, 'too useful to be removed', 'remained to feel that they were in bondage to an alien race. They knew that they were despised as barbarians by men who had robbed them of their lands.'[44] So modern Ulster with its terrible legacy of hatred and death came into being, in the name of union, peace, and civilisation.

Jonson's official comment on James's Irish policies is in his *Irish Masque at Court*, which he wrote for the second marriage of Lady Frances Howard with Somerset at Christmas and New Year 1612–13, after her scandalous divorce from Essex. Once the King was seated, actors from the King's company dressed up as Irish footmen rushed in looking for King 'Yamish'. When they find him, they address him:

> – Pleash ty shweet faish, vee come from Ireland.
> – Vee be Irish men, and't pleash tee.
> – Ty good shubshects of Ireland, an't pleash ty mayesty.
> – Of Connough, Leymster, Ulster, Munster.   (ll. 48–53)

They tell the King, 'Be not angry vit te honesh men, for te few rebelsh, and knavesh . . . For, by Got, tey love tee in Ireland.' They dance 'to the bagpipe and other rude music' and then their Irish masters enter, wearing Irish cloaks. They dance 'to a solemn music of harps'. A 'civil gentleman' of Ireland then brings in a Bard and speaks thus:

> Advance, immortal Bard, come up and view
> The gladding face of that great king, in whom
> So many prophecies of thine are knit,
> This is that James of which long since thou sung'st,
> Should end our country's most unnatural broils.
> And if her ear, then deafened with the drum,
> Would stoop but to the music of his peace,
> She need not with the spheres change harmony.
> This is the man thou promised should redeem,
> If she would love his counsels as his laws,
> Her head from servitude, her feet from fall,
> Her fame from barbarism, her state from want,
> And in her all the fruits of blessing plant.   (ll. 153–65)

The Bard sings to two harps, urging the Irish masquers to bow in full obedience – 'You'll feel yourselves changed by-and-by.' During this song the masquers drop their Irish cloaks, and reveal themselves in their 'masquing apparel'. This is the sign that by obedience and subjection they have become civilised. They have dropped their outlandish and separatist garments and accepted not merely the English dress but participation in the formal ceremony of the masque at court, in which the English court strove to give symbolic expression to the nation's very being.

Jonson was ever an enthusiast for the idea of Great Britain, as for example he shows in a poem for King Charles's birthday in 1632.

> This is King Charles his day. Speak it, thou Tower,
> Unto the ships, and they from tier to tier,
> Discharge it 'bout the island in an hour,
> As loud as thunder, and as swift as fire,
> Let Ireland meet it out at sea, half-way,
> Repeating all Great Britain's joy, and more,
> Adding her own glad accents to this day.   (*HS*, VIII, p. 249)

Before he became an official mouthpiece, however, Jonson unwisely shared in writing a play dealing very satirically with England's new British partners north of the border, and with the extension of her empire in Virginia. This was the play *Eastward Ho!*

'Eastward Ho!'

In February 1610 William Crashaw, father of the poet, and a contentious divine, preached a famous sermon in London before Lord de la Warr, Lord Governor and Captain General of Virginia, when the latter was about to set sail to bring succour to the ailing colony at Jamestown. The Virginia Company had received its charter in 1606 and what turned out to be the first permanent settlement of Englishmen on the American continent was established in the following year. After the total disappearance of Ralegh's 1587 colonists on Roanoke Island, there had been many attempts to gain a foothold. Ralegh himself sent off Samuel Mace on yet another reconnaissance of Virginia in 1602. In the same year, Bartholomew Gosnold led an expedition to northern Virginia – later called New England. They had trouble on return with Ralegh's exclusive claim over the entire area. Martin Pring explored the Cape Cod area in 1603. He was followed in 1605 by Captain George Weymouth, whose expedition, partly to reconnoitre for a Catholic colony, was financed by the Earl of Southampton and Lord Thomas Arundell among others. None of these ventures was able to establish a colony. The Virginia Company aimed further south, nearer Ralegh's earlier colony. The troubles of the Jamestown colonists were largely of their own making. They were constitutionally incapable of the simple enough matter of sowing corn, and of the much more difficult but essential task, enjoined upon them, of creating a *modus vivendi* with the Indian inhabitants on whose goodwill and assistance their lives depended. E. S. Morgan, in his brilliant book, *American Slavery, American Freedom: The Ordeal of Colonial Virginia* (1975), tells the frightening story of the punitive expedition of George Percy, brother of the Earl of Northumberland (pp. 73–4). The idea was to punish Powhatan, the powerful Indian ruler, for returning 'proud and disdainful answers' to enquiries whether he had harboured a runaway Englishman. Percy took a troop to the nearest tribe he could find, killed a dozen or so Indians, captured the queen and her children, burned the houses and cut down the corn. In the boat going home men protested against carrying the captives, so the children were thrown overboard and their brains blown out in the water. On return to the settlement, Percy was told that he should not have brought the queen back alive. He declined to burn her alive, and she was stabbed to death. Morgan comments wonderingly on the 'suicidal impulse' to 'destroy the corn that might have fed them and to commit atrocities upon the people who grew it'. Morgan's book has important implications for *The Tempest* and we shall come back to it.

In 1609 nine ships set out from England with huge reinforcements of men and provisions for the colony. Even more important, however, was the presence of Sir Thomas Gates and Sir George Somers; they had been appointed under Lord de la Warr to govern the colony and were going ahead of the General. The ship containing the commissioners was wrecked in the Bermudas. Many months later, Gates made his way to Jamestown and found everything in confusion. The only person capable of organising the colonists, John Smith, had given up and left for England. The decimated colony had still not grown corn, and they could not support the new settlers. Gates and Somers resolved to abandon the colony. But as they were sailing down the river, a ship came into sight. It was one of Lord de la Warr's ships. The new governor had arrived, and the colony survived.

The Virginia Company was very sensitive about criticism of the Jamestown venture, and did their best to encourage faith in the plantation of America at a time when scepticism seemed justified by events. In 1610, other pamphlets besides Crashaw's sermon were published. One was *A True and Sincere Declaration of the Purpose and Ends of the Plantation begun in Virginia ... Set forth by the authority of the Governors and Councillors established for that plantation*. Another was *A True Declaration of the estate of the Colony in Virginia with a confutation of such scandalous reports as have tended to the disgrace of so worthy an enterprise*.

Published by advice and direction of the Council of Virginia.[45] The aims of colonisation are explained as, first, the spread of the Christian religion; second, the easing of the burden of an overflowing population; third, the winning of necessary raw materials; fourth, the establishment of defensive positions. The *True Declaration* concludes: 'The same God that hath joined three kingdoms under one Caesar will not be wanting to add a fourth, if we would dissolve that frosty iciness which chilleth our zeal and maketh us so cold in the action.' A later writer, Robert Johnson in 1612, brought in both Agincourt and the Armada to whip up fervour for the colonial cause, suggesting that nothing less than the commitment of the whole nation as shown on those occasions needed to be shown again now.[46]

Crashaw's sermon is a great patriotic appeal on behalf of the Virginia enterprise.

Hereby we shall honour ourselves and strengthen ourselves by propagating our own religion. Hereby we shall mightily advance the honourable name of the English nation . . . Hereby we shall mightily enrich our nation . . . and be less beholding to other nations for their commodities.

The enterprise had, however, 'three great enemies', and they were the Devil, Papists, and Players. Given the cast of Crashaw's mind, this is not such an odd combination, for he was strongly anti-theatre and anti-Catholic, but it is none the less very surprising to find the theatre appearing in this political context. They are 'enemies to this plantation and do abuse it'.

They abuse Virginia, but they are but players. They disgrace it; true, but they are but players, and they have played with better things, and such as for which, if they speedily repent not, I dare say vengeance waits for them.

Crashaw had no difficulty in imputing motives to the players' abuse of Virginia.

I will tell you the causes. First, for that they are so multiplied here, that one cannot live by another, and they see that we send of all trades to Virginia, but will send no players, which if we would do, they that remain would gain the more at home. Secondly . . . because we resolve to suffer no idle persons in Virginia, which course if it were taken in England, they know they might turn to new occupations.[47]

This last sentence is laughable, for the main cause of the near-disaster of the infant colony was the disinclination of the many gentlemen among the voyagers to erode the privilege of their status by actually working. But the implication is clear: Crashaw held the traditional view that as players followed no trade they were not properly members of society, but 'a superfluous sort of men'. The further implication is interesting: as players were supposed to scoff at religion, and degraded royalty and authority by mimicking it, and were not dutiful workers in society, they would inevitably be opponents of a great national enterprise, which was also a religious endeavour. Neither Catholics nor players were to Crashaw's mind properly members of the community, and they would not be expected to be enthusiastic supporters of the expansionist endeavours of the Protestant nation.

Crashaw speaks of the players *abusing* Virginia, and in 1612 Robert Johnson, in the Epistle Dedicatory of *The New Life of Virginia*, spoke of 'the licentious vein of stage poets' accompanying those who 'have whet their tongues with scornful taunts' against the Virginia enterprise.

The cause of all this resentment must be mainly if not solely the play *Eastward Ho!*, a collaboration between Jonson, Marston, and Chapman, acted by the Children of the Revels and published in 1605. It gave offence to authority because it contained gibes at the Scots; Marston and Chapman were imprisoned and Jonson gave himself up to join them. They seem to have got off without trouble though they had been threatened with mutilation, and Jonson gave a feast to celebrate the release. The play (an excellent one anyway) thrived on the scandal. It was reissued without the offending passage, and there were two further editions during the same year. The main gibe at the Scots had gone, but the satirical treatment of colonial endeavours remains. The story is about Sir Petronel Flash, a gentleman who has taken advantage of James's sale of honours to acquire a knighthood. In a passage which the printer failed to excise, a gentleman mimics a Scottish accent and says, 'I ken the man weel, he's one of my thirty pound knights' (IV.i.178). Deeply in debt, Flash has decided to stake everything on an expedition to Virginia. Whatever other reasons were given, genuinely or hypocritically, for adventuring to the New World, the riches to be got, running from gold down to soap-ashes, were the unvarying motive.

In order to finance his expedition, Flash exploits the social ambitions of a goldsmith's wife for her daughter Gertrude and marries her, falsely representing that she will become not only a Lady but the mistress of a family castle. His expedition has been kept absolutely quiet (II.ii.165; III.i.54–60) for the three reasons that he has no charter, that he has equipped the expedition on credit, and that his wife must not know he proposes to desert her as soon as her property is his own. Here a well-wisher is speaking to a money-lender:

> All he could any way get is bestowed on a ship now bound for Virginia, the frame of which voyage is so closely [secretly] conveyed that his new lady nor any of her friends know it. Notwithstanding, as soon as his lady's hand is gotten to the sale of her inheritance, and you have furnished him with money, he will instantly hoist sail, and away.
>
> *Security.* Now a frank gale of wind go with him. Master Frank, we have too few such knight adventurers. Who would not sell away competent certainties to purchase (with any danger) excellent uncertainties? Your true knight-venturer ever does it. Let his wife seal today, he shall have his money today.
>
> (III.ii.163–75)

His wife is tricked into signing a bond which makes over her property and she is bundled into a coach to go to the non-existent castle. However, when the voyagers assemble at Billingsgate they get drunk, take boat for their ship at an adverse time, and are tossed into the Thames before they ever reach their ship. They are arrested and jailed, and the end of the comedy releases them, Virginia forgotten.

The main reference to the Scots is in an extended passage (III.iii) giving a satirical account of the riches of Virginia, which freely draws on *Utopia* and Hakluyt – 'their chamber pots are pure gold . . . and for rubies and diamonds, they go forth on holidays and gather 'em by the sea-shore'.

And then you shall live freely there, without sergeants, or courtiers, or lawyers, or intelligencers; only a few industrious Scots perhaps, who indeed are dispersed over the face of the whole earth. But as for them, there are no greater friends to Englishmen and England, when they are out on't, in the world, than they are. And for my part, I would a hundred thousand of 'em were there, for we are all one countrymen now, ye know, and we should find ten times more comfort of them there than we do here.

Eastward Ho! is a witty and intelligent comedy, with some excellent characters and some superb scenes, debunking everything in sight except perhaps honest Touchstone the goldsmith. Its attitude to union in this passage is characteristic of its derisive tone. What the poets and their king hymned so ecstatically is seen as a matter of too many bloody Scotsmen around the place. Virginia is seen as a lure for the needy and the desperate who seek to get rich quick; adventuring overseas is the province of bankrupts, confidence-men, and shady financiers.

It is not a balanced view about union and empire which *Eastward Ho!* represents, but it is a necessary aspect of the truth, an antimasque to the official solemnity. That Crashaw should be furious at mockery like this is easily understandable, and the resentment of those like Gates and Somers, wrecked in Bermuda, or John Smith in Jamestown, facing all sorts of dangers and labouring tirelessly to make the thing work, will be more than justified. But this play has the acuteness of Lear's fool. 'Come, boys!' shouts the sea-captain, 'Virginia longs till we share the rest of her maidenhead' (III.iii.14). There is indeed a sexuality – without much bliss in it – in the exploration, possession, and exploitation of the fair land they called Virginia. Donne had the image the other way round. 'Oh my America, my new found land', he says of a woman's naked body. But it's the same insight.

The question remains, *who* was responsible for this 'alternative vision' of the great enterprise of national expansion? Both Chapman and Jonson appear to repudiate responsibility for the passages which gave most offence. Chapman said that the 'chief offences are but two clauses, and both of them not our own' (*ES*, III, p. 255). Jonson said in a letter to Salisbury that since his 'first error' (which might be one of several; see below, pp. 135–6) he had 'attempered' his style, and asked whether in his books he had ever 'given offence to a nation, to any public order or state, or any person of honour, or authority' (*HS*, I, p. 195).

Jonson's style is certainly less evident in the play than those of Marston and Chapman. The principal Virginia scene is generally ascribed to Chapman, the man who in 'De Guiana Carmen Epicum' of 1596 wrote in heroic terms of Ralegh's Guiana voyage,

> Riches, and conquest, and renown I sing,
> Riches with honour, conquest without blood,
> Enough to seat the monarchy of earth,
> Like to Jove's eagle, on Eliza's hand.
> Guiana, whose rich feet are mines of gold,
> Whose forehead knocks against the roof of stars,
> Stands on her tip-toes at fair England looking,
> Kissing her hand, bowing her mighty breast,
> And every sign of all submission making.
> To be her sister, and the daughter both
> Of our most sacred Maid . . .
> . . .   .
> Go forth upon the waters, and create
> A golden world in this our iron age.
> . . .   .
> And now a wind, as forward as their spirits,
> Sets their glad feet on smooth Guiana's breast,

Where, as if each man were an Orpheus,
A world of savages fall tame before them,
Storing their theft-free treasuries with gold.
. . .   .
And there do palaces and temples rise
Out of the earth, and kiss the enamour'd skies,
Where new Britannia humbly kneels to heaven,
The world to her, and both at her blest feet,
In whom the circles of all Empire meet.[48]

Whoever wrote the passage about the Scots, Jonson and Chapman collaborated with Marston in a satirical comedy which had at its centre a derisive view of expeditions to the New World. The paradox of Chapman's two voices parallels the paradox of Jonson's two voices, which are the main subject of Chapter 6. It is satisfying that *Eastward Ho!* (purged of its offensiveness, of course) was given at court in the same year as the *Irish Masque* (1614). The epic and the burlesque visions co-exist as they always have done and always will do.[49] It is the stifling of either voice which is the great crime, and it is the greatness of Shakespeare that he could nearly always find room for both visions within the same play, as he did about the New World in *The Tempest*.

'The Tempest'

The status of *The Tempest* as a New World play is not infringed but enhanced by Prospero's island being right in the middle of the Mediterranean. For the play without any shadow of a doubt continuously raises issues about the confrontation of the Old World with the New and by the indefiniteness of the geography it brings that confrontation back into Europe and everywhere else.

Shakespeare's known and possible links with those associated with the Virginia Company and the Jamestown colony have been very closely pursued,[50] and at least two writers have pictured him sitting in the congregation listening to Crashaw's sermon and resolving to present the theatre in a better light by writing *The Tempest*.[51] He used the pamphlets written about the 1609 wreck of Gates and Somers in the Bermudas to help with his own shipwreck, and Philip Brockbank has shown how the sombre accounts of human problems in those pamphlets may have affected the morality of the play.[52] His use of Montaigne's rosy view of primitive innocence in Brazil widens the picture. It would be impossible for Shakespeare not to know well from written records what life had been like for Europeans in touching on or attempting to settle in the New World, quite apart from conversation with voyagers themselves. Nevertheless the sharpness of his perception of the main issues of conflict in the colonial situation is surprising; it certainly astonished the French social psychologist Mannoni, who was investigating earlier in this century the psychological attitude of the coloniser and the colonised in Madagascar when he read *The Tempest* and discovered that his findings were already summed up there. He called his book *Prospero and Caliban: The Psychology of Colonisation.*

Throughout, *The Tempest* is dealing with claims to territory – more so than *Henry V* or *Cymbeline*. Prospero has been dispossessed of his dukedom of Milan, and the action of the play is his endeavour to force the usurper, his brother Antonio, to restore it to him, and, moreover, by marrying his daughter to the heir of the King of Naples, to unite Milan and Naples. But, in taking over the island, Prospero has dispossessed Caliban, who bitterly rejects Prospero's acquisition as theft and treachery (I.ii.331–2; III.ii.43–4). Yet Caliban's right to the island is, like Prospero's, only by reason of accidental arrival: his mother Sycorax was deported from Algiers and marooned on the island. Ferdinand, on the island, reflects that he has now inherited Naples, since he saw (as he thought) the King his father drowned. Antonio takes the first opportunity to tempt Sebastian to murder his brother and so obtain the kingdom of Naples. Stephano decides to claim the island: 'Trinculo, the king and all our company else being drowned, we will inherit here.' Caliban recruits them in a plot to murder and dispossess Prospero.

These complexities, and above all the parallel of Prospero dispossessed by Antonio with Caliban dispossessed by Prospero, make the English claim to France as it is portrayed in *Henry V* a coarse and simple issue. The situation is of course made much more intricate by the different levels of civilisation of Prospero and Caliban. The difference is very much greater than the difference between Roman and British civilisation as shown in *Cymbeline*. Prospero, gifted with all that human intellect can achieve in understanding and in power over the environment, arrives by accident not design at what the Folio wrongly calls 'an uninhabited island' and there is confronted with the least developed (or most debased) of men, a 'salvage and deformed slave', lacking even language; Caliban. The educated intruder treats the savage inhabitant generously and receives his help until he has evidence that he cannot trust him. Thereafter the relations are bitter,

with Caliban labouring for Prospero under duress. The labour is
essential for Prospero, and only severity and punishment can enforce
it.

> *Caliban.* This island's mine, by Sycorax my mother,
>   Which thou tak'st from me. When thou cam'st first
>   Thou strok'st me, and made much of me; wouldst give me
>   Water with berries in't, and teach me how
>   To name the bigger light, and how the less,
>   That burn by day and night. And then I lov'd thee,
>   And show'd thee all the qualities o' th' isle,
>   The fresh springs, brine-pits, barren place and fertile.
>   Curs'd be I that did so! All the charms
>   Of Sycorax, toads, beetles, bats, light on you!
>   For I am all the subjects that you have,
>   Which first was mine own king. And here you sty me
>   In this hard rock, whiles you do keep from me
>   The rest o' the' island.
> *Prospero.*   Thou most lying slave,
>   Whom stripes may move, not kindness! I have us'd thee,
>   Filth as thou art, with human care, and lodg'd thee
>   In mine own cell, till thou didst seek to violate
>   The honour of my child.
> *Caliban.* Oh ho, Oh ho! would't had been done!
>   Thou didst prevent me; I had peopled else
>   This isle with Calibans.
> *Prospero.*[53]   Abhorrèd slave,
>   Which any print of goodness wilt not take,
>   Being capable of all ill! I pitied thee,
>   Took pains to make thee speak, taught thee each hour
>   One thing or other. When thou didst not, savage,
>   Know thine own meaning, but wouldst gabble, like
>   A thing most brutish, I endow'd thy purposes
>   With words that made them known. But thy vile race,
>   Though thou didst learn, had that in't which good natures
>   Could not abide to be with. Therefore wast thou
>   Deservedly confin'd into this rock,
>   Who hadst deserv'd more than a prison.
> *Caliban.* You taught me language, and my profit on't
>   Is, I know how to curse. The red plague rid you
>   For learning me your language.   (I.ii.331–65)

E. S. Morgan, in the book mentioned earlier, describes the growth
of English attitudes to the native Americans. From Peter Martyr,
Englishmen learned that there were two kinds of native in the new
world: friendly, tractable people like the Arawaks (worked to death
by the Spaniards in Hispaniola) and hostile, unlovely people like the

Colaiste Mhuire Luimneach (library stamp)

Cannibals whom Columbus had found on certain Caribbean islands. Drake had formed the policy of employing the co-operative peoples oppressed by the Spaniards as allies, and the English got the name of liberators, and opponents of the brutal harshness of Spanish rule. Indeed, in the early 1580s, still believing in the class of co-operative Indian, English colonial policy contained nothing about forced labour, the standard Spanish custom. Hakluyt had assured Elizabeth that when it was known that the English used 'the natural people' with humanity and courtesy they would revolt from the Spaniard. It was specifically enjoined upon colonists 'that no Indian be forced to labour unwillingly'. Morgan describes (chiefly from D. B. Quinn's Hakluyt Society volumes on the Roanoke Voyages) the unhappy course by which, during Ralegh's first colony of 1585–6, the Indians changed in English eyes from the co-operative to the intransigent, from Ariel, almost, to Caliban. John White's famous drawings of the Indians express a dignity which seems actually to have been in the Indians and which White and Harriot perceived. But perhaps both races expected more of each other, and themselves, than either was able to fulfil. The Indians looked on the white men as gods, and the white men were already convinced of their own superiority, and of their destiny to establish themselves as rulers in the land. But these gods could not even learn what the Indians tried to teach them in order to survive. They came to look less and less godlike, even as the Indians came to look less and less like willing contributors to the new order in the new world. Ralph Lane was running the colony too much like a military community – and indeed he had cause to worry about discipline, being, as he said, 'amongst savages . . . [with] . . . wild men of mine own nation' – very much as Prospero saw himself. Unfortunately, Ireland had provided the training ground for what to do with a recalcitrant native community – 'whom stripes may move, not kindness'. Mutual suspicion grew up, and Lane began to act *ad terrorem*. In a punitive expedition, he murdered the Indian king, Wingina, and his advisers. Ironically, a few days later, Drake arrived with a cargo of Indians and Negroes liberated from Spanish oppression. Lane had had enough, and chucked his hand in; the colony was abandoned just before Grenville's squadron arrived with supplies. Morgan points out that no source gives any account of what happened to the liberated victims of the Spaniards.

It may well seem that Shakespeare comes in with Lane against Harriot (who believed that 'some of our company towards the end of the year showed themselves too fierce') and accepts, of Indians as of Irish, that if they do not do what English occupying forces tell them they are rebels who must be punished into submission. But Shakespeare, I think, uses the relationship of Prospero and Caliban to suggest that the difficulties of Ralph Lane may be the difficulties of authority anywhere in the world. There is a touch of Prospero in Shakespeare's Henry IV, wearily contemplating the vicissitudes of things and the perpetual need to control the malice active in his kingdom – which his own deeds are indirectly responsible for. He has little confidence that life has any meaning, but he knows that order in society is imperative, and that government is his responsibility and burden. Henry IV is an unlovable man. A figure of restraint and containment, he is less sympathetic than those whose enthusiasms and indulgences he has to curb; Hotspur, Falstaff, and his own son. The strain of governing, of containing and directing the very different energies of Ariel, of Caliban, of Ferdinand and Miranda, is manifest throughout *The Tempest*. All want freedom in their different ways, and the ruler cannot afford to give it to any of them, until he abdicates (which in time he does).

Rights to territory are a fundamental question in *The Tempest* – or what would happen to Prospero's own claim to Milan? – and Caliban's assertion that he has been deprived of his rights by Prospero is sympathetically presented. His claim seems linked to that small but saving poetic centre which Shakespeare gave to his soul, however brutish his steps to regain his kingdom seem. But on the island for a time the question of rights is overridden by the pragmatic question of the need for a fit ruler to contain the wilfulness and anarchy of mankind. Shakespeare accepts that Prospero is a man by nature and education better able to rule and Caliban a man more fitted to serve, just as Henry IV was a man better able to govern England than Richard II was, however much less his right. If Prospero's heavy authority had no object other than Caliban, the play would have a very different moral. But there is also the malice and greed of the civilised white man, breaking out in the attempt by Sebastian and Antonio to murder the King of Naples, which Prospero is able to frustrate. This attempt is an act of unprincipled political ambitiousness which has for motive none of the grievance which led to Caliban's plot to murder Prospero. And, again, to balance the badness of Caliban is the drunken and ineffective murderousness of Stephano and Trinculo. To read the Bermuda pamphlets is to be deeply depressed by the nature of the civilised European, and especially his tendency to mutiny and murder; and Brockbank has rightly pointed out the importance this picture of constant disorderliness may have had as Shakespeare worked on *The Tempest*.

Shakespeare's acceptance of the unlovable authority-figures like Prospero and Henry IV is something we cannot help recoiling from, but the force of the acceptance is surely in the unlovableness, and in the honesty with which the appeal of all that has to be sacrificed is presented. Restraint, and control, and suppression are not attractive, and the emotional appeal of that which rises up against them is probably never better shown than in Ariel's longing for freedom – which in this fanciful play can be granted in the end. The victory of Prospero is a victory over the self, and that Shakespeare should be convinced that so distasteful a victory is necessary is what makes the career of Prince Hal so difficult to feel happy about.

The harshness shown to Caliban is distressing, but there is no tincture of colour-prejudice in it. The vagueness about what Caliban actually is, is important. He is not an Indian, but a mysteriously begotten scion of the old world, a deformed human. He is one of us, the thing of darkness we acknowledge ours: our heart of darkness. So, equally, he may be an Indian or an Irishman. In so far as he is an Indian, Shakespeare rejects that he is better than we are. He brings in Montaigne's view that naturally man is good, and that civilised society is the cause of human savagery, and obviously he does not accept it. Caliban tried to rape Miranda, and that assault is to be compared with the ceremonious betrothal, and the refraining from sexual intercourse before marriage, in the relations between Ferdinand and Miranda. But civilised behaviour is not the constant property of civilised man: far from it. It is the goal of the best civilised man, but civilised men in general are as prone to evil as uncivilised. Cloten's attempt to rape Imogen parallels Caliban's attempt on Miranda. Prospero finds himself in a position where he has to rule, whether he is an intruder or not. Those whom he has to chasten and improve if he can are Old World as well as New World, white as well as brown or black.

Alien rule justifies itself in *The Tempest* because it is positive rule, and not because there is any sense of mission or destiny that Prospero should come to the nameless island, rule it, develop it, exploit it, or Christianise it. This last is achieved without much positive proselytising within the play, and Caliban at the end of the play is left on the

island, his own master, intending to 'seek for grace' while Prospero
and the others sail back to Italy. Prospero had no wish to come to the
island, and when he has a dukedom to return to he is thankful to leave,
empty-handed. I find it a great oddity that A. D. Nuttall should in one
of his essays insist with such force that Caliban accompanies Prospero
back to Milan – as though he were one of those Indians regularly
brought back at these times to show wondering Londoners – and
speak so vehemently against those who accept what everyone has
accepted for centuries – that Caliban stays on the island.[54] Caliban
belongs to Prospero on the island because he is necessary to him on
the island. Prospero has no need whatsoever for him in the ducal
palace at Milan, any more than, his great endeavour over, he has need
of Ariel. The parting from Caliban is of some importance. *The Tempest*
is in a great many respects a New World play, but it is not a colonial
play. It portrays no interest whatsoever in the abiding passion of so
many disciples of Hakluyt and Ralegh – the expansion of the empire
to the New World and the maintenance of rule there. Shakespeare
shows extraordinary insight into the difficulties of the commerce
between colonisers and natives but there is no observable enthusiasm
for maintaining a permanent presence on Caliban's island.

5

THE HIDDEN KING:
SHAKESPEARE'S HISTORY PLAYS

Whom should he follow but his natural king?
(3 Henry VI, I.i.82)
– Speak, citizens, for England. Who's your king?
– The king of England, when we know the king.
(King John, II.i.362–3)

The sequence of plays on English medieval history up to the death of
Richard III, which Shakespeare wrote between about 1590 and 1599,
is perhaps the greatest *sequence* of plays in the world, and probably no
one has made a more powerful drama from his nation's history.
Although since the days of Lily Bess Campbell, E. M. W. Tillyard,
and John Dover Wilson[1] we have all been anxious to protect Shakespeare from the charge of being the propagandist of Tudor autocracy,
meek accepter of its rewritings of history, and philosopher of its strong
right arm, there isn't a shadow of doubt that much of the energy of the
sequence comes from a sense of progress, or better, of emergence, by
which the English nation is seen coming from the dark of the Wars of
the Roses into the light of the Tudor dynasty – with the reign of
Elizabeth as a time when achievement was surpassed only by the
promise of the future. This sense is clearest in that half of the sequence
which Shakespeare wrote first, the three Henry VI plays, and *Richard
III* – the 'first tetralogy'. At the end of *Richard III*, the future Henry
VII appears as the divinely sent saviour of England, rescuing her
from long years of misrule, national humiliation, civil war, and
tyranny.

England hath long been mad, and scarred herself –
The brother blindly shed the brother's blood,
The father rashly slaughtered his own son,
The son, compelled, been butcher to the sire.
All this divided York and Lancaster,
Divided in their dire division.

Oh now let Richmond and Elizabeth,
The true succeeders of each royal house,
By God's fair ordinance conjoin together!
And let their heirs, God, if Thy will be so,
Enrich the time to come with smooth-faced peace,
With smiling plenty and fair prosperous days!   (V.v.23–34)[2]

The second sequence, dealing with the earlier historical period
(*Richard II*, the two Henry IV plays, and *Henry V*), also ends with the
emergence of the strong king who unites England, subdues her
enemies, and brings peace. But although critics have often seen this
second sequence as a steady movement up to the triumph of King
Henry V, the vehement nationalism of the final play is surely a
narrowing rather than an opening out. The louder the trumpets blow,
the coarser the music becomes. In the two preceding plays, the two
parts of *Henry IV*, Shakespeare used the quadrangle of forces represented by Hotspur, Falstaff, Prince Hal, and Henry IV for a profound exploration of the ways of human fulfilment. In *Henry V* he
reverted to an altogether shallower system of measuring human life.
This narrowing of the perspectives inevitably qualifies and criticises a
view of history as an onward march. It is not surprising that Shakespeare should take a more complex view of history as he grew older,
and in any case the England of the later nineties was not a land to
encourage optimism. There were serious economic privations, the
Queen was becoming more difficult and repressive, and worries about
the succession increased as she aged.[3]

What seems most arrestingly to mark the change of mood about
the march of history in the second tetralogy is the matter-of-fact
Epilogue spoken by the Chorus at the end of *Henry V*, about 'this star
of England'.

                    Fortune made his sword,
        By which the world's best garden he achieved,
        And of it left his son imperial lord.
        Henry the Sixth, in infant bands crowned King
        Of France and England, did this king succeed;
        Whose state so many had the managing
        That they lost France and made his England bleed,
        Which oft our stage hath shown. And, for their sake,
        In your fair minds let this acceptance take.

The second tetralogy is symmetrical with the first in that it ends with
England emerging triumphantly from anarchy to peace under a
strong king. But quite deliberately the ending of the eighth play takes

us right back to the beginning of the first – Part One of *Henry VI*, written eight or nine years before – which opened with a ceremonious lament over the coffin of Henry V, and very quickly showed the loss of that king's French conquests. By directing us back to the beginning of *Henry VI*, Shakespeare does more than politely remind us that if we want the next sixty-five years of English history he has already written them up, early in his career. Like Joyce in *Finnegans Wake*, he makes the close of his long saga its beginning also, so that we may see the progress of history to be circular, not linear. One does not have to accept Jan Kott's view of either history or the Histories to agree with him that the plays when seen as a whole have a dominant cyclical pattern.[4] No one, I take it, assumes that when he was twenty-six Shakespeare decided to write eight plays on English history from 1389 to 1485, beginning with the later reigns and then writing the earlier part. The configuration which he eventually achieved, however, by going like a crab backward, is remarkable. The historical conclusion of the series, the Battle of Bosworth, by appearing in the middle of Shakespeare's writing, looks to anyone who reads or sees the plays now in the order in which they were written as only a momentary respite in the ugly story of violence and misery. And this sense of precariousness in the peace which Richmond brings is strongly emphasised by Shakespeare's insistence on the temporary and transient nature of Henry V's triumphs in the last lines of his last play, sending his hearers back in their minds to recall the anarchy and discord, so quickly to follow, which was the subject of his very first play.[5]

A further effect of the epilogue of *Henry V* is to remind us that, while it is quite legitimate for an historical dramatist to conclude his play at a moment of actual triumph or peace, the feeling which he may give of the achievement being final and the peace permanent belongs to the experience of art. The exhilaration and sense of blessing which come from the resolution of problems at the close of a play are not to be belittled, and only a fool scoffs at happy endings. But history does not flow like a play. The first two parts of *Henry VI* are remarkable in their attempt to proceed as though they were governed by the rules of history rather than those of art. Thereafter Shakespeare did something greater and gave us a sense of history in a sequence of plays which individually have the rhythm of works of art. By deliberately calling us back from the exhilaration of the triumphant ending of the play *Henry V* to a recollection that history is always ready to go on with its depressing story, Shakespeare reminds us of the existence of the two worlds, art and history, without compromising either.[6]

Shakespeare's history plays are part – the major part – of a body of historical drama which provided a feeling of a national awareness, even of national identity, among Englishmen at a time when their nation was emerging as a great power. Although inevitably something of the concept of a national destiny, a sense of the development of the nation from weakness to strength, is apparent in the plays, and particularly at the end of *Richard III*, the idea of emergence is considerably qualified and quietened if we look at the series as a whole.[7]

It remains there, however. The plays are born from a spirit of national self-realisation and pride, and they do not disown their origin. It remains there in quite another way, however: transmuted from belief into longing. What finally supports the Histories as a whole is not the belief that the awfulness of the past is over and that better times are on the way but the longing that this should be so. The belief that the king has come who will alter our lives and protect us is transformed into the hope that he will come. The happy endings become not statements that the course of history has changed, but fragile moments of expectation.

The transmutation requires that to some extent history becomes symbol. The historians presented Shakespeare with a picture of the history between Bolingbroke's rebellion against Richard II in 1399 and Henry Richmond's assumption of the throne in 1485 as largely a matter of continuous contention for the crown. (And thereafter of course there was more of the same thing, with Lambert Simnel and Perkin Warbeck, Lady Jane Grey and Mary Queen of Scots.) Dramatic tradition, in the political morality play, presented him with the idea of England as *Respublica*, a suffering being fought for by allegorical figures of vice and virtue. And the political hagiolatry of the Tudors presented him with an idea of kingship as something mysterious in its holiness and its power.[8] One starts from love of country, which I take to be undisputable bedrock in Shakespeare. (It is a different thing from nationalism.[9] Nationalism can exist without it, and love of one's country may often oppose what nationalism proposes.) Next, the happiness of the country becomes identified with the presence of her true king. As Wilson Knight put it, 'Royalty and England tend to involve each other.'[10] The efficiency of a king's administration is not the most important thing about him; his legitimacy is much more important, and legitimacy is a spiritual thing. At some levels of comprehending Shakespeare's history plays, the person of the king almost vanishes. True kingship may be 'a metaphor for a harmony of the personality, the unity of being and doing when private person and public office are one'.[11] And the spiritual harmony of the English people may be portrayed symbolically by the people's acknowledgement of and loyalty to the rightful sovereign. It is this condition which is hymned at the end of *Richard III*. Art can give us the vision of this condition: history never reaches it. In the Histories, England is always moving hopefully towards this condition or despairingly moving away from it. The two major endings of the tetralogies, as I have presented them, show the perpetual restless movement of history pulling towards the absolute beneficence of peace under the true king. This haven is never really gained. It is always in the past and always in the future.

Deposition and the unending anarchy of rival claimants for the throne, which are the main subjects of Shakespeare's Histories, exist on three levels. On one level they were a simple explanation to an English audience of their antecedents, acting out the grim historical consequence of uprooting in Richard II the last undisputed heir of William the Conqueror, until at last a dynasty came strong enough to secure itself against challenge. On the second level, they commended the common political morality of the time, that complete acceptance of the undoubted right of the monarch to rule was the only sure protection against the final horror of civil war. On the third level, with sacred royalty under attack from ambitious barons, or foreign kings, or from an impostor monarch, they provided fierce symbolic pictures of the state of human society, bewildered, lost, divided against itself, wounding itself, looking for salvation and being punished with false gods. Time and again Shakespeare pictured the contention for the crown as the lethal self-division of the family.

> The conquerors
> Make war upon themselves, brother to brother,
> Blood to blood, self against self.   (*Richard III*, II.iv.61–3)

> And in this seat of peace, tumultuous wars
> Shall kin with kin and kind with kind confound.
> Disorder, horror, fear, and mutiny
> Shall here inhabit, and this land be called
> The field of Golgotha and dead men's skulls.
>   (*Richard II*, IV.i.140–4)

What Shakespeare seems to have discovered during the writing of

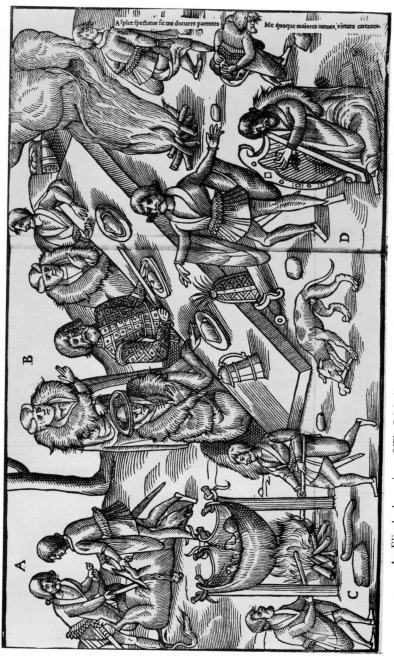

Aspice spectator sic me docuere parentes

Me quoque maiores omnes, virtute carentes.

An Elizabethan view of The Irish *file* or poet reciting before his lord, accompanied by a harpist

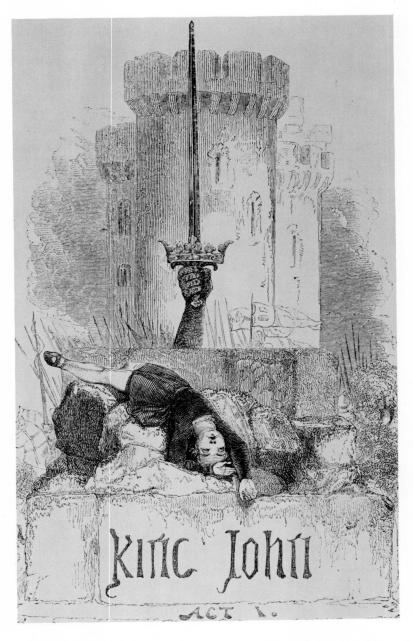

The death of Arthur in Shakespeare's *King John*, as drawn by Kenny
Meadows, 1843

The House of Fame
Drawing by Inigo Jones for Ben Jonson's *The Masque of Queens*, 1609

Cathleen ni Houlihan at the Abbey Theatre. Drawing by Ben Bay

the Henry VI plays is the polarity within the Tudor conception of monarchy, and, seeing this as a disabling self-contradiction, he began to objectify its antagonisms in the two parties of the contention for the crown. The concept of Old Kingship begins to settle on Henry VI, a pious man of peace, deeply concerned for the land he has inherited. The Duke of York is the New King, masterful, ambitious, competent, concerned with empire and conquest.[12] So the contest for the crown, signifying the painful effort of a divided England towards spiritual self-realisation, comes to be pictured as a contest between Old Legitimacy and New Efficiency. I think it was Shakespeare's realisation of the essential nature of the conflict during the writing of the first tetralogy which drove him further back into history to write about Richard II, whose reign, the acknowledged *fons et origo* of the Wars of the Roses, made it possible to draw the lines of the conflict with much more sharpness and clarity. I also believe that the realisation drove him to move quite outside the sequence and write *King John*, in order to crystallise the issues in greater freedom.

I think that the usual dating of *King John*, between the two tetralogies, is correct, and therefore the play follows the anonymous *Troublesome Reign of King John*; it is, indeed, a very deliberate and pointed rewriting of that play, so coarse and confident in its patriotism and anti-Catholicism. The critical change, which governs all the others, was to take away John's title to the throne, to make him a *de facto* and not a *de jure* king, usurper of the rights of Arthur, son of John's deceased elder brother Geoffrey. E. A. Honigmann says, 'John's "usurpation" is Shakespeare's fiction, for his "right" is not seriously questioned in the chronicles.'[13] Indeed, Holinshed says firmly that before his death Richard I assigned the crown to his younger brother John, and made the nobles swear loyalty to him.[14] Because John is not the rightful king, Arthur and his French backers appear in a quite different light – in *The Troublesome Reign* Arthur is a puppet of the French. Arthur's right in *King John* is established in the poetry of the French king, who speaks simply to John of the rights of primogeniture and the will of God.

> Thou from loving England art so far
> That thou hast underwrought his lawful king,
> Cut off the sequence of posterity,
> Outfaced infant state, and done a rape
> Upon the maiden virtue of the crown.   (II.i.94–8)

An important section of his speech which follows suffers from some textual confusion. As given in the Folio it is punctuated as follows. (The French king has been pointing out Arthur as the embodiment in little of the dead Geoffrey.)

> That Geoffrey was thy elder brother born,
> And this his son, England was Geoffrey's right,
> And this is Geoffrey's in the name of God:
> How comes it then that thou art called a king,
> When living blood doth in these temples beat
> Which owe* the crown, that thou o'er-masterest?
>
> (II.i.104–9)

Many editors assume that in the third line the Folio's words are right and the punctuation wrong. They put a stop after 'And this is Geoffrey's', and make 'In the name of God' the commencement of the succeeding question. This is unsatisfactory because 'England was Geoffrey's right, / And this is Geoffrey's' does not have a clear meaning. The rhythm of the syntax and the ideas suggest a build-up of the invocation of divine authority for the claims of Arthur, and it is less forceful to make 'In the name of God' an adjuration to John. I suspect that the third line ought to read:

> And it was Geoffrey's in the name of God:

with the compositor performing the common error of dittography – starting the line with the opening of the previous line. If there is deeper corruption, it is possible the line should read:

> And thus is Arthur's in the name of God.

Whichever reading we adopt, however, the solemnity of the French king's indignation is powerful. R. L. Smallwood in the commentary to the New Penguin edition points out how far Shakespeare is going in emphasising the validity of Arthur's claim. England was never Geoffrey's right, since when he died his father, Henry II, and his elder brother, Richard Coeur-de-Lion, were both alive.

By contrast with the eloquence on Arthur's behalf, John has nothing to appeal to except – tersely enough – his possession of the crown. The challenge of the two parties to the city of Angiers to admit its king is a fine piece of symbolic ceremony. The city is not disputing that it is rightly England's:

> We are the king of England's subjects:
> For him, and in his right, we hold this town.   (II.i.267–8)

* As in several of the extracts from the play which follow, 'owe' = 'own'.

But they do not know who the true king is: they will admit whoever proves to be their king. Assertions of title are not valid.

> *King John.* Whose party do the townsmen yet admit?
> *King Philip.* Speak, citizens, for England. Who's your king?
> *Citizen.* The king of England, when we know the king.
> *King Philip.* Know him in us, that here hold up his right.
> *King John.* In us, that are our own great deputy . . .
> . . .   .
> *Citizen.* A greater power than we denies all this
>
> (II.i.361–8)

The citizens are strongly affected by the myth of *rex abscondicus*. There is a king to whom they belong, and they are quite confident that he really exists. Though he has not yet appeared, they will know him immediately and unequivocally when he does. This walled town in France is an emblem of England itself.

At this juncture there is an intervention from the Bastard, Philip Faulconbridge. He is the third person in the play with the royal blood of England in his veins, and unlike John and Arthur he is in the direct line of descent, being the son of Richard I. But not by his lawful wife. In strong contrast with his later behaviour, he makes the utterly irresponsible proposal that the contending parties should join in flattening this exasperating town, and John assents with alacrity.

> I like it well! France, shall we knit our powers
> And lay this Angiers even with the ground,
> Then after fight who shall be king of it?   (II.i.398–400)

Here once more as so often in this play is the crystallisation of a major theme of the Histories. Kingship is a sacred office, and on it depends the well-being of the community. There is no end to the competition for this great office. As they compete, the contenders destroy the community they seek to rule. The Bastard's scheme, however, prompts the expedient which the townsmen bring forward to save themselves, the dynastic marriage between the Dauphin and Blanche, which the Bastard so roundly condemns as 'commodity'. Self-interest explodes King Philip's altruism, which brought him into the field (as the Bastard says) as 'God's own soldier', and diverts him from 'a resolved and honourable war' (ll. 566, 585). So Arthur, true heir to the English crown, is left deserted and helpless, with his mother crying out to the King of France in another of those resonant sentences:

> You have beguiled me with a counterfeit
> Resembling majesty, which, being touched and tried,
> Proves valueless.   (III.i.99–101)

When the papal legate enters to demand John's obedience, John resolutely defies him and asserts the Reformation principle of national sovereignty.

>   No Italian priest
> Shall tithe or toll in our dominions;
> But as we, under God, are supreme head,
> So under Him, that great supremacy
> Where we do reign, we will alone uphold,
> Without th' assistance of a mortal hand:
> So tell the Pope, all reverence set apart
> To him and his usurped authority.   (III.i.153–60)[15]

'It is John's finest hour,' says Smallwood. As France wilts and finally submits to Rome's orders, breaking the new league with England, John calmly accepts the military consequences of his defiance, and leads his army to victory – capturing Arthur, the chief threat to his position. Shakespeare's somewhat cheeky borrowing of *The Troublesome Reign*'s standard New-Monarchy kit just at this point may remind us of the patriotic defiance which the Queen and Cloten in *Cymbeline* showed to the Romans. What seems an admirable display of sturdy national courage is questioned by the moral quality of the speaker, and by his eventual fate in the play. A patriotic audience, responding enthusiastically in either play to familiar nationalist sentiments, is puzzled at the end. The fact that the quality of John's stand is questioned by his later misdeeds, his later weakness, and his later submission to Rome does not, naturally, mean that Shakespeare would have preferred submission to Pandulph. But John's ability to uphold the needs of England is transient. At times all that the country needs is boldness and a strong arm, and these John at this juncture provides. And even here his rôle as national hero, which Shakespeare produced by turning on the tap from *The Troublesome Reign*, has the bluster of its origin. His policy, and his presentation of that policy, are neither wrong nor admirable.

From then on, everything is decline. To secure his own position John must have Arthur put to death. The scene of the attempt to blind the boy, much more than the scene of the boy's actual death, is the climactic scene of sacrilege which serves as focus for the whole play. The violence offered to the child-king is beyond any conceivable need of John. Apparently John's régime not only depends on the extinction of the true inheritor of holy kingship, but it is necessary for him, as it was for Mortimer with Edward, to defile and degrade the true king. Hubert and the executioners are not in the end prepared to inflict the suffering required by the king, and their compassion emphasises the cruelty of their master.

John has another means of securing his position – a second coronation. He had earlier asked, 'Doth not the crown of England prove the king?' (II.i.273), and this new coronation is a damning indication of the falseness of his kingship. The crown and all ceremonies associated with it have sacramental value. They are the outward adjuncts and visible testimonies of the royalty within. Henry V was wrong to despise them as mere external trappings.[16] King John is wrong to believe in them as efficacious in themselves. The barons are greatly troubled by an act which is both sinister and offensive – the repetition of a ceremony that has already been performed in its due season. 'You were crowned before!' Salisbury worries chiefly about the disregard for the meaning of time-honoured customs.

> In this the antique and well-noted face
> Of plain old form is much disfigured.
> And like a shifted wind unto a sail
> It makes the course of thoughts to fetch about,
> Startles and frights consideration,
> Makes sound opinion sick and truth suspected,
> For putting on so new a fashioned robe.   (IV.ii.21–7)

There is a religious disquiet here, and the way in which the abuse of ceremony in this scene follows the harrowing ill-treatment of the royal child in the preceding scene adds to the emblematic quality of this play. It is the barons' unease about this ceremony, coupled with their anxiety about the fate of Arthur, which begins their alienation from John. When they hear the news (untrue, in fact) that Arthur is dead, they find where their allegiance properly lay. Pembroke says:

> I'll go with thee,
> And find th'inheritance of this poor child.
> His little kingdom of a forcèd grave.
> That blood which owed the breadth of all this isle
> Three foot of it doth hold – bad world the while!
>   (IV.ii.96–100)

Arthur kills himself escaping from prison. John is lucky not to have his blood directly on his hand, but he is indirectly responsible. It is over

his corpse that the Bastard makes his deeply moving lament for
England. It is of the greatest importance and though so well known
must be quoted.

> I am amazed, methinks, and lose my way
> Among the thorns and dangers of this world.
> How easy dost thou take all England up!
> From forth this morsel of dead royalty
> The light, the right, and truth of all this realm
> Is fled to heaven; and England now is left
> To tug and scamble and to part by th' teeth
> The unowed interest of proud-swelling state.
> Now for the bare-picked bone of majesty
> Doth dogged war bristle his angry crest
> And snarleth in the gentle eyes of peace.
> Now powers from home and discontents at home
> Meet in one line; and vast confusion waits,
> As doth a raven on a sick-fallen beast,
> The imminent decay of wrested pomp.   (IV.iii.140–54)

(In the third line of the extract, the Bastard is speaking to Hubert,
who is lifting the dead boy. The Folio punctuation runs this line on
with the next, but it can hardly be right.)

The Bastard is stunned by the sight of the dead body, and the
cheerful irreverent loyalty which has so far inspired him will no longer
serve. This death is a harder thing to adjust to than 'commodity'. 'I
am amazed' – not astonished, but brought to a halt in confusion and
uncertainty – 'and lose my way'. New values and new loyalties
supervene. John's regal position – about to collapse – is 'wrested
pomp'. No speech in the Histories puts more clearly the idea of the
identification of the realm with the true king, and its health with his
health. The corpse of this defenceless boy is 'all England' (see Plate
2). His soul, leaving earth for heaven, is 'the life, the right, and truth of
all this realm'. Nor, in spite of many rivals, does any speech in the
Histories put quite so graphically the 'vast confusion' of the country
when it lacks its king.

John, whose 'strong possession' could for a time justify loyalty and
protect the country even though his title was 'wrested', is finished.
And Arthur is dead. It is the Bastard himself who provides the answer
in this impasse. In his Introduction to the New Penguin edition,
Smallwood makes much of the Bastard's self-abnegation in not pressing his own claim to the crown and the nation's loyalty at this
juncture. Certainly, when one compares his behaviour with that of
York in *Henry VI*, his dedication to England rather than to self is

remarkable. The barons, outraged, can think only of destroying the
man who has misled them, and join forces with the French invaders.
The Bastard remains with John and tries to galvanise him with his
own spirit (V.i.44–61). But John gives up. 'Have thou the ordering of
this present time!' With this commission, the Bastard works brilliantly. The all-embracing need is the integrity of England, and on
behalf of England and the royal blood that is in him he puts up the
magnificent pretence that there is a fierce and warlike John behind
him, pretends that his own stirring eloquence is an index of John's
continued strength. It is interesting that he begins his great speech to
the French army and the English rebels with the impersonality of:

> Now hear our English king,
> For thus his royalty doth speak in me.   (V.ii.128–9)

And it is perhaps to this fictional image which the English barons
respond when they learn that only the fate of traitors awaits them if
France wins. They will return 'to our great King John' (V.iv.57)!
They do so in time for John to forgive them before he dies. It is now,
and only now, that Prince Henry appears to provide a convenient
focus for the loyalty of a reunited England in the Bastard's speech at
the close of the day.

> This England never did, nor never shall,
> Lie at the proud foot of a conqueror
> But when it first did help to wound itself.
> Now these her princes are come home again,
> Come the three corners of the world in arms
> And we shall shock them. Naught shall make us rue
> If England to itself do rest but true.   (V.vii.112–18)

How is England to rest true to itself? The heroic Bastard who since the
anagnorisis over Arthur's corpse has been the very spirit of England
has first focused loyalty on the propped-up image of a dying king. Is
Prince Henry a convenience of art, or another product of the Bastard's extraordinary skill in creating a centre of loyalty out of nothing?
For in Shakespeare's rendering of history, Prince Henry is only the
son of an unlawful king, and those who had read Holinshed knew that
during Henry III's long reign England was anything but settled and
happy under its monarch. The ending of *King John* is not evasive, and
not ironic; but the last line is a conditional clause whose fulfilment the
rest of the play and the rest of the Histories show to be pretty well
impossible.

Shakespeare's respect for historical fact in *King John* has yielded to his wish to create a trio of men who have some claim to succeed Richard I. The Bastard is simply non-historical and, as we have seen, Shakespeare sharply reduced John's right to the throne and increased Arthur's. The beloved country, England, has a centrality which is undeniable. She is ruled by a man who is not the rightful king, who persecutes and drives to his death the boy who *is* the rightful king. John can support England for a while but his strength is all outside. He crumbles and fails England when she most needs help. The royal blood flows in the Bastard, and he too can support England for a time, but he's not the true king either, and all one can say is that the play ends before Prince Henry fails. The poetry and the structure of *King John* tend to generalise its meanings, and those meanings have to do with the frustrations of the search for true royalty in the national community, when the condition of life is one of self-wounding caused by new ambitions extinguishing old sanctity.

We may perhaps now look back to the *Henry VI–Richard III* cycle of plays which Shakespeare had written before. A mark of the brilliance of his early powers is the arresting way in which all the unease of the early events in Part One of *Henry VI* – the disunity, the pettiness, the collapse of the overseas empire in spite of the courage of the English – is 'explained' when Richard Plantagenet, future Duke of York, visits the dying Mortimer in prison (II.v) and learns who he is, as the old rebel takes him back through history and tells of the deposition of Richard II and the repeated attempts to replace the line of the usurper Bolingbroke by the rightful heir – the latest of whom is now Richard Plantagenet. This Spenserian scene, with the young hero visiting the old weary sage in his cave to learn the truth of his identity and the nature of his quest, takes us not only backwards in time but inwards. We are moving towards the efficient cause of the country's distress, not made clear till now even in the Temple garden scene: namely, the instability of the kingship.

During the succeeding three plays, as the contention for the crown grows more and more serious, Henry VI is increasingly cast as the ineffective relic of past sanctity, with York, followed by his son Richard of Gloucester, filling the power vacuum with his ambition and energy. My description of the antipathy between Old Legitimacy and New Efficiency is no more than a gloss on the binary principle which Yeats saw as governing Shakespeare's Histories in his great essay 'At Stratford-upon-Avon' in 1903 (discussed in Chapter 8, pp.

205–9). I accept the Yeatsian metaphor of the vessel of porcelain and the vessel of clay as appropriate to the reading of Shakespeare's Histories. Yeats's definition of the struggle of Shakespeare's warring kings is a means for us to explore an attitude to nation which in their different countries and different centuries the two men had in common.

The opposition between Henry VI and the Yorkists is less clear than the similar opposition between Richard II and Bolingbroke because Henry's title has its distant dubiety, and because the contest is spread through the thick incidents of two whole plays. But the similarities are profound. Henry is the lawful monarch who yet is so politically feeble that he is weakening the country – even giving away the empire in the unforced surrender of Anjou and Maine. It is not just ineptitude, of course, but defeatism. He doesn't want to be king, as he keeps complaining (e.g. Pt 2, IV.ix.1–6). He is worried about his title. He gives away his inheritance to York (Pt 3, I.i.175). He believes he's bad for England (e.g. Pt 3, IV.vi.19–25). Above all he foresees his own destruction. In the brilliant scene of the finding of Gloucester dead in bed (Pt 2, III.ii), Henry swoons because his intelligence and insight show him not only that the Protector has been murdered, but that the death prefigures his own. Asked to view the body, he says:

> That is to see how deep my grave is made,
> For with his soul fled all my worldly solace,
> For seeing him I see my life in death.   (III.ii.150–2)

The vacuum caused by the absence of strong rule tempts masterful men to fill it. By the side of the lack of will of the saintly Henry grows the determination of York to gain the crown. York's ambition is soon overtaken by his son Richard of Gloucester's, a man whose intoxication at the prospect of the crown which Henry despises is influenced by Tamburlaine's.

> And, father, do but think
> How sweet a thing it is to wear a crown,
> Within whose circuit is Elysium,
> And all that poets feign of bliss and joy.
> (Pt 3, I.ii.28–31)

It is when Henry has already been deposed once, but has been re-crowned by Warwick, that he catches sight of Henry, Earl of Richmond, the future Henry VII.

> Come hither, England's hope.
>
>   *Lays his hand on his head.*
>   If secret powers
> Suggest but truth to my divining thoughts,
> This pretty lad will prove our country's bliss.
> His looks are full of peaceful majesty,
> His head by nature framed to wear a crown,
> His hand to wield a sceptre, and himself
> Likely in time to bless a regal throne.   (Pt 3, IV.vi.68–74)

It could be said that this sort of thing comes pretty easily. Dr Johnson's note on these lines was as follows:

He was afterwards Henry VII. A man who put an end to the civil war of the two houses, but not otherwise remarkable for virtue. Shakespeare knew his trade. Henry VII was grandfather to Queen Elizabeth, and the King from whom James inherited.

But Shakespeare's language is so ludicrously inappropriate as regards that crafty Welshman, the real Henry Tudor, as to suggest that his mind is working at a different level from that of either flattery or documentary history. The poetry of this passage is quickened by the *idea* of national emergence, not the particulars of things, and this idea is itself elevated way above not only the Tudors, but the world of events altogether, finely expressing the dream world of longing for the time when all is peace. The imagery of 'his head by nature framed to wear a crown' is particularly interesting, with its Cinderella fancy that the symbol of royalty awaits its *natural* claimant. The most important thing about the passage, though, is that it is spoken by Henry VI, as the priestly divination of expiring royalty, prophesying the coming of the new king, who will replace him and bring new strength. At the same time, by the laying on of hands, he ensures true succession.

This metaphor of true succession exists side by side with the other metaphor which we have looked at in *Edward II* and *King John*: succession by the brutal extinction of the old inheritor. First, the young Prince Edward, Henry's son, is ritually murdered at Tewkesbury by the daggers of the three sons of York (Pt 3, V.v.38–40). Next, the old king in the Tower, finding himself alone with Richard of Gloucester, knows, as he had foreseen at the death of Humphrey Duke of Gloucester years before, that his life is required as a sacrifice.

> So first the harmless sheep doth yield his fleece,
> And next his throat unto the butcher's knife.
> What scene of death hath Roscius now to act? (Pt 3, V.vi.8–10)

The obligatory ceremony of his own murder he images first as butch-
ery and then as theatre. It is both.

The development of Richard of Gloucester's ambition during Part
Three of *Henry VI* is clearly intended by Shakespeare as a comment on
Tamburlaine. Tamburlaine was enormously handsome and attractive;
with a personality which inspired devotion, and an absolute directness in his behaviour. (He may double-cross Cosroe, but what he
presents to the world is not an image of himself but himself.) He
coveted a nobility of life and love, based on great power and wealth; to
achieve this was to be a king. Richard has the same passion for the
circlet of bright gold. But he is deformed, ugly, misshapen, repellent
to men and women. In the great speech which Shakespeare gives him
in Part Three (III.ii.124–95), his ugliness is his motive to power, since
there is no other success in life open to him, and since a position of
command allows him to lord it over those who can succeed in love and
wherever a 'daily beauty' commends itself.

> Since this earth affords no joy to me
> But to command, to check, to o'erbear such
> As are of better person than myself,
> I'll make my heaven to dream upon the crown,
> And whiles I live, t' account this world but hell,
> Until my mis-shaped trunk that bears this head
> Be round impalèd with a glorious crown.
>
> (Pt 3, III.ii.165–71)

Richard's 'soul's desire' for the crown, which in the first part of
Tamburlaine was the natural goal of human excellence, becomes the
compensation of the socially inadequate person, the vindictive assertion of the deprived self. Richard is so far removed from legitimate
inheritance of the crown that he feels he does but 'dream on
sovereignty' (l.134). His wonderful depiction of his struggle towards
kingship as:

> one lost in a thorny wood,
> That rends the thorns and is rent with the thorns,
> Seeking a way and straying from the way, . . .   (ll.174–6)

is followed by his declaration of method – to frame his face to all
occasions and 'change shapes with Proteus for advantages'. Here
again the change from *Tamburlaine*, from directness to deviousness, is
marked. The inspiration and the procedures of kingly ambition are
both made sorry things.

Richard III is a very special study by Shakespeare of a particular kind of ambitious person, but the opposition of his ruthless efficiency to Henry's saintly helplessness gives it a 'morality' air, and we are entitled to consider Richard as a genuine member of that distinguished group of new kings whose position is maintained by murder, including King John and Macbeth. His father York was a nicer man, and ended bravely, but still he too is accompanied by a black shadow, not of his own deformity, but of Cade's rebellion, a seductive and sinister mirror of his own grim plans to gain the throne. Indeed, Cade's rebellion forms part of his own grand scheme (Pt 2, III.i.355–9). Cade too is a claimant for the crown, and he too has a tortuous argument of lineal descent. Though he is the very image of brutish disorder and destruction, opposed to all established law and custom, he operates under a banner of nationalism and patriotism. The country has been betrayed by the authorities, and it is the intellectuals who are behind it all.

Dick. And furthermore, we'll have the Lord Say's head for selling the dukedom of Maine.
Cade. And good reason, for thereby is England main'd and fain to go with a staff, but that my puissance holds it up. Fellow kings, I tell you that that Lord Say has gelded the commonwealth and made it an eunuch: and more than that, he can speak French: and therefore he is a traitor.
                                                                                        (Pt 2, IV.ii.160–7)

Cade. What canst thou answer to my majesty for giving up Normandy unto Monsieur Basimecu, the Dauphin of France? Be it known unto thee by these presence, even the presence of Lord Mortimer, that I am the besom that must sweep the court clean of such filth as thou art. Thou hast most traitorously corrupted the youth of the realm, in erecting a grammar school . . .   (Pt 2, IV.vii.27–34)

This black-comedy version of kingly ambition closes with the death of Cade at the end of Act IV. The heroic version opens Act V.

> *York.* From Ireland thus comes York to claim his right,
> And pluck the crown from feeble Henry's head.
> Ring bells aloud, burn bonfires clear and bright,
> To entertain great England's lawful king.
> Ah sancta majestas, who would not buy thee dear?
> Let them obey, that knows not how to rule.
> This hand was made to handle nought but gold.
> I cannot give due action to my words
> Except a sword or sceptre balance it.
> A sceptre shall it have, have I a soul,
> On which I'll toss the flower-de-luce of France.
>   (Pt 2, V.i.1–11)

This is a fine expression of the exalted enthusiasm of the contender for the crown, which ends with the bitter mockery of the 'she-wolf of France' as she crowns him with a paper crown before stabbing him. However, the Yorkists win in the end, and Edward IV reigns. Richard of Gloucester is more successful than his father in carving his way to the throne, but his reign of darkness comes to an end on Bosworth Field. Derby enters bearing the crown.

> Courageous Richmond, well hast thou acquit thee.
> Lo here, this long usurpèd royalty
> From the dead temples of this bloody wretch
> Have I plucked off, to grace thy brows withal.
>
> (*Richard III*, V.v.3–6)

The hidden king emerges, briefly enough, to invoke God's blessing on a newly united England, as we have seen.

I suggested that, having written the *Henry VI–Richard III* tetralogy, Shakespeare felt it necessary to go back to the accepted beginning of the disordered times which the Tudors did indeed bring to a close and write *Richard II*, and that the rewriting of *The Troublesome Reign of King John* gave him the opportunity of isolating some of the issues which he was seeing were fundamental to the main historical cycle. The *Richard II–Henry IV–Henry V* group of plays gives us a clear picture of a contest between two types of kingship, medieval and modern.[17] Richard II discovers the true meaning of his sacred inherited royalty too late to prevent the reaction which his earlier irresponsibility set in motion. The mystical idea of kingship is something Shakespeare treated with great care and great sympathy in *Richard II*.[18] The inverted ceremony of the deposition, followed by degradation and finally murder, represents the replacement of the old order of kingship as sacrilege, iconoclasm, and defilement. It is useless offering to choose between Richard and his supplanter Bolingbroke. Richard wasted and divided his country but he had a supremacy which the more efficient Bolingbroke simple cannot acquire: a true title to the throne and a real if belated understanding of his relationship with his people and with God, totally different from Bolingbroke's shrewdness in managing people. The country has to suffer the inevitable consequences of the outrage on royalty in the years of misery of contention for the disputed crown. Henry V, the imperialist king, does all which the new kingship can do to unite and inspire the English people and extend England's greatness. But everyone has the feeling of spiritual limitation in King Henry, though Yeats is unnecessarily rough with him. And the cycle of national self-wounding as the nation tries to decide who is the true king is, I have suggested, only very temporarily suspended.

In her book, *Tragic Form in Shakespeare* (1972), Ruth Nevo makes an interesting and I think valid contrast between the two attitudes to England shown in Richard's saluting the earth on his return from Ireland, and in Gaunt's attack on Richard for his conduct as king. Here are a few lines of Richard's speech:

> I weep for joy
> To stand upon my kingdom once again.
> Dear earth, I do salute thee with my hand,
> Though rebels wound thee with their horses' hoofs.
> As a long-parted mother with her child
> Plays fondly with her tears and smiles in meeting,
> So, weeping, smiling, greet I thee, my earth,
> And do thee favours with my royal hands. (III.ii.4–11)

Richard, says Ruth Nevo, 'is invoking an ancient, sacramental magic. It is prenational, a-historical; it is the sacred, animistic bond between king and land – the *corpus mysticum* which includes and transcends both political kingdom and physical earth . . .' (pp. 74–5).

Gaunt's speech really should be quoted in full, but it is very long and very famous.

> This royal throne of kings, this sceptred isle. . .
> This fortress built by Nature for herself. . .
> This happy breed of men, this little world,
> This precious stone set in the silver sea,
> Which serves it in the office of a wall. . .
> This blessed plot, this earth, this realm, this England,
> This nurse, this teeming womb of royal kings . . .
> This land of such dear souls, this dear dear land,
> Dear for her reputation through the world,
> Is now leased out – I die pronouncing it –
> Like to a tenement or pelting farm. (II.i.40–60)

'Gaunt's patriotism,' writes Ruth Nevo, 'takes the form of a national pride in the virtues and achievements of an historical nation-state, its martial valour, its renown abroad, its strength and independence . . . Gaunt's patriotism is anachronistic, far more Elizabethan than feudal' (p. 75).

I think this is yet another piece of evidence (since the contrast may well not have been intentional) that Shakespeare's mind as he wrote the history plays was at a deep level always working at the bifurcation in the Elizabethan idea of kingship and setting the primordial against

the modern. Each side makes tremendous claims on one's loyalty –
one feels it now. Tempted towards the side of the saintly failures, we
remember how shockingly Henry VI and Richard II misgoverned.
Tempted towards the other side, we remember that it includes not
only King John but Richard III and Macbeth. *Macbeth* is the most
extraordinary version of the myth of the hidden king. The country is
now Scotland not England (which is taken to be at peace under her
true king). Here again is the bloody desecration of sacred kingship in
order that a man should realise his wild, secret dreams of the glory
and power of kingship. Nowhere does Shakespeare more sympathetically portray the inwardness of an ambitious bid for the crown, but
nor does he anywhere portray so vividly the horror of the necessary
murder, the disease and suffering of the land deprived of its true king,
and the spiritual shipwreck suffered by the usurper. At the end, once
again, the hidden king makes his brief appearance in Malcolm, whom
Macduff addresses.

> Hail King, for so thou art. Behold where stands
> Th'usurper's cursed head. The time is free.
> I see thee compassed with thy kingdom's pearl,
> That speak my salutation in their minds,
> Whose voices I desire aloud with mine.
> Hail King of Scotland.
>
> *All.*   Hail King of Scotland.   *Flourish.*

The sense of history as continuous self-laceration under rival
contenders for the crown gives to Shakespeare's affirmations of the
true king – Malcolm, or Henry V, or Henry VII – a disabling fragility.
Every monarchical achievement comes to look temporary, every
peace ephemeral. The idea of progress within such a vision can never
be more than a tentative suggestion. There may seem to be a giant
paradox in the attitude to nation suggested by Shakespeare's history
plays. He is quite clearly inspired by pride in his country. But the
nation which is sometimes seen marching towards its deliverance and
realisation under the Tudors is most often seen as a threatened or a
suffering land looking for a spiritual kingship which it can never find.
The sense of losing something of ineffable importance is often conveyed in the fates of the doomed kings of old, unfitted to survive in a
world of opportunism and go-ahead nationalism. Sometimes, as
when Shakespeare makes his King John assume Henry VIII's clothes
as supreme head of the church, it almost seems as though Shakespeare is attacking the Reformation and its kings. But I think that

Wyndham Lewis was right in the brilliant – and infuriating – pages of
The Lion and the Fox to claim that an important element in Shakespeare's universality was 'the complete eclecticism and confusion of
his time', when 'every influence of the old and new world met and
parleyed'.[19] The Elizabethan idea of kingship looked both ways:
Shakespeare, seeing the antipathies, made a rich contention of kings
from it in his history plays, and he too looked forward and back. Only
I think that, with Yeats, he looked backwards more than forwards in
describing the communal longing for the coming of the hidden king.

6

BEN JONSON

Introductory

Modern criticism of Jonson rightly emphasises how complex, ambiguous, and contradictory he is and how difficult it is to give straight answers to questions about his vision, his attitude, his meaning, whether we are talking of his individual pieces or his writing as a whole. Jonson is never plain and direct. There are ironies within ironies and subtleties within subtleties in every play, and no one has any confidence any more in saying (for example) that Crites in *Cynthia's Revels* is (or is not) an author figure,[1] that Ovid in *Poetaster* is exiled from Rome with Jonson's approval;[2] or, in a larger sphere, that Jonson did (or did not) believe that satire improved society;[3] that he did (or did not) flatter James in his masques.[4] When we try to survey his work as a whole, in satire, tragedy, court entertainment, and public poetry, bafflement is complete. It seems impossible to bring its contradictions within a comprehensible frame. These wider contradictions, made worse of course because they rest on the narrower uncertainties about the significance of individual works, are of four main kinds. First there is the contradiction between the brilliance of imagination and invention, in language, in character, in incident, set against the repeated failure of most of his plays to 'convince' either their original audience or modern readers as successful works of art. He has exactly two sure-fire successes, *Volpone* and *The Alchemist*, and three slightly less dependable ones, *Every Man in his Humour*, *Epicoene*, *Bartholomew Fair*. Jonson both despised popular esteem and exclaimed against the public's failure to like his plays.[5] He constantly submitted and resubmitted himself to the public's approval, and by pre-Brechtian sabotage of illusion and suspense refused to let the public have what it wanted.[6] He is one of our most brilliant writers, one of the most important figures in English literature, yet few actually enjoy the greater part of what he wrote.[7]

The second contradiction is between Jonson's majestic idea of the poet's rôle in society and the fact that he wrote mostly 'comical satires', court entertainments, occasional poems. Only two tragedies, no epic. Even his collection of literary criticism is largely translation. The third major area of contradiction is between his fostering of the values of an ordered, civilised, monarchic state, and the deep insurgency of his recurrent vision of society as anarchic and authority as pathetic and futile. The fourth contradiction is between the vehemence of his onslaught on vice, and the gusto with which he gave an abounding vitality to the vicious in his plays.

These areas of contradiction are of great importance in discussing Jonson's relation with the British nation. But it must first be pointed out that in spite of the difficulty, or impossibility, of seeing Jonson whole, the equivocations, tensions, and oppositions which so test our powers of negative capability are contained within a union of the man with his writings which is more solid and important than we usually find. Jonson himself, famously, insisted on 'the impossibility of any man's being the good poet without first being a good man' (*HS*, v, p. 17). The relationship is not so simple and beautiful as that, but every play sends us back to the man Jonson, working out what his function in English society was, every masque shows us a poet at the centre of a court which was the centre of a nation. Indeed, one could say that just as his court masques were (as it has been so eloquently and abundantly demonstrated by D. J. Gordon and his disciples Orgel and Strong) not so much shows or entertainments but political facts, literally involving foreign states in the persons of their squabbling ambassadors, depicting the king as he sat there, merging the symbolic image of the nation with the actual people who led the nation as the aristocratic masquers mingled in the dancing with the audience; just as the majority of his poems are public or occasional poems, written to and about his friends and patrons, commenting on what was going on around him; so the imaginative world of his plays blends and fuses with the life that Jonson was leading: comments on, explores, and defines himself and his England.[8] This fusion is not something that we discover. Jonson shouts it at us in the prologues and interruptions in which illusion is smashed and the play is candidly discussed.[9] Self-definition is most prominent in the group of earlier plays before the reshaping of his literary life in 1602, *Every Man Out of his Humour*,

Cynthia's Revels, and *Poetaster*, but there are few plays which are not in some ways models of what existed beyond the theatre. Both *Sejanus* and *Bartholomew Fair* are transmogrifications of England. In some ways you can say that Jonson is the most self-concerned writer in English apart from Wordsworth; but you must then also say that the concern is with the self in relation to a living society. There is certainly a self-absorption in Jonson: the sort of thing that properly exasperated Dekker. 'You must have three or four suits of names, when like a lousy pediculous vermin th'ast but one suit to thy back. You must be called Asper, and Criticus, and Horace. Thy title's longer a-reading than the style o' the big Turk's: Asper, Criticus, Quintus, Horatius, Flaccus.'[10] But there is a sublimity in his egotism as in Wordsworth's. He reaches out to a knowledge of man through a study of himself as a poet writing in England under King James.

The contrarieties and the equivocal 'message' in Jonson's writings are therefore not only the signs of a keenly intelligent writer who can always see (like a Sophist) beyond an affirmation to its equally plausible contradiction (though they are that), but also a witness to Jonson's own uncertainty about the place and function of the poet in English society under Elizabeth, James, and Charles.[11]

The one area on which there is an absolute silence in the archives of English drama is that of the circumstances in which the Renaissance dramatists came to write for the common stage. Marlowe, Kyd, Shakespeare, Jonson, Fletcher, Middleton, Massinger, Ford give us no inkling what pressures, what aspiration, what hope or despair, what drift or accident led them to undertake their first work for the professional theatre. The nearest we get to an archive is Greene's taunt on Shakespeare – 'an upstart crow, beautified with our feathers', who 'supposes he is as well able to bombast out a blank verse as the best of you' and supposes he is 'the only Shake-scene in a country'.[12] This is Chrisoganus crying out against Posthaste. Shakespeare is presumably an actor, a member of a travelling troupe, who has begun to prepare scripts for his own fellows to act. The question then pushes itself back: was it choice or necessity which made him a common player? What Greene implies was Shakespeare's entry into dramaturgy may also have been Jonson's. His own father, a gentleman who had become impoverished and had entered the ministry, died just before Jonson was born in 1572 and Jonson was 'brought up poorly' (*HS*, I, p. 139). After his Westminster schooling under Camden

(Jonson told Drummond) he was put to a craft, 'I think was to be a wright or bricklayer, which he could not endure' (*HS*, 1, p. 139). He enlisted as a soldier and fought in the Low Countries. He did not tell Drummond what led him to become a stage-poet. Dekker's *Satiromastix*, whose object is not truth but ridicule, has clear views on this as it abuses Jonson for his vanity and social ambition ('Horace did not screw and wriggle himself into great men's familiarity, impudently, as thou dost' (V.ii.254–6). He had become a strolling player: 'thou hast forgot how thou amblest (in leather pilch) by a play-wagon, in the highway, and tookst mad Jeronimo's part, to get service among the mimics' (IV.i.130–2). 'I ha' seen thy shoulders lapt in a player's old cast cloak, like a sly knave as thou art; and when thou ranst mad for the death of Horatio, thou borrowedst a gown of Roscius the stager . . . and sentst it home lousy, didst not?' (I.ii.354–8). By 1597, Jonson was on Henslowe's books as a writer.[13] By 1602, he had written about a dozen plays (of which only five are extant) for Henslowe's companies, for the Chamberlain's men, and for children's companies. From 1602, Jonson's literary life took on a quite different complexion. His plays, *Sejanus, Volpone, Epicoene, The Alchemist, Catiline, Bartholomew Fair*, were spread out at much greater intervals (six plays in eleven years up to 1614). He lived with patrons: Sir Robert Townshend, the Lord d'Aubigny, Sir Robert Cotton, Sir Robert Sidney at Penshurst, Sir Henry Goodyere in Warwickshire, Sir Robert Wroth. He came to be on unusually intimate terms with a large number of the greater nobility, including the Earl of Pembroke (who gave him a small pension), the Countess of Bedford, and the Countess of Rutland. For aristocratic patrons like these Jonson would occasionally write entertainments for special occasions, for which he was well paid.[14] His major literary work, however, during James's reign, apart from the plays already mentioned, was done at court in the revels season between Christmas and Lent. In the Christmas season of 1604–5, the *Masque of Blackness* ushered in his great series of court masques which he in collaboration with Inigo Jones provided during James's reign. He received a royal pension of 100 marks from 1616, later increased, and in 1621 was granted the reversion of the Mastership of the Revels (though the post itself never came to him).

Jonson was dropped as writer of court masques for the first five years of Charles's reign, though he was recalled in 1631 for two masques. He returned to stage-plays after a nine-year break with *The Staple of News* in 1626. Though he died (in 1637) after much illness, neglect, and poverty, he had risen to an unusual height of national distinction for a man of letters. It was thought an honour to be the dedicatee of one of his works;[15] the universities of Oxford and Cambridge gave him honorary degrees; he published his plays in folio in 1616 as his *Works* – which vexed or amused those who had known him in his less palmy days; for a young poet to be sealed of the tribe of Ben, as one of his sons, was a distinction. Another former common player, Edward Alleyn, had achieved wealth and importance, and was able to establish the great school and hospital at Dulwich. But Jonson's eminence was of another kind, and his distinction had nothing to do with money, or acting ability. It was as a writer for public performances that he achieved his unique position in the nation.[16]

A vision of Jonson basking in royal approval ought to be qualified by the recollection of Jonson's keen experience of the sharper edge of authority. Very early in his career he had a hand in a satiric comedy, *The Isle of Dogs* (not extant). The Privy Council, having been informed that this was 'lewd', and contained 'very seditious and slanderous matter', arrested some of the actors and those of the writers they could lay their hands on. Jonson was in prison for several weeks, and he claimed that two undercover agents were put with him as fellow-prisoners to extract intelligence from him (*HS*, I, p. 139). In 1598, Jonson fought a duel with an actor, Gabriel Spencer, killed him, and was arrested, branded, and imprisoned. He avoided execution by claiming benefit of clergy. In prison he was visited by a Catholic priest, who converted him, and he remained a Catholic for twelve years. Three of his plays in the early years of the seventeenth century caused him trouble for supposed politically dangerous matter. He was cited to appear before Lord Justice Popham for *Poetaster* in 1601 (an intervention led to the examination being dropped). He was summoned before the Privy Council by the Earl of Northampton for *Sejanus* in 1603; it is not on record that he suffered any penalty. In 1605, however, he was in prison for some months for his share in *Eastward Ho!* Immediately after the Gunpowder Plot in the same year, Jonson, a Catholic who had known some of the conspirators well (*HS*, XI, p. 578), was given a warrant by Cecil to get in touch with a priest who was reported to be willing 'to do good service to the State'. The priest would not come forward, however, and Jonson reported his failure to make contact in a letter to Cecil in which he asserted his loyalty, saying, 'For myself, if I had been a priest, I would have put on wings to such an occasion, and have thought it no adventure, where I might have done (besides his Majesty and my country) all Christianity so good service.'[17] In 1606, Jonson was charged as a recusant and a Catholic proselytiser at the Consistory Court in London: once again no penalty is known.

Jonson told Drummond that he was 'accused' upon *The Devil is an Ass* (1616) and (apparently) that the King 'desired him to conceal' some feature of the play (*HS*, 1, pp. 143–4). There was a more serious accusation by the Privy Council in 1628 that he was the author of verses praising Felton for assassinating Buckingham. Jonson was examined by the Attorney General and exonerated. Finally, oaths in *The Magnetic Lady* brought Jonson to answer to the Court of High Commission in 1632: he put the blame on the players.

These brushes with authority clearly indicate the unpleasant closeness of the court poet to major national happenings like the Gunpowder Plot and the assassination of Buckingham, the extreme concern of the state about the stage as a potentially dangerous political platform, and Jonson's own experience of the means by which the state attempted to identify and destroy its enemies. Shakespeare having presumably neither the temperament nor the desire to pursue the aggressively competitive course which lodged Jonson in his chair as the court poet equally avoided the situations of danger which Jonson ran into because of his religion, the outspokenness of his plays, or his violence.

Jonson's theory of the relationship between prince and poet

The relationship between poet, monarch, and state was a subject which Jonson theorised about in prefaces and dedications, objectified in the dramatic situations of his plays, and lived out in his work at court. The relationship is a complex perspective, and it may be that the least interesting element is the theoretical formulation of the poet's function which Jonson would make from time to time. Yet these statements give us a convenient suggestion of the quality of the aspirations which led Jonson first to dramatise the poet in society in the 'comical satires' and then to enter the court, like Chapman's Bussy d'Ambois, on the gamble that it might work in practice.

In two places in particular, the dedication of *Volpone* in 1604, and in the posthumously published *Timber or Discoveries*, Jonson strongly voiced the widely shared Renaissance ideal of poetry, which reached perhaps its finest expression in Sidney's *Apology for Poetry* (written about 1580). This view of the poet and his function was built up from the wisdom of the sages and poets of the past from Plato and Aristotle through to the early humanists. Its syncretic quality is shown by the very form of *Discoveries*, which is chiefly translations and recordings of Jonson's readings in the classics and the humanists. The great tradition as it culminates in Sidney is that what matters in life is 'virtuous action', that for all individuals, but particularly for those who must govern others and direct the community, wise action depends on a full mind, on learning, on a knowledge of the best that has been thought in the world. The poet is a creature specially favoured among men; not merely is his gift a divine gift, but his imagination is in some way an avenue by which divine truth reaches men. The poetic gift is only potentiality: hard work at acquiring human knowledge and learning, the discipline of eloquence, and poetic craft are required before the poet can play his proper rôle, and that rôle is the dispensing of wisdom and knowledge in the form of images which men find more attractive and persuasive than learning in any other guise.

The major theme of *Discoveries* is the civilising power of letters – of all literature but especially poetry – in the life of the individual and in the conduct of the state. Poetry and learning are inseparable, poetry and morality are inseparable, individual and communal morality are inseparable. In the dedication to *Volpone* he says the poet is 'able to inform young men to all good disciplines, inflame grown men to all great virtues'. The poet is 'the interpreter and arbiter of nature, a teacher of things divine no less than human, a master in manners; and can alone, or with a few, effect the business of mankind'.

It is this last phrase which Jonson gives more emphasis to than any other English Renaissance writer, even Spenser and Milton: the idea of the poet as an active participant in the direction of human affairs, sitting as Seanchan had formerly had the right to sit, at the very council table of the king.

The most important theoretical statement of Jonson's is a translation, in *Discoveries*, of a sentence by Juan Luis Vives, the Spanish humanist (1492–1540). It is headed *Mutua auxilia*.

Learning needs rest: Sovereignty gives it. Sovereignty needs counsel; Learning affords it. There is such a consociation of offices between the Prince and whom his favour breeds, that they may help to sustain his power, as he their knowledge.   (*HS*, VIII, p. 565)

Vives was not talking about poetry and drama; indeed, he was an anti-theatre man. But Jonson makes explicit that the truest man of learning is the poet.

I could never think the study of wisdom confined only to the philosopher, or of piety to the divine, or of state to the politic. But that he which can feign a commonwealth (which is the poet), can govern it with counsels, strengthen it with laws, correct it with judgements, inform it with religion and morals, is all these.   (*HS*, VIII, p. 595)

It is a very common idea in Renaissance poetics that the rulers of mankind have traditionally honoured poets. Boccaccio, arguing that poets needed solitude and peace, hastened to point out that they were nevertheless honoured in courts and camps, and gave as examples Ennius accompanying Scipio on his campaigns, and Petrarch's intimacy with the Emperor Charles, King John of France, and King Robert of Naples.[18] Spenser in *The Shepherd's Calendar* (October eclogue), lamenting the decay of poetry, wrote:

> O peerless poesy, where is then thy place?
> If nor in princes' palace thou do sit
> (And yet is prince's palace the most fit),
> Ne breast of baser birth doth thee embrace.

Neither in Boccaccio nor Spenser is there talk about *counselling* princes. But Spenser in the same eclogue, lamenting that 'great Augustus long ago is dead', continued:

> And all the worthies liggen wrapped in lead
> That matter made for poets on to play.

This reciprocity, of princes protecting poets who celebrate their patron's deeds, is underlined in E.K.'s gloss.

He sheweth the cause why poets were wont be had in such honour of noble men; that is, that by them their worthiness and valour should through their famous poesies be commended to all posterities. Wherefore it is said that Achilles had never been so famous as he is, but for Homer's immortal verses.

It was traditional, based on Aristotle's authority, that the major task of the best poets was to represent the noble actions of distinguished men, and Puttenham's *Art of English Poesy* helps us to see how honouring the great doings of kings can be associated with counselling them. In Chapter 8 of his first book, talking of the esteem in which princes have held poets, Puttenham writes:

Nor this reputation was given them in ancient times altogether in respect that poesy was a delicate art, and the poets themselves cunning prince-pleasers, but for that also they were thought for their universal knowledge to be very sufficient men for the greatest charges in their commonwealths, were it for counsel or for conduct, whereby no man need to doubt but that both skills may very well concur and be most excellent in one person.[19]

While this is Jonsonian (and Yeatsian) in seeing the poet honoured as government adviser, it seems to separate the tasks of writing poetry and counselling the king. Jonson would presumably not have been averse to accepting a post as an adviser to the king, but his aim (we infer) was not that of Lyly, who wished to use court poetry only as an entrée to other employment, nor that of being the paid entertainer enlivening the royal evenings. It is to be a counsellor *as he is a poet*; that is the heart of the matter. That boldest of claims, which reminds us of Yeats's chiasmus on the mutual interdependence of literature and nationality, ran: 'There is such a consociation of offices between the Prince and whom his favour breeds, that *they may help to sustain his power, as he their knowledge.*'

A prince's power will be sustained if he knows what he is and what he should do. There is a strong hint in E.K.'s gloss on Spenser's October eclogue that the greatness of the heroes of the past was actually created by the poets who celebrated their actions.

Wherefore it is said that Achilles had never been so famous as he is, but for Homer's immortal verses . . . And also that Alexander the Great coming to his tomb in Sigeus, with natural tears blessed him that ever was his hap to be honoured with so excellent a poet's work: *as so renowned and ennobled only by his means.*[20]

The heroic ideal is created by the poet because he knows what virtue is and he celebrates it where he finds it in the doings of outstanding men; and this ideal is kept alive in the tradition of poetry. Not only is Homer's Achilles still available in the poetry of old but the imagination of succeeding poets, working in the tradition, recreates the heroic image and spells out to a lesser age what it should strive after, as Yeats created his Cuchulain figure to energise a new Ireland.

> For in the genius of a poet's verse
> The King's fame lives.

So wrote Jonson in his 'Epigram to the Household' in 1630. Inigo Jones's elaborate House of Fame, for Jonson's *Masque of Queens*, 1609 (reproduced in Plate 3), had 'for the lower columns . . . the statues of the most excellent poets, as Homer, Virgil, Lucan, etc., as being the substantial supporters of Fame. For the upper, Achilles, Aeneas,

Caesar, and those great heroes which those poets had celebrated'. In
the text, Heroic Virtue describes the house,

> whose columns be
> Men-making poets, and those well-made men
> Whose strife it was to have the happiest pen
> Renown them to an after-life, and not
> With pride to scorn the muse and die forgot.[21]

It is the poet who recognises virtue and by celebrating it in those who
show it creates fame for them and a model for others. By honouring
the great when their deeds are worthy the poet may be said to *counsel
them*, because he thus instructs them in what is truly noble and what is
base, and thus also sustains their power. Great men, says Augustus
in *Poetaster*, are 'hollow statues' if they lack 'Promethean stuffings
reached from heaven' (V.i.15–16). Surrounded with images of greatness and wisdom, the prince is fashioned in that image.[22]

As Spenser, this time in *A View of the Present State of Ireland*, says:

.In all ages, poets have been had in special reputation . . . for besides their
sweet inventions and most witty lays, they are always used to set forth the
praises of the good and virtuous . . . so that many brave young minds have
oftentimes, through the hearing the praises and famous eulogies of worthy
men sung and reported to them, been stirred up to affect like commendations,
and so to strive unto the like deserts.[23]

Almost always coupled with the grander view of the nature and
function of the poet is the lament for the rottenness of the present state
of poetry. Meretricious poets are esteemed, real worth is neglected.
Aristocrats are not like Maecenas, kings are not like Augustus. But
the times are always bad; the poet is always having to force himself
like Jonson and Yeats into the national centre and create the greatness that he does not find. Elizabeth never took a professional poet so
much into the bosom of the court as James took Jonson, and James
was incapable of the elevation which the theory required. Hence the
eagerness with which the poets turned to Prince Henry and tried to
turn him into a youthful Alexander or Augustus. It was also part of a
time-honoured recognition of the nature of the poetic praise of men in
high office that you could tactfully improve your man by picturing
him somewhat nearer the ideal than he really was.[24] This leads us into
a very treacherous area in connection with the ethics of flattery which
will be examined later. The immediate point is to show how Jonson's
vision of the poet as one whose counsel maintains the king in power is
the culmination of a traditional view that poets, working at the side of

princes, while they deferentially pretend to do no more than com-
memorate heroism, are actually creating the heroic ideal in their art
and perpetuating it for the guidance of less talented generations.

The comical satires, 1599–1601

Jonson put three 'comical satires' on the stage between 1599 and
1601, *Every Man Out of his Humour*, *Cynthia's Revels*, and *Poetaster*. These
plays have as a common factor of all and the ultimate aim of each the
definition of the relationship between poet and monarch. The plays
are self-reflexive in that Jonson, considering his own future, examines
and promulgates his ideas by writing plays about a poet-intellectual
coming into a relationship with the ruler of his nation, but they
are neither autobiographical nor wish-fulfilment plays.[25] They are
mock-ups or models; the place of art in society is investigated in a play
about the place of the artist in society.

Every Man Out of his Humour is altogether too sophisticated and
intricate to succeed, and it is thoroughly unfortunate that the original
ending, which crowned and explained the work, had to be scrapped.
The play directly answers or complements the *Histriomastix* which was
discussed in an earlier chapter. Macilente is a re-creation of the
neglected humanist Chrisoganus; he is much more deeply immersed
in Envy, and when the Queen-Elizabeth figure appears at the end of
the play he is not forgotten or left out as he was in the earlier play.
Unfortunately, objection was apparently taken to an impersonation
of the Queen appearing on a common stage. Jonson had to change the
ending, and he thereby deprived the play of its final meaning. When
he had the play printed, however, in 1600, he added as an appendix
not only the original ending but an invaluable defence of it.[26]

It will be remembered that the presenter of the play is Asper, a
man 'of an ingenious and free spirit, eager and constant in reproof,
without fear controlling the world's abuses'. *Every Man Out of his
Humour* is Asper's play. He goes to change and he reappears in the
body of the play as Macilente, 'a man well-parted, a sufficient scholar,
and travelled, who (wanting that place in the world's account which
he thinks his merit capable of) falls into such an envious apoplexy,
with which his judgement is so dazzled and distasted, that he grows
violently impatient of any opposite happiness in another'. During the
course of the play, Delirio, a merchant, takes pity on the embittered
and splenetic Macilente and manages to secure the interest of

Fastidious Brisk, who says that if Macilente can get himself a decent
suit of clothes he will 'carry him to court' and 'prefer him to some
nobleman of good place' (II.vi.68–84). Macilente is a totally ungrateful, disloyal, and malicious man. He goes beyond not only Alceste but
Gregers Werle in causing trouble by inhumane candour – telling his
benefactor Fastidious how he's despised at court, and Delirio how his
wife's abused him. His low point is gratuitously poisoning Puntarvolo's dog, and then coolly lying about it (V.i.81–5; V.iii.26–8;
V.v.21). But this is also his crisis, for the poisoning is symbolic. He
purges himself of the poison of Envy by pouring it into a dog – who
slowly dies of it (V.iii.58). After the dog incident, everyone changes.
Puntarvolo, the effeminate owner, proves himself a man and beats
Carlo Buffone, who proves himself a coward, Brisk is disgraced, and
Delirio has, alas, no reason to continue uxorious.

In the revised version which Jonson was forced to write, Macilente
simply says that all his envy is spent.

> Now is my soul at peace,
> I am as empty of all Envy now
> As they of merit to be envied at.
> My humour (like a flame) no longer lasts
> Than it hath stuff to feed it.   (V.xi.54–8)

It is not possible to reconstruct the original version exactly from what
Jonson has left us, but the main issue is clear. A figure representing
Queen Elizabeth appeared 'against expectation' *before* Macilente had
purged himself of all envy. Indeed, Jonson narrates it, he 'was now
come to the Court with a purposed resolution (his soul as it were new
dressed in envy) to malign at anything that should front him'. The
wonder of this sudden regal apparition 'strikes him to the earth dumb
and astonished. From whence, rising and recovering heart, his passion thus utters itself':

> Blessed, divine, unblemished, sacred, pure,
> Glorious, immortal, and indeed immense –
> O that I had a world of attributes
> To lend or add to this high majesty!
> Never till now did object greet mine eyes
> With any light content; but in her graces
> All my malicious powers have lost their stings.
> Envy is fled my soul at sight of her
> And she hath chased all black thoughts from my bosom
> Like as the sun doth darkness from the world.
> . . .   .

And I have now a Spirit as sweet and clear
As the most rarefied and subtle air,
With which, and with a heart as pure as fire,
Yet humble as the earth, do I implore,   *He kneels.*
O Heaven, that she (whose figure hath effected
This change in me) may never suffer change
In her admired and happy government;
May still this island be called Fortunate.

At the end of his speech, of which this is only an extract, a trumpet sounds a flourish and Macilente steps out to address the audience.

Well, gentlemen, I should have gone in, and returned to you as I was Asper at the first, but (by reason the shift [of clothes] would have been somewhat long, and we are loth to draw your patience any farder) we'll entreat you to imagine it.

Macilente *is* Asper, before he was changed by meeting the Queen. The change is meant to be sensational, ridiculous, incredible. The poison engendered by society's neglect and the gallants' scorn is poured into a dog, and the sight of the Queen transforms him into the free spirit controlling the world's abuses.

   In the justification of his cancelled ending, having argued that there were precedents for introducing a representation of the Queen, Jonson continued:

2 It is to be conceived, that Macilente being so strongly possessed with envy (as the Poet here makes him) it must be no slight or common object, that should effect so sudden and strange a cure upon him as the putting him clean Out of his Humour.

3 If his imagination had discoursed the whole world over for an object, it could not have met with a more proper, eminent or worthy figure than that of her Majesty's, which his election (though boldly, yet respectively) used to a moral and mysterious end.

By 'mysterious' he means having an inner, concealed meaning. It is not far to seek. Macilente loses the humour which as with the others was essentially a concealment of himself. His learning, intelligence, moral fervour turned into most unpleasant channels until he was transformed into his true self, at court in the eye of the Queen.

   Of course, Jonson hoped that this allegory might have its personal application. His fourth defence for having presented on stage the 'prosopopeia' of the Queen was this:

4 His greediness to catch at any occasion that might express his affection to his Sovereign may worthily plead for him.

If it is the Queen herself in person whom Macilente catches sight of
and kneels before, the hint is strong that if she has enjoyed the play she
may transform its author by her favour. The Chamberlain's men
played at court on the day after Christmas, 1599, and on Twelfth
Night. But in spite of the confidence of E. 'K. Chambers and the
Clarendon Press editors,[27] the only evidence that *Every Man Out of his
Humour* was ever performed before Elizabeth is the reprinting in the
1616 Folio of the cancelled original version of the ending with the
heading 'Which, in the presentation before Queene E. was thus
varied'. In the speech, the words of Macilente, 'whose figure hath
effected/This change in me' (see above), are changed to 'whose
presence hath effected/This change in me'. On at least one other
occasion Jonson wrote lines for a court performance which never took
place.[28] It is hard to believe that in the Quarto printed in 1600 Jonson
would not have made some mention of the presence of the Queen in
person during his defence of the impersonation of her if the Christmastide court performance had been a reality. But it will not diminish
the clear meaning of the play if the Queen, as shape-changer of
discontented intellectuals, was present in impersonation only.

The existence of *Cynthia's Revels*, which shows a complete rethink-
ing of the dramatic structure required to figure the poet/monarch
relationship and was written for an entirely different kind of dramatic
company, a company of children, might be held to indicate that
Jonson had not in the earlier play been able to make his point to
Elizabeth. Evidence suggests that this play *was* played at court, and
there is, unfortunately, also some evidence that it was not a success,
not only from the biased Dekker, but in the sad title-page quotations
from Juvenal's Seventh Satire: 'Quod non dant proceres, dabit his-
trio. Haud tamen invideas vati quem pulpita pascunt.' (What noblemen won't give, the actor will. Don't envy the poet who is supported
by the stage (*HS*, IX, pp. 189–9).) It is a pity it was not more
successful, because it is a strange and beautiful play, a delicate
conception with some of Jonson's best writing and some of his
loveliest songs. Even the elephantine growths which in the 1616 Folio
version were added to the much leaner and sparer Quarto version of
1601 contain some brilliant passages, like Moria's description of
sexual promiscuity at court (IV.i.140–57).

In this play the end which crowns the work is determinedly and
repeatedly pointed out from the beginning. Cynthia has proclaimed
revels at her court, which she is to grace in person, and everyone is

looking forward to them. There is no story. There are courtiers,
affected and foolish, who have either drunk of the fountain of Self-
Love or intend to do so, and two observer-figures, a 'retired [sc.
retiring] scholar', Criticus in the Quarto and Crites in the Folio, and
'the lady Arete, or Virtue, a poor nymph of Cynthia's train, that's
scarce able to buy herself a gown' (Induction, 90–1). The courtiers
are hit pretty severely; the 'two essential parts of the courtier' we are
told are 'pride and ignorance' (II.ii.77). The ignorance shows itself
offensively in scorning the scholar (II.ii.90).

In III.iv, Crites protests at length to Arete of the corrupt vanities of
the courtiers, and Arete replies:

> Patience, gentle Crites.
> This knot of spiders will be soon dissolved,
> And all their webs swept out of Cynthia's court,
> When once her glorious deity appears
> And but presents itself in her full light.
> Till when, go in, and spend your hours with us . . .
> Think on some sweet and choice invention, now,
> Worthy her serious and illustrous eyes,
> That from the merit of it we may take
> Desir'd occasion to prefer your worth,
> And make your service known to Cynthia. (III.iv.87–92; 95–9)

This double aim of the reformation of the court and Cynthia's acceptance of her new poet is to be made single in time. Crites worries that
the masque which he is to perform will be ruined by the nature of the
only available performers, the awful courtiers. Arete firmly tells him
of his error in a speech which is most important for Jonson's theory of
the masque (V.v.15–33). The discipline and ceremony of the masque
impose order on the discordant elements which contribute to it – here
the revellers themselves, the foolish courtiers,

> especially
> When they are not presented as themselves
> But masked like others.   (V.v.26–8)

And, she adds, *not* to 'incorporate' them within the masque is to
promote anarchy and disease. So the masque is a means of imposing
order and a sense of society on a disorderly court, and the masquers
are improved by the impersonations they undertake.

Before the masque begins, Arete takes the opportunity of mention-
ing Crites to Cynthia, as the neglected and deserving man who has
planned the royal entertainment. But Cynthia has her eye on him
already.

> We have already judged him, Arete;
> Nor are we ignorant, how noble minds
> Suffer too much through those indignities.   (V.vi.101–3)

In between the two masques there is a double recognition. In the first masque, Cupid, masked as his anti-self, Anteros, has presented Cynthia with a crystal orb, a 'symbol of perfection', which will show 'whatsoever the world hath excellent'. In the crystal, Cynthia on stage perceives the 'real' Cynthia, Queen Elizabeth. (It may be that at court performances she ostentatiously looked through the crystal at the Queen sitting in state.) And at this very moment, Crites is summoned:

> What shape? what substance? or what unknown power
> In virgin's habit, crowned with laurel leaves
> And olive branches woven in between,
> On sea-girt rocks, like to a goddess shines?
> O front! O face! O all celestial sure
> And more than mortal! Arete, behold
> Another Cynthia, and another Queen,
> Whose glory (like a lasting plenilune)
> Seems ignorant of what it is to wane!
> Not under heaven an object could be found
> More fit to please. Let Crites make approach.   (V.viii.4–14)

There is a ceremonious and somewhat pompous ritual of presentation (by Arete), acceptance (by Cynthia), devotion (by Crites). The man is 'not of usual / earth / But of that nobler and more precious mould / Which Phoebus' self doth temper'. Cynthia says he is now 'our Crites', exempted from the common multitude.

> Henceforth be ours, the more thyself to be.   (l. 35)

In the two masques, the courtiers act out their 'neighbour virtues', those good qualities which they have corrupted into vices. Even self-love can be an aspiration after honour. It is clear from V.x that simply taking part in a masque is not enough to restore the fallen courtiers. Cynthia, seeing through their masks to their real qualities, passes them over to her new poet for reformation. Crites orders that they should repair to 'the well of knowledge, Helicon',

> Where purged of your present maladies,
> (Which are not few nor slender) you become
> Such as you fain would seem: and then return,
> Offering your service to great Cynthia.   (V.xi.153–6)

The poet is the supplier of knowledge which corrects the courtier. The

centre of moral improvement is the revels which the Queen orders
and the poet supplies. The dedication to the court which Jonson wrote
for the 1616 Folio makes no more pretence about the true nature of
courtiers than the play itself does, but, like the play, it is optimistic
about the possibility of improvement. It is addressed to 'The Special
Fountain of Manners: The Court':

Thou art a bountiful and brave spring, and waterest all the noble plants of
this Island. In thee the whole Kingdom dresseth itself, and is ambitious to use
thee as her glass . . . It is not powdering, perfuming, and every day smelling of
the tailor that converteth to a beautiful object: but a mind, shining through
any suit, which needs no false light either of riches or honour to help it. Such
shalt thou find some here, even in the reign of Cynthia (a Crites and an
Arete).

. . .   .

Thy servant, but not slave,
Ben. Jonson.

Courtiers need learning in the best sense to become the pattern of
civilised behaviour for the nation. The poet is used by the monarch to
teach manners and wisdom by his art. Until the poet is recognised by
the monarch he has no real being: until the poet begins his work at the
royal court, the courtiers are not themselves.

We are dealing in *Cynthia's Revels* with a fantasy showing the
movement to an ideal position in which the mutual needs of prince,
poet, and court are satisfied. There was also for the Renaissance poet
an historical period which acted as a touchstone or a bitter memory,
the age of Rome under Augustus, and this is the subject of Jonson's
third poet/monarch play, *Poetaster* (1601).

Once again the dramatic strategy is completely altered. There are
three poets in the play: Ovid the love-poet, Horace the satirist, and
Virgil the great writer of the national epic. Horace has many resemb-
lances to Jonson himself, and of course Dekker and Marston so
figured him in their reply. But the three great Roman poets are used
by Jonson not to characterise himself or others but to indicate different aspects of poetry. (On the offensive side it is different, and there is
no need to dispute the identification of Demetrius with Dekker and
Crispinus with Marston.)

Ovid is the enthusiast, the servant of 'sacred poesie', on fire with
'the high raptures of a happy Muse'. He is as impulsive in love as in
poetry and it is a matter for debate among commentators how far
Jonson approved of his banishment by Caesar for 'soothing the

declined affections/Of our base daughter' after the wild and daring masque of the gods.[29] Ovid certainly represents the dangerous side of poetry, but he is no poetaster, and I think D. M. Bevington is right that Jonson's point in the banishment really concerns the autocratic power which even a civilised and benevolent despotism is likely to use in controlling art. 'Ovid's banishment is a warning of what intelligent artists may expect from a court grown too powerful in silencing free expression.' Augustus was to blame in countenancing the banishment.[30] Certainly, the paranoia of the state – the state reckoned to be the most favourable of all towards art – about the threat of sedition in literature is a major point in *Poetaster*. It emphasises Jonson's awareness of what was discussed in Chapter 2 – the necessary co-existence of control with encouragement in the monarchy's adoption of the theatre. Jonson's excellent portrait of the conspiracy-sniffing magistrate Lupus is really rather courageous. Lupus believes 'these players are an idle generation, and do much harm in a state' (I.ii.37), and finding that a list of properties for a forthcoming play contains 'a crown, and a sceptre' cries out rebellion and treason and sets a prosecution on foot.

Whatever the verdict on Caesar's treatment of Ovid, there is no doubt of his commitment to poetry and the encouragement of poets. He voices the idea that the poetic imagination is the creator of the greatness it celebrates. 'Sweet poesy' is

> of all the faculties on earth
> The most abstract and perfect; if she be
> True born, and nursed with all the sciences.
> She can so mould Rome, and her monuments,
> Within the liquid marble of her lines,
> That they shall stand fresh and miraculous
> Even when they mix with innovating dust.   (V.i.18–24)

This is in the fifth act, and there is a ceremonious entry of Virgil:

> *Eques.* Virgil is now at hand, imperial Caesar.
> *Caesar.* Rome's honour is at hand then. Fetch a chair
>   And set it on our right hand; where 'tis fit
>   Rome's honour, and our own, should ever sit.   (V.i.68–71)

The king's threshold is crossed. Virgil reads part of his national epic in the emperor's presence. But *Poetaster*, celebrating the discomfiture of bad poets and the exaltation of the good, was only a play. *Poetaster* was followed by 'an apologetical dialogue' (printed in the 1616 Folio but 'only once spoken on the stage' and apparently forbidden 'by

authority' from being printed with the Quarto) in which Jonson
fulminated against the misconstructions put on his plays.

> And since the comic Muse
> Hath proved so ominous to me, I will try
> If tragedy have a more kind aspect.   (ll. 222–4)

For a year or more Jonson wrote no plays at all. He gave up his direct
bid for court favour by means of plays which showed the necessity of
royal patronage, and sought patronage among the friendly nobility.
His next play was *Sejanus His Fall*, a tragedy and one of the most
powerful of his plays, about a reign of terror conducted chiefly against
the intelligentsia by the tyrannical puppet of the ruler. The ultimate
authority in the state has shifted from Augustus to Tiberius, a lax,
self-indulgent, and cruel man who, with the aid of a corrupt and weak
senate, makes Sejanus's pogrom possible. His most effective act of
responsible government is to destroy Sejanus and replace him with
the equally vicious Macro. *Sejanus His Fall* was acted in 1603, and it
must have been before Elizabeth's death on 24 March because the
theatres were then closed for a whole year. It is Jonson's farewell to
Cynthia. The first audience at the Globe hated it, and hissed it off the
stage.

The court poet

Under James, Jonson became the national poet and his work fills us
with disquiet. If he had succeeded with Elizabeth, the position would
not be so bad. It is one thing to write praises for Elizabeth, who was a
great stateswoman; it is another thing to do it for James, whom
nobody can admire. The problem is not the same as that which some
people have with Yeats or Eliot – liking the poetry but not liking the
political views which often inform it. It is a deeper problem, in which
conduct and literary criticism are inextricably mixed. In the fiction,
the neglected wit Macilente behaves very unpleasantly when he is
poor and solitary. When he is properly recognised, he is Asper.

He is of an ingenious and free spirit, eager and constant in reproof, without
fear controlling the world's abuses. One whom no servile hope of gain, or
frosty apprehension of danger, can make to be a parasite, either to time, place,
or opinion.   (*HS*, III, p. 423)

Jonson's continuance as court poet depended on his writing things
pleasing to his royal and aristocratic employers. This stern and

obdurate man, who refused to flatter the public and give them the
kind of play they wanted, who was concerned to present things as they
really were and not as most people fancied they were, concerned
above all to illuminate that distance between a man's true nature and
his own conceit of himself, this man must now spend his life in literary
cosmetics, presenting ignoble people with the image which their
vanity required, using his great learning for the greater glory of fops,
criminals, nonentities, and incompetent statesmen. 'What think'st
thou of a masque?' asks a character at the beginning of *The Maid's
Tragedy* (?1610), 'Will it be well?'

> – As well as masques can be.
> –   As masques can be?
> – Yes, they must commend their king, and speak in praise
>   Of the assembly, bless the bride and bridegroom
>   In person of some god: they're tied to rules
>   Of flattery.

The masque which follows has a hideous ironic distance, in its ful-
some characterisation of the King and of the loveliness of the wedding
of the bride and groom, from the actual situation immediately afterwards revealed in the bridal chamber when Amintor learns his marriage is merely a convenience to serve the King's lust.[31]

Since the whole of the rest of this chapter explores what in the
fullest way we understand by 'flattery' in Jonson's work for king and
court, some few examples may be given here for a rough identification
before we enter the very difficult regions we have to investigate. Here
first is Jonson's Epigram XXXVI, 'To the Ghost of Martial'.

> Martial, thou gav'st far nobler epigrams
> To thy Domitian, than I can my James;
> But in my royal subject I pass thee –
> Thou flatter'dst thine, mine cannot flatter'd be.

The eulogy of James (to his face) in *Prince Henry's Barriers*, celebrating
the investiture of the Prince of Wales in 1610, is as follows:

> But all these spurs to virtue, seeds of praise
> Must yield to this that comes. Here's one will raise
> Your glory more, and so above the rest,
> As if the acts of all mankind were pressed
> In his example. Here are kingdoms mixed
> And nations joined, a strength of empire fixed
> Conterminate with heaven; the golden vein
> Of Saturn's age is here broke out again.
> Henry but joined the roses that ensigned

Particular families, but this hath joined
The rose and thistle, and in them combined
A union that shall never be declined.
Ireland, that more in title than in fact
Before was conquered, is his laurels' act.
The wall of shipping by Eliza made,
Decayed (as all things subject are to fade),
He hath new built, or so restored that men
For noble use prefer it afore then:
Royal and mighty James, whose name shall set
A goal for all posterity to sweat
In running at, by actions hard and high;
This is the height at which your thoughts must fly.
He knows both how to govern, how to save,
What subjects, what their contraries should have,
What can be done by power and what by love,
What should to mercy, what to justice move;
All arts he can, and from the hand of Fate
Hath he enforced the making his own date.
Within his proper virtue hath he placed
His guards 'gainst fortune, and there fixed fast
The wheel of chance, about which kings are hurled,
And whose outrageous raptures fill the world.

(*HS*, vii, pp. 333–4)

A briefer and more visionary address is the hymn to Pan, who images
James, in *Pan's Anniversary*, for the King's birthday, 1620.

Pan is our all, by him we breathe, we live,
We move, we are; 'tis he our lambs doth rear,
Our flocks doth bless, and from the store doth give
The warm and finer fleeces that we wear.
        He keeps away all heats and colds,
        Drives all diseases from our folds,
        Makes everywhere the spring to dwell,
        The ewes to feed, their udders swell;
        But if he frown, the sheep (alas),
        The shepherds wither, and the grass.
Strive, strive to please him then by still increasing thus
The rites are due to him, who doth all right for us.

(*HS*, vii, p. 535)

Here are two fairly standard poems complimenting statesmen:

To Robert, Earl of Salisbury.
What need hast thou of me? or of my Muse?
Whose actions so themselves do celebrate?
Which should thy country's love to speak refuse,
Her foes enough would fame thee in their hate.

'Tofore, great men were glad of poets: now,
I, not the worst, am covetous of thee.
Yet dare not, to my thought, least hope allow
Of adding to thy fame; thine may to me, .
When in my book men read but Cecil's name,
And what I write thereof find far and free
From servile flattery (common poets' shame)
As thou stand'st clear of the necessity.

To William, Earl of Pembroke.
I do but name thee Pembroke, and I find
It is an epigram on all mankind;
Against the bad, but of and to the good:
Both which are asked, to have thee understood.
. . .   .

But thou, whose noblesse keeps one stature still,
And one true posture, though besieged with ill
Of what ambition, faction, pride can raise;
Whose life, even they that envy it must praise;
That art so reverenced, as thy coming in,
But in the view, doth interrupt their sin;
Thou must draw more: and they, that hope to see
The commonwealth still safe, must study thee.

(*HS*, viii, pp. 40; 66)

All these extracts are perfectly normal, conventional exercises in well-established genres: the praise of the monarch in the court pageant, and the complimentary poem to a major statesman. They are put here at this point only to illustrate the kind of work which is to be done when the monarch has accepted the poet. The question is not, 'Did Jonson flatter?', because he certainly did, for years on end. Nor is the question, quite, 'Does it matter if he did?' The question is of understanding his works of flattery (chiefly the masques) and his works of non-flattery (chiefly his satires), of understanding each in the light of the knowledge that he wrote the other. *Volpone* and *The Alchemist* and *Bartholomew Fair* are not the same as they would be if we did not know that he had written *Hymenaei* and *Love Freed from Ignorance and Folly*. Equally, *Hymenaei* and *Love Freed* become quite different when they are seen as companion pieces and contemporaries (respectively) of *Volpone* and *The Alchemist*. Jonson is not different from other writers in that his work is all of a piece, and that no part can be fully understood without relation to the whole. There is a difference in degree, perhaps, which I remarked on earlier, and there is a difference in the strange cross-cancelling tendency of different works. The rest-less, shifting, shimmering, integral plane which contains the creating mind, the created single work, its occasion, its original audience, its present audience, preceding and succeeding works, is more forcibly present to us in a writer who is both so public and so self-absorbed as Jonson, and yet the integrity or wholeness of that plane is exaspera-tingly difficult to comprehend. But there is no retreat from the in-tegral plane into the refuge of the autonomy of the work of art. It is no use pretending that we do not have knowledge which we actually possess. To suppose we can judge *The Alchemist* or *Hymenaei* as though it existed in splendid isolation is to fabricate a State of Innocence.

Jonson achieved something like the position in society which his theory of poetry and his early plays would suggest he had wished to achieve in order that his art might reach its proper potential and do the most public good. What did he do with his position?

It seems destiny rather than an accident that the other pillar of drama at this time, Shakespeare, should by his choice of life so emphatically *not* raise the kind of enquiry raised by Jonson. His days of writing for aristocratic patronage were early, and all his life he was only too ready to mould his art in obliging deference to public taste and compose plays 'as you like it'. He would not hold up a play, as Jonson did, while two characters laugh at the audience's restiveness over not getting the sort of thing they liked.[32] His greatest and most original work was done by employing rather than defying audience expectation. Flexible and easy-going as regards pleasing the public, he showed no interest in pleasing the great, apart from the occasional compliments in *A Midsummer Night's Dream*, *Macbeth*, and *Cymbeline*. Shakespeare's most extended discussion of his own profession act-ually explores the moral implications of the patron–client relationship which he steadfastly avoided, in *Timon of Athens*. The Poet is one of those who crowd about Timon in the first scene seeking his largesse. He is rehearsing a few moral lines:

> When we for recompense have praised the vile,
> It stains the glory in that happy verse
> Which aptly sings the good.   (ll. 335–65)

The Painter, who knows his man, drily suggests that he is busy with 'some dedication/To the great lord'. The Poet pooh-poohs this – he is perpetually as high-minded in what he says about his art as he is mercenary in what he does with it. Poetry is a 'gum which oozes', a 'gentle flame' that 'provokes itself' – not a studied thing. The poem he is going to give Timon is a very moral thing about Fortune throned on a high hill. A man is ascending that hill, but when he falls all his sycophants and hangers-on desert him. It is, as the Painter says, a pretty common idea. It is a lofty traditional warning to great men, and the Poet offers it to Timon for money. The surly Apemantus thinks it degrades Timon to be willing to receive flattery and to pay for it (I.i.225–7). Most unexpectedly and unfortunately for the Poet, his moral picture is borne out to the letter. Timon falls and is allowed to fall by those whom he has helped. When it is reported that in his exile he has found gold, the Poet and Painter rush to the scene. 'You shall see him a palm in Athens again', says the Painter, 'and flourish with the highest. Therefore 'tis not amiss we tender our loves to him . . .' (V.i.10–12). Unfortunately neither of them has a work available to present to Timon, and more unfortunately Timon comes out of his cave and overhears the Poet as he is fabricating an unwritten work.

I am thinking what I shall say I have provided for him. It must be a personating of himself; a satire against the softness of prosperity, with a discovery of the infinite flatteries that follow youth and opulency.

(ll. 192–203)

Here is more high-minded philosophy offered with the same cynicism as at first. Timon says aside, 'Must thou needs stand for a villain in thine own work? Wilt thou whip thine own faults in other men?' And of course, violently, he sends them packing.

We don't think that Shakespeare excluded himself from the charges he lays against the Poet – that morality in art is easily dispensed and is a good saleable commodity, and that one may be knowledgeably guilty of the vices which one preaches against in one's art – nor that Shakespeare in any way has Jonson in mind. But it is not possible to think of Jonson's rôle without discomfort when reading the Poet passages in *Timon*.

There is a whole range of possible views on Jonson as court poet and masque writer. It would be possible to take a political view, and say that Jonson should never have mixed himself up with James and his court, and that to write masques was a prostitution of his talents. It was the old puritan view, which became the old whig view, that the grossly expensive and lavish masques were the symbols of the decadence, corruption, and wrong-headedness of expiring royalism.[33] A more sympathetic view, which can be found in Gifford and the early

volumes of Herford and Simpson's big edition, is that Jonson had
little choice. He had to live; it was an honour to be chosen to write for
royalty; his masques are beautiful, subtle and delicate conceptions –
but they are marred by the contemptible adulation which he was
forced to insert. Flattery was the price he had to pay for being allowed
to write.

> The Masque-writer was subject to a control more arbitrary and more abso-
> lute than any exercised by the play-house manager or by his public.
>   (HS, II, p. 275)

> We have to face the fundamental flaw of the whole Masque-genre, – the
> radical insincerity which a man of genius writing for the entertainment of his
> sovereign can only in the rarest cases escape.   (HS, II, p. 288)

There are not many critics who take the political stance now, either
because they are sentimental royalists or because they are apolitical,
but it is important not to forget it. As for excusing Jonson for the
blemishes of adulation, the revolution in criticism of the masques,
brought about by the pioneer work of A. H. Gilbert and D. J. Gordon
in the forties[34] and the later work of Stephen Orgel,[35] has so changed
our understanding of the nature of the genre that in the eyes of many
critics flattery must seem quite irrelevant. Jonson is seen as (in
various ways) fulfilling himself as a writer and in his own conception
of the poet's function through his engagement in the masque. I shall
be looking at these views very shortly. But a recent book by D. B. J.
Randall, wholly devoted to one masque of Jonson's – *The Gypsies
Metamorphosed* – sensibly reminds us that the problem of flattery has
not gone away and that not only is it a continuing problem for us, but it
'constituted a continuing problem for Jonson'.[36] *The Gypsies Metamorphosed* was a special sort of entertainment arranged by Buckingham
for James at Burley-on-the-Hill. Jonson was paid £100 (Lanier got
£200 for the music). James was so delighted by the entertainment that
it was repeated for him twice, once at Belvoir and later at Windsor.
Randall is right to say that Jonson knew of the corruptness surrounding the great favourite Buckingham and we hope he is right to say that
he disapproved of it (p. 31). Briefly, Randall's thesis is that in portray-
ing Buckingham and his family as gypsies Jonson was in fact giving us
his contemptuous view of their real status. Their transformation
towards the end of the entertainment into courtiers mimes James's
transformation of 'a devilishly charming rogue' and 'his ragtag pack
of friends and relations' into the higher nobility. 'Without flattery,

Jonson could not have functioned at court at all, but by using it thoughtfully he could depict and recommend real virtue in terms of the court' (p. 154). The question which Randall unfortunately does not successfully answer is how on earth James and his favourite did not perceive this meaning of the masque. There was enough praise of James and enough humour in the work to protect Jonson 'in the event that anyone, the King included, was so foolish as to cry out that his shafts had struck home' (p. 165). Randall also plays with the idea that James and the performers were too drunk to take in what Jonson was implying! 'Jonson met with resounding success'; Randall notes (p. 105) that, besides the £100 from Buckingham, the question of a knighthood and the Mastership of the Revels was consequent upon James's delight with the invention. 'Jonson must have felt elated at having pulled the whole thing off.' It is a delicate problem whether it is not *more* despicable to take money for flattery if that flattery is in fact intended to be seen by the knowing as a sneer. I don't like Jonson's elation at his successful trick at all, but I don't think the trick took place. The contractual tone of the work is the amused condescension of great men in demeaning themselves to act as gypsies. The whole of this brilliant masque is sprightly, light, and pleasant; its easy, good-humoured familiarity is shown in the splendid litany for the King:

> From a needle or a thorn
> I'the bed at ev'n or morn
> Or from any gout's least grutching,
> Bless the sovereign and his touching. . .

The lightly mocking air quite occludes the possibility of a secondary saturnine mocking as the 'meaning' of the masque in any useful sense of the word 'meaning'.

Yet what has entered Randall's mind may have entered Jonson's. 'And a pack of gypsies they *are*!', he may have muttered at some point. It is fundamental that we remember all the time Jonson's own keen awareness of the difficulties and perplexities of his position, and his capacity for self-derision. The most remarkably disenchanted view of his own endeavours given by Jonson is *A Tale of a Tub*. The importance of this work has been overlooked because of the strange acceptance by the Oxford editors that it was basically a very early play of Jonson's which he revised late in life in order to include in it an attack upon his erstwhile collaborator in the great series of Jacobean masques, Inigo Jones. So the play comes as the very first text in that vast, indispensable, and so often unhelpful edition. But nearly everyone now accepts it as belonging to the year 1633 when it was allowed for the stage after cuts had been made at the instigation of the indignant Jones.

The play was written, the Prologue tells us, 'To show what different things/The cotes of clowns are from the courts of kings'. It presents a wholly derisive view of authority. It is set back in the reign of Queen Mary and the kingdom is confined to a small area of London on St Valentine's Day. The prime trickster is Canon Hugh, the vicar of St Pancras. The other authority figures are Squire Tub and Justice Preamble, but above all the pompous, self-important, and stupid High Constable of Kentish Town, Toby Turf. Turf is trying to marry his daughter Audrey Turf to John Clay (a right earthy couple they are) and the play consists of the interruptions caused by Canon Hugh's tricks to stop the wedding and sell this most unattractive bride both to Squire Tub and to Justice Preamble. Much is made of the royal authority invested in High Constable Turf.

> *Turf.* Do's any wight parzent her Majesty's person,
>   This Hundred, 'bove the High Constable?
> *All.*   No, no!
> *Turf.* Use our authority, then, to the utmost on't.   (I.iv.53–5)

In IV.i, there is a fine etymology:

> *Cyning* and *Staple*, make a Constable:
>   As we'd say, a hold or stay for the King.   (ll. 55–6)

The author of this improving derivation is Diogenes Scriben, D'oge for short, the literary member of an extraordinary little court which surrounds High Constable Turf, and also includes In-and-In Medlay the handiman, who presumably was invented by the unintimidated Jonson to replace the banned Vitruvius Hoop. As certainly as Medlay stands for Inigo Jones, D'oge Scriben stands for Jonson himself. He has the rôle in this little court of both poet and genealogist. Very much like the Irish bard, he ministers to the High Constable's esteem by harping on his valiant ancestry.

> *Scriben.*   I can give you, Sir,
>   A Roman story of a Petty Constable
>   That had a daughter that was called Virginia,
>   Like Mistress Audrey, and as young as she. . . .
>   . . .   .
> *Turf.*   That, that, good D'ogenes!
>   A learned man is a chronicle!

> *Scriben.*   I can tell you
> A thousand, of great Pompey, Caesar, Trajan,
> All the High Constables there.
> *Turf.*   That was their place;
> They were no more.
> *Scriben.*   Dictator, and High Constable
> Were both the same.   (III.vi.10–13; 16–21)

The masque at the end of the play is for Squire Tub and not for the High Constable, and it's prepared by Medlay who elbows out Scriben. It is a parody of a court masque and it images the action of the play which is itself a derisive image of the English court.

A Tale of a Tub is indeed the work of an embittered and discarded man. But concentration on the satirical portrait of Inigo Jones, jealous of literary collaboration in masque-making (V.ii.29–40), has directed attention away from the fact that this play presents a contemptuous retrospect not only of stage architects, but of masques, court poets, courts, and kings. Authority is portrayed with scorn; perpetually weak, needing self-gratification, easily duped. Neither poet nor architect honours himself in honouring either High Constable or Squire. The Church is a pandar, and Justice corrupt. *A Tale of a Tub* stands at the exit from Jonson's court-writing, as *Sejanus* stands at the entrance.

Jonson's masque for January 1624, *Neptune's Triumph for the Return of Albion*, was intended to celebrate the return of Charles and Buckingham from Spain in the previous October after the failure of negotiations for the Spanish marriage. Here was a rather difficult celebration for a court poet, in that the empty-handed return had been both a major defeat of James's plans and a matter of national rejoicing. In the event, the masque was never performed, because one of the recurring disputes over precedence among the ambassadors proved irreconcilable.

The masque opens with the Poet being met by the Master-Cook. Their dialogue is so important that a large quotation from it is required.

Poet. You are not his Majesty's confectioner, are you?
Cook. No, but one that has as good title to the room, his master-cook. What are you, sir?
Poet. The most unprofitable of his servants, I, sir: the poet. A kind of a Christmas engine, one that is used at least once a year for a trifling instrument of wit, or so.
Cook. Were you ever a cook?

Poet. A cook? No, surely.

Cook. Then you can be no good poet, for a good poet differs nothing at all from a master-cook. Either's art is the wisdom of the mind.

Poet. As how, sir?

Cook. Expect. I am by my place to know how to please the palates of the guests; so, you are to know the palate of the times, study the several tastes, what every nation, the Spaniard, the Dutch, the French, the Walloon, the Neapolitan, the Briton, the Sicilian can expect from you.

Poet. That were a hard and heavy task, to satisfy Expectation, who is so severe an exactress of duties, ever a tyrannous mistress, and most times a pressing enemy.

Cook. She is a powerful great lady, sir, at all times, and must be satisfied. So must her sister, Madam Curiosity, who hath as dainty a palate as she, and these will expect.

Poet. But what if they expect more than they understand?

Cook. That's all one, Master Poet, you are bound to satisfy them. For there is a palate of the understanding as well as of the senses. The taste is taken with good relishes, the sight with fair objects, the hearing with delicate sounds, the smelling with pure scents, the feeling with soft and plump bodies, but the understanding with all these, for all which you must begin at the kitchen. There the art of poetry was learned and found out, or nowhere, and the same day with the art of cookery.

(*HS*, vii, pp. 683–4)

A little later, when the Poet has explained the device of the masque that is to come, the Cook asks, 'But where's your antimasque now, all this while?' 'Faith, we have none', replies the Poet.

> None, I assure you, neither do I think them
> A worthy part of presentation,
> Being things so heterogene to all device,
> Mere by-works, and at best outlandish nothings.

(*HS*, vii, p. 688)

The Cook won't have this, and so he produces the two antimasques, one of a host of comic characters who come out of a large cooking pot, and another of sailors. Now, as Herford and Simpson point out, 'the Poet is not to be identified with Jonson' (II, p. 326), who had so enthusiastically and brilliantly developed the rôle of the exuberant antimasque. Orgel, agreeing, argues that the Cook's discussion of the 'palate of the understanding' is Jonson's insistence on the appeal of the masque to all the senses, using all resources to affect the spectator's understanding. He suggests that Jonson shows the Poet and Cook as complementary: 'Antimasque and masque have a genial relationship in this work, and the cook's invention can be accepted in the spirit of play and assimilated with ease into the larger world of the poet's creation.'[37]

This is surely correct, but it leaves us still with a joint poet-figure, a Siamese twin of Poet and Cook, one half of whom does the serious part of the masque to order as an underpaid hireling trotted out every Christmas, forced against his conscience to obey Expectation, 'a tyrannous mistress, and most times a pressing enemy'. The other half is a complaisant and flexible creature who, totally unlike the Jonson of the public stage, is prepared to meet his audience with what it wants, and hopes to reach their understanding that way. (Orgel had earlier pointed out that the strong development of the rumbustious antimasque was due to the tastes of the King.)[38] There is a 'debate' quality in the conversation of the Poet and the Cook: both attitudes of mind must have been present in Jonson, that is to say (a) he was under orders and he hated it and (b) he was under orders, but accepted subservience and was prepared to do his best and utilise the constraints to the best advantage. Either way, poet or cook, he was not a free man.

One of the most beautiful of Jonson's masques to read is *The Vision of Delight*, presented at court for Christmas 1617. The scene to begin with is an urban street. Delight brings in Night, and Night brings in Fantasy, to create in waking dreams the 'various shapes of things' to please the mind. Fantasy produces one of the Hours, and the scene changes to the bower of Zephyrus. A character called Wonder marvels at the transformation: 'Grows/The wealth of nature here, or art?' (ll. 141–2). Fantasy rather unkindly remarks, 'How better than they are are all things made/By Wonder!' and brings in yet a further and more wonderful transformation – *'the bower opens, and the masquers discovered as the glories of the spring'*. Wonder asks,

> How comes it winter is so quite forced hence,
> And locked up under ground?
> . . .   .
> How is't each bough a several music yields?
> . . .   .
> Whose power is this? what god?
> *Fantasy.*   Behold a king
> Whose presence maketh this perpetual spring,
> The glories of which spring grow in that bower,
> And are the marks and beauties of his power.
>
> (ll. 179–80; 192; 199–204)

In the wintry city of London, the King creates spring: its glories are his courtiers. But all this is a 'waking dream' produced by Fantasy and ecstatically described by Wonder. Fantasy at her entrance offers dreams of every sort:

> It is no one dream that can please these all;
> Wherefore I would know what dreams would delight 'em. (ll. 58–9)

She then speaks an amazing nonsense speech, as brilliant as it is opaque (ll. 60–114). Orgel has worked hard at it and claims it is a debate between lechery and gluttony. I very much doubt this. It seems to me an inscrutably dark piece on the subject of the masque – the power of the mind to create its own world. It glimmers into near sense every now and again.

> Your whale he will swallow a hogshead for a pill;
> But the maker o' the mousetrap is he that hath skill.
> . . .   .
> You will say now the morris bells were but bribes
> To make the heel forget that ever it had kibes.   (ll. 83–4; 95–6)

I interpret 'the maker o' the mousetrap' as the devisers of the masque, Jonson and Jones (Orgel says it is 'slang for lecher'). You don't need to swallow a hogshead for a pill when their art can transform winter into spring. And in the second couplet I quote they innocently deny that the morris bells of this entertainment at court are designed to make us forget our real chilblains. The spring is created by art. But the spring is a metaphor for the beneficence and power of the king. The glories of the spring are the king's own noblemen. Is this the waking dream of Fantasy? Or is it art which creates the spring, and *we* who apply this figuratively to James's reign? In its questioning *The Vision of Delight* seems to me, in a wonderfully good-humoured and deft way, far more 'seditious' than *The Gypsies Metamorphosed*, and far more questioning of the value of the masque than anything else in the masques themselves.

In a well-known passage of his poem to Sir Robert Wroth, Jonson praises him for not spending his time in city and court:

> Nor throng'st (when masquing is) to have a sight
>   Of the short bravery of the night;
> To view the jewels, stuffs, the pains, the wit
>   There wasted, some not paid for yet!   (*HS*, VIII, pp. 96–7)

For years, because he had to, or felt he had to, or because he wanted to, Jonson contributed to that form of festivity which here he praises Wroth for avoiding. There is one masque of Jonson's in which he

meets head-on the frequent and unassailable objections to the col-
ossal extravagance of the masque, so lavish and costly and so soon
over. This is *Love Restored*, 1612. The commentaries on the masque are
irritatingly silent about what lies behind it. Herford and Simpson say
that this slight and unpretentious masque came into being because of
controversy over financial expenditure on the masque; but they do
not specify. It does not appear that Inigo Jones designed it. There is a
characteristic Jonsonian 'outer-gate' entrance to the work, with one of
the actors telling the audience that it looks as though there'll be no
show tonight. Plutus, god of money, masquerading as Cupid,
appears. 'I will have no more masquing; I will not buy a false and
fleeting delight so dear.' Those who worship money regard it as
misspent on the frivolity of masques. 'I will endure thy prodigality nor
riots no more; they are the ruin of states. . . . Let 'em embrace more
frugal pastimes . . . Away; I will no more of these superfluous exces-
ses.'

Robin Goodfellow, exuding the vitality of country sports, has
arrived to see a court masque, and to join in if permitted. He is able to
see that this Cupid is an impostor. Money is now reigning in the
world, not Love. Love lives frozen to death because of the tyranny of
money. But Robin Goodfellow and the King will restore things.

I'll bring you where you shall find Love, and by the virtue of this Majesty,
who projecteth so powerful beams of light and heat through this hemisphere,
thaw his icy fetters and scatter the darkness that obscures him. Then in
despite of this insolent and barbarous Mammon, your sports may proceed,
and the solemnities of the night be complete without depending on so earthy
an idol.   (ll. 193–200)

Plutus scornfully replies: 'Ay, do, attempt it! 'Tis like to find most
necessary and fortunate event, whatsoever is enterprised without my
aids.' The real Cupid enters with the masquers, throws off his furs in
the radiance of the court. Of Mammon, he says:

> The majesty that here doth move
> Shall triumph, more secured by love
> Than all his earth, and never crave
> His aids, but force him as a slave.   (ll. 247–50)

It would seem very likely (the expenditure on record being very
low indeed) that *Love Restored* was done on the cheap, and was
therefore a proof that the court could have its vital festivities without
the huge expenditure which caused such annoyance. But there seems

a real disingenuousness somewhere. Court masques are a highly artificial, formal and expensive entertainment by definition. Merry country pranks and jollities which one might associate with Robin Goodfellow have very little if anything to do with the Renaissance court masque. There is a false analogy in the protest that mere money values have taken over and are cancelling out the world of pastimes in both country and court. The comparatively low expenditure of 1612 is not a proof that in their essence masques are very simple and needn't cost money. The expenditure may be less, and presumably it would be possible to maintain economy in the future, but Plutus in his sarcasm is absolutely right, ''Tis like to find most necessary and fortunate event, whatsoever is enterprised without my aids.' It is this recognition that the masque depends on money – *some* money – that leads to the dubiousness of the passage from Cupid's final speech which I have quoted. Majesty depends on love, not money, and Majesty will never crave the aid of money 'but force him as a slave'.

It is clear Jonson found it impossible to free the masque from Plutus's grip. He moves from the gesture of banishing money to the idea that they will use money like a slave. This lofty idea that money is dirty, but one has got to have it, is exactly the Antonio complex – borrowing money from the disgusting Shylock to fit out Bassanio for his wooing – or is it the Brutus complex – using money from bribes and condemning the taking of bribes? Monarchy believed that it affirmed its identity by the magnificent display of the annual masques. Display needed money, and money had to come from merchants and trade generally. In January 1618, when James was in money difficulties, Nathaniel Brent wrote to Sir Dudley Carleton:

Your lordship heard before this time that the merchants of Middelburg and the East Indies have undertaken to furnish the Exchequer with £50,000. Of which his Majesty hath been pleased to assign for Ireland £12,000; for the arrearages of the artillery £8,000; for Marquess Hamilton £8,000; for my Lord D'Aubigny £4,000; for my Lord Hay £3,000; for my Lord Haddington £2,000; and £4,000 for the Prince's masque. All which he will most graciously perform if there be not too much difficulty found in the collecting of it.   (*HS*, x, p. 577)

The crown depended on what the subject gave and with too large a slice of that money tried to create an image of itself as independent of votes of supply and those low traders in the city. Both the economy exercised in 1612 and the argument of *Love Restored* fail to convince us that Jonson's knowledge in the poem to Wroth was not his better knowledge.

Modern studies of the Jacobean masque have taught us that the essential and distinguishing quality of this kind of performance is its merging with the life of those who are present as spectators. Professional actors and musicians carry the show forward but the high point is reached with the revelation of the masquers themselves, the high nobility of the land, disguised in the magnificent costumes suitable to whatever myth or heroic fable is being enacted. They dance on their own and then at the climax they join in dancing with their fellows in the audience. The King, who is the centre of the fable being enacted, is in the centre of the hall. He is both the mythic being celebrated in the masque and James, King of Britain. He sits in the centre of his most powerful subjects, who dance together, some in heroic guises and some in more everyday shape.

At the same time that scholars have made clear to us this very exciting idea of the fusing of the image and real presence in the masque, they have recognised that the very act of merging creates for us the sense of a great chasm between the heroic image and the quality of the people who identify with it. In his fine study of the 1618 *Pleasure Reconciled to Virtue* at the end of *The Jonsonian Masque*, Stephen Orgel ingeniously builds on that famous explosion of the King, 'drunk and sleepy' at the very high point of the masque, dissatisfied with the brevity of the dancing, 'Why don't they dance? What did you make me come here for? Devil take you all, dance!' (*HS*, x, p. 583). James's crude intervention, says Orgel, 'must have returned the contemporary audience to the realities of life at court rather abruptly, but it did so only a little earlier than the masque itself'. The final poem of the masque sends the masquers back to the craggy landscape of the scene where (in the fable) Virtue is to be striven for.

> There, there is Virtue's seat.
> Strive to keep her your own;
> 'Tis only she can make you great
> Though place, here, make you known.   (ll. 345–8)

Jonson knows what courtiers are really like, and here, Orgel says, Jonson the satirist makes himself known to us, aware of the distance between the ideal and the real. 'This masque asserts with equal strength both the power of the individual will to overcome disorder and the insubstantiality of the ideal vision. The final song clearly implies the difficulties and uncertainties attendant upon the choice of virtue as a way of life.'[39]

The question of the relationship between image and person in Jonson's masques, which we must now examine, takes us to the heart of Jonson's work as poet of a nation.

It was a time-honoured concept that the praise of great men which was the prime subject for poetry (see above, pp. 138–41) could be tactfully used to indicate the magnanimous virtue which a nobleman or prince *ought* to have.[40] Two essays by American scholars in the forties, A. H. Gilbert in *Philological Quarterly* in 1943, and E. W. Talbert in *PMLA* in 1946, argued that Jonson's masques should properly be seen in this tradition of educating great men while appearing to praise them. The basic text is from Bacon's essay 'Of Praise'.

Some Praises come of good wishes, and respects, which is a form due in civility to kings and great persons, *Laudando praecipere*; when by telling men what they are, they represent to them what they should be.

The idea was well put by Jonas Barish in 1960: the masque was 'a mirror for magistrates in which the king sees himself transfigured by the virtues he ought to possess'.[41] Jonson appears to accept the principle of *laudando praecipere* in his poem to John Selden.

> Though I confess (as every Muse hath erred,
> And mine not least) I have too oft preferred
> Men past their terms, and praised some names too much,
> But 'twas with purpose to have made them such.   (*HS*, VIII, p. 159)

The tone of this is interesting: it is not a boast that Jonson has tried to improve people, but a confession of a mistake that came about from a justifiable wish to improve. The context of this passage is about overpraising books through affection to their authors, wounding good judgements 'through favouring what is there not found'. The passage which I have quoted, ending 'But 'twas with purpose to have made them such', continues (with my italics):

> *Since, being deceived,* I turn a sharper eye
> Upon myself, and ask to whom, and why,
> And what I write; and vex it many days
> Before men get a verse, much less a Praise.

It becomes clear that this passage is very far from a justification of educating by praising, and that Jonson holds that praise is properly due only to worth. There is another relevant passage which is worth examining, from the dedication to Pembroke of the *Epigrams.*

If I have praised, unfortunately, anyone that doth not deserve, or if all answer not in all numbers the pictures I have made of them, I hope it will be forgiven me, that they are no ill pieces, though they be not like the persons.

Here again praise which has not actually been earned is considered regrettable; what Jonson does argue, however, is that the poem can be a worthy poem even if the person ostensibly the subject does not measure up to his description, and this argument we shall shortly have to turn to. The whole complex problem in the *Epigrams* of the relation between ideals of virtue and named individuals was discussed in a valuable long essay by E. Partridge in 1973, which is also a useful exposition of the relation between the poet, virtue, great men, praise, and fame discussed above.[42] But I think that in the end the tradition *laudando praecipere* is somewhat empty and theoretical. Jonson was always aware of the predicament he was in through interweaving a platonic ideal of human worth with the actual doings of his noble patrons at the Jacobean court, and he had more difficulty than his critics in absolving himself from the charge that the result was indistinguishable from the bad faith of adulation.

> Since men have left to do praiseworthy things,
> Most think all praises flatteries.

Such is the honest start to a poem to the Earl of Suffolk (*Epigrams*, LXVII) which continues as barefaced flattery. There is no way of reading the poem except in the light of the knowledge of its opening, any more than there is of reading the *Epigrams* as a whole except in the light of the self-disgust of his address 'To My Muse' (LXV).

> Away, and leave me, thou thing most abhorred,
> That has betrayed me to a worthless lord.

Poverty will be his new Muse, he continues,

> She shall instruct my after-thoughts to write
> Things manly, and not smelling parasite.

The poem concludes with a 'turn' of defiant ingenuity which one hopes is ironically intended.

> But I repent me: Stay! Whoe'er is raised
> For worth he has not, he is taxed, not praised.

When we look at most of the praise which is given in poems and masques to James and his family it is straightforward panegyric, and it seems to me that the educational potential for the recipients is totally outweighed by the real damage which flattery does.

Look on this state, and if you yet not know
What crown there shines, whose sceptre here doth grow,
Think on thy loved Aeneas, and what name
Maro, the golden trumpet of his fame,
Gave him, read thou in this: a prince that draws
By example more than others do by laws,
That is so just to his great act and thought,
To do not what kings may, but what kings ought;
Who out of piety unto peace is vowed,
To spare his subjects, yet to quell the proud
And dares esteem it the first fortitude
To have his passions, foes at home, subdued.

                    (*The Haddington Masque*, ll. 212–23)

Jonson took enormous trouble with his masques. They are deeply intricate as well as (often) surpassingly beautiful. The elucidation of their esoteric layers of meaning has been left largely to commentators of the second half of the present century. There is no doubt that Jonson, as he seems to have argued in *Cynthia's Revels*, hoped that taking part in his masques would improve the minds and morals of the nobility. This appears to be the meaning in his strongest commendation of his own masques, the dedication to *Hymenaei*, 1606. He compares the short-lived glory of the masque as performance to the long life of its meaning in the understanding.

This it is hath made the most royal princes and greatest persons, who are commonly the personaters of these actions, not only studious of riches and magnificence in the outward celebration or show, which rightly becomes them, but curious after the most high and hearty inventions to furnish the inward parts, and those grounded upon antiquity and solid learnings; which, though their voice be taught to sound to present occasions their sense or doth or should always lay hold on more removed mysteries.   (*HS*, vii, p. 209)

Jonson published his masques: he was proud of them and believed they had a moral value extending far beyond the circle of those who took part in them. As with the poems which he had in mind in the dedication of his *Epigrams* 'they are no ill pieces', whatever might be thought of the persons who took part in them, or whom they celebrated.

The most famous separation of a masque from the persons who occasioned it is connected with *Hymenaei*, composed for the wedding of Lady Francis Howard (daughter of the Earl of Suffolk) and the Earl of Essex (son of Queen Elizabeth's executed favourite). The masque was published in quarto in 1606, with the names of those whom it

celebrated: *Hymenaei: or the Solemnities of Masque, and Barriers, magnifi-
cently performed . . . at Court: To the auspicious celebrating of the Marriage-
union between Robert, Earl of Essex, and the Lady Frances, second Daughter to
the most noble Earl of Suffolk*. But when the masque was republished in
Jonson's *Works* in 1616, the names of the persons were expunged, and
it became *Hymenaei, or the Solemnities of Masque and Barriers at a Marriage*.
By that time, details of perhaps the most famous or infamous scandal
in English history were beginning to emerge. The marriage of Frances
Howard to Essex was a political move, encouraged by James and
Salisbury, to bring Essex into an alliance with the Howards and the
Cecils (a second daughter of Suffolk was to marry a Cecil). He was
fourteen and she was thirteen. They did not then sleep together, and
in fact Essex went away travelling without the wedding being con-
summated. When he returned nearly two years later, Frances Howard had fallen in love with Robert Carr, the new favourite of James.
She kept her husband at bay by some means or other, possibly drugs,
and eventually managed to get a sordid divorce through pleading
Essex's impotence. James actively encouraged this repellent intrigue
and divorce, which disgusted all decent men and women. To his great
discredit, Lancelot Andrewes was one of the four bishops who bowed
to royal pressure and gave his verdict for Frances Howard and the
annulment of her marriage. She married Carr, now Viscount Rochester, at the end of 1613, and Ben Jonson wrote *A Challenge at Tilt* to
celebrate it. (The occasion of this also was suppressed on publication.) Rochester was made Earl of Somerset. Two years later, in the
autumn of 1615, the repulsive details began to circulate about the
death of Somerset's friend, Sir Thomas Overbury, in the Tower in
1613. He had in fact been poisoned at the instigation of Frances
Howard, for being an opponent of her remarriage. The Folio of
Jonson's *Works* was at this time printing, but he was able before
publication in 1616 to remove the names of those celebrated from
both the wedding masques for Frances Howard. Somerset and his
wife were tried and found guilty in the spring of 1616.

In his brilliant and famous essay of 1945, '*Hymenaei*, Ben Jonson's
Masque of Union', D. J. Gordon scarcely mentions the wedding
couple. He feels that the fact that the marriage was a political matter
helped Jonson in filling the masque with political concern, but otherwise it appears that personalities are irrelevant. Marriage is important, because the image is used by Jonson for the mystical union of
kingdoms by James, seen as an aspect of the divine unity of the world,

but it is not important who was married. '*Hymenaei* is not only a formal wedding masque; *Hymenaei* is a dramatic and symbolic representation of the Union of the Kingdoms.'[43]

It is a question how far this depersonalising of the masque should go. For Jonson there was quite clearly an 'ideal' quality in it; it was platonically what a wedding masque in a particular society should be, and Frances Howard and the Earl of Essex merely happened to be there to fill the vacant places. Indeed the final philosophical view of union on the personal and political levels as manifestation of a richer transcendental harmony is independent also of James's attempts to unite England and Scotland.

Of the Epithalamium which ended the masque Jonson wrote:

After them, the musicians with this song, of which then only one staff was sung; but because I made it both in form and matter to emulate that kind of poem which was called *epithalamium*, and by the ancients used to be sung when the bride was led into her chamber, I have here set it down whole, and do heartily forgive their ignorance whom it chanceth not to please, hoping that *nemo doctus me iubeat thalassionem verbis dicere non thalassionis* [no learned person will order me to write a wedding song not in the words of a wedding song].

Jonson shows himself in this note striving to bring into the lives of those witnessing and later reading the masque an understanding of the ideal model of the wedding celebration, found out by learning and made alive by his art. It was clearly an offence to him that his work should have been truncated in performance, for whatever reason. Yet as we read what was left out, this strong lyrical celebration of the sexual consummation of the marriage and of the conception of a child, we can see all sorts of reasons why it should have been decided to cut a song which would have been very right and proper in most circumstances but thoroughly embarrassing and inappropriate for the child-marriage in question. *Hymenaei* is stately and beautiful, didactic and visionary. It is, if you like, a *true* image of the full meaning of concord in the life of man, a wedding as symbol of harmony in the individual life, harmony and growth in the married life, peace between kingdoms, peace under God. Its truth was not assailed by the constant inappropriateness which has depressed or amused most readers since 1616 – its original inappropriateness to the child-couple, and to the qualities of James as a successful international statesman. One surely is left with a double response. On the one hand, yes, this *is* the fulfilment of the bardic ideal: here is the king and his court, and a marriage of young people on whose future behaviour (as they are the king's highest servants) the prosperity of the kingdom rests. Let them all learn from this celebration what the sages of the world throughout history have taught of the golden chain from heaven linking all human activities, and joining them to the divine purpose. And on the other hand there is a sense of depersonalisation and dislocation, a feeling of the uselessness of this mysticism in face of the sheer ineluctable fact of weakness, hate, stupidity, discord. As in the individual sphere Frances Howard refused bodily union with her husband, so in the political sphere, that husband Essex became the leading general in the parliamentary army that destroyed the kind of monarchical rule which James and his son set up.

But they are ever good men, that must make good the times; if the men be naught, the times will be such.   (*HS*, VIII, p. 571)

So wrote Jonson, under the heading 'Principes et Administri' in *Discoveries*. It is the same idea, as regards kings, as the continuum between a man and his poetry – 'the impossibility of any man's being the good poet without first being a good man'. It was Jonson's misfortune that the king whose threshold he crossed was James I, a king who, though he was quick-minded, shrewd, and learned, was also self-important, self-indulgent, self-protective; timid, coarse, lazy; ungrateful, disloyal, dishonest; suspicious, intriguing, insecure. As the adulation in the masques seems the worse as it is directed to James rather than to Elizabeth, so the nobility of the concepts conveyed by the masques seems the more irrelevant because of the lack of worth in James and those whom he fostered.

Bacon is another man like Jonson whose work shows an intense awareness of the unlovely realities of political life and who yet seems in his reverent attitude to James either to be blind to the weakness of the man, or to contrive some mental separation of the person and the office. It is an uncomfortable matter in our assessment of Jonson, first that his announced view, which I have just quoted, spoke of the wrongness of disconnecting the moral worth of the individual ruler from the worth of his government and authority, and second that one of the things we most value Jonson's plays for is their brilliant probing of the gap between what men are and the pretended life built for them by themselves or by others – as with Sir Epicure Mammon or Volpone.

Stephen Orgel has a brilliant title for his most recent study of the Jonsonian masque, *The Illusion of Power*. The masque is for Jonson a powerful symbolic show; but to Charles the masque gave an illusion of a power he did not possess. In an earlier work, Orgel wrote, 'Every masque is a ritual in which the society affirms its wisdom and asserts its control of its world and its destiny. The glories of the transformation scene express the power of princes, bringing order to human and elemental nature, partaking thereby of the divine.'[44] But Charles mistook the image for the reality. 'Power was asserted only through analogies, faith affirmed only through symbols . . . If kings will be philosophers, they had better not be Platonists. After a decade of ideals, a disenfranchised Parliament at last declared its authority by virtue of the realities of its power, and the absolute rule of the Stuart monarchy was revealed as a royal charade, a theatrical illusion.'[45]

> Did that play of mine send out
> Certain men the English shot?

Yeats knew of the dangers in a national poet's creation of heroic images which breed a new life in the minds of others.

> When Pearse summoned Cuchulain to his side,
> What stalked through the Post Office?

There is a counter-truth in Jonson's writing, and the wholeness of his meaning is not solely in either the excoriation of the satires or the heroic loftiness of the masques. In 1614, when Jonson was at the height of his powers as a writer of court masques, his *Bartholomew Fair* was acted (on its second night) before the King at court. The authority figure in this play is the bemused magistrate Adam Overdo, constantly deceived as he tries to watch over his little kingdom, rid it of iniquities and reward the deserving; he finally gives up and invites everyone to a feast at his house. How far James saw his own authority mocked, it is impossible to say; if he identified at all, he could excuse the freedom of the court jester since there's little if any direct application of Overdo to James. It is often said that the antimasques show Jonson's awareness of the world of disorder and licence which is finally contained within the harmonies of the closing of the main masque.[46] I am not sure that I feel very much threatened by antimasques. The real antimasque in this sense is *Bartholomew Fair*, in which the inadequacy of self-important authority to reduce the teeming richness of sensual mischief to order is so marvellously shown. And Jonson thought it right for his king to see the play.

The progress of the authority figure in Jonson's plays makes a remarkable study, from the benevolent jocularity of Justice Clement in *Every Man in his Humour*, ultimately reliable, through to the total stupidity and helplessness of Toby Turf in *A Tale of a Tub*. In the three comical satires discussed earlier in this chapter we have the unassailable figure of the monarch, Cynthia or Augustus, to resolve all problems and restore all loss. It is after 1603 that the authority figure appears only to be questioned – the Venetian court which is so corrupt and almost by accident finally brings Volpone and Mosca to book, Lovewit in *The Alchemist* returning home as judge and making common cause with the criminal, Overdo in *Bartholomew Fair*. What is as interesting as the development of the authority figure is the seeming need of it. Plays which lack it, like *Catiline*, seem the weaker thereby. It is *Sejanus* which most powerfully conveys the significance of authority figures in the plays, and is, it seems to me, a key to much else in Jonson.

Sejanus is a tyrant play – and very brilliantly it portrays a reign of terror to which most bow in fear but which a very few have courage to defy.

> We have no shift of faces, no cleft tongues,
> No soft and glutinous bodies, that can stick,
> Like snails, on painted walls . . .   (I.i.7–9)

In the usual type of tyrant play, like *Richard III*, a vicious man gains control of the state, but pride, fortune, and the continuing efforts of good men weaken him, until a new force of good comes along (Henry Richmond, or Malcolm in *Macbeth*) to overthrow him and take his place.

But Jonson's mind required a figure of ultimate authority, irremovable and God-like, and the governors who succeed each other are in secondary authority, taking their commission from the ultimate figure. So behind Sejanus the tyrant there is Tiberius the emperor. Tiberius as Ultimate Authority is woken up from inattendance; he exerts his power, destroys Sejanus, and then slothfully turns back to self-indulgence.[47] Behind Tiberius there is nothing; no God, no Fortune, nothing. This figure of the final arbiter who can be relied on – just – to come and protect his suffering people in the nick of time is a brilliant conception. Sejanus the tyrant was a cancer growing riotously in the benevolent host tissue of the Emperor. Tiberius created Sejanus, and Sejanus served him as well as used him. And when he has relieved suffering humanity by destroying Sejanus he returns to his orgies, leaving behind him Macro, who is going to be every bit as bad as the tyrant he has succeeded.

Tiberius is a man who knows what his duties are. He is princeliness corrupted. It is a corrupted, fitful, wayward, and erratic authority which takes the place of God or Providence. *Sejanus* comes at the fag-end of Elizabeth's reign and I think it shows a widespread sense of disillusion and bitterness. It also seems to me to show Jonson's intense need for a father and protector in the seat of government. For the sense is of a double betrayal: first that Sejanus should have so much power and do such evil, and secondly that when the Saving Figure moves into the arena, he is incalculable, undependable, a joker. Such an emphasis on betrayal by authority surely indicates a yearning for authority.

Most people felt an air of promise and hope with the coming of James. It is impossible to think that anyone of the understanding and intelligence of Jonson, anyone with his keenest of eyes for the fool, knave, self-deluder, and hypocrite should not have read James for what he really was quite early in his reign. And I would suggest that we have to read his masques in praise of James not only as coming from a man able to delineate authority in its cruelty and treacherous unreliability as in *Sejanus* and in its pathetic ineffectualness as in *Bartholomew Fair*, but also as coming from a man who feels himself a second time betrayed in what he might expect from his sovereign. He had got, as he crossed the threshold, a pretty good living – better than he could get by relying solely on the professional stage. He has the opportunity of voicing the kind of poetic morality which the untrammelled Asper might voice, but its human context must surely have been the source of constant bitterness and self-reproach. As I read them, the great beauty of those late scenes in the masques, when peace and plenty are assured under a stable, wise, and selfless monarchy, is not decreased when those scenes are taken not as descriptions of James, nor as injunctions to James, nor as promises of what may yet be, but as visions of a dream of order and peace that have no dwelling except in the poetic imagination. A tragedy like *Sejanus*, and a comedy like *Bartholomew Fair* with its striking figure of the madman, Trouble-All, insisting that nothing be done without a warrant from the magistrate, are both, to me, made more powerful as the disenchanted views of an imagination that could create such enchantments as the best of the masques.

THE ROYAL PRETENDERS: FORD'S *PERKIN WARBECK* AND MASSINGER'S *BELIEVE AS YOU LIST*

That Policy hath never yet prevailed (though it hath served for a short Season) where the Counterfeit hath been sold for the Natural, and the outward Shew and Formality for the Substance.

Sir Walter Ralegh, *Seat of Government*[1]

The purpose of this chapter is to suggest some possible reasons why two of England's leading dramatists, about the year 1630, should each have been moved to write a play dealing very sympathetically with the appearance of a pretender to a throne, who is in the end defeated. The dramatists are John Ford and Philip Massinger, and the plays are *The Chronicle History of Perkin Warbeck: A Strange Truth* and *Believe As You List*. A connection between the two plays was noted by Peter Ure in an appendix to his Revels Plays edition of *Perkin Warbeck* in 1968. He thought that, since the plays were given by rival companies at rival theatres, one might have been written to match the other, but he could not decide on a precedence. The date of Massinger's play can be fixed quite definitely: the original version, which was banned and is not extant, was completed by 11 January 1631; the revised version was licensed for acting on 6 May 1631.[2] The date of *Perkin Warbeck* is not known; it was in print in 1634 and was probably written a year or two before that.

A sketch of the action of the two plays may be helpful at the outset. In Ford's play, Perkin Warbeck, claiming to be Richard, Duke of York, son of Edward IV, supposedly murdered in the Tower by Richard III, appears at the Scottish court of James IV, and is accepted there. He wins to wife Lady Katherine Gordon, who has the royal blood of Scotland in her veins. Henry VII successfully persuades James to renounce his protection of Warbeck. Warbeck's landing in Cornwall is a failure: he is captured and brought to face Henry VII. He and his low-born followers are led off to execution. At

no point in the play, by word or hint to others, or in soliloquy, is
Perkin Warbeck shown having any doubt of the truth of his claim to
royalty; and at no point does Ford introduce an incident or speech
decisively indicating his own opinion of the claim.

Massinger's play, in the rewritten version which alone is extant,
shows Antiochus, King of Lower Asia, returning to his kingdom
twenty-two years after his defeat and supposed death at the hands of
the Romans (in the second century BC). In his fight for recognition he
is constantly opposed by the indefatigable Roman envoy, Flaminius.
The Carthaginian senate, honest enough to recognise him, is too
nervous to countenance and support him. Prusias, King of Bithynia,
shelters him until persuaded by Flaminius of the political danger of
his protection. Antiochus is imprisoned, humiliated, tempted, but
will not confess he is an impostor. There is a moment of recovery when
a proconsul recognises him and denounces the cruel Flaminius, but
his defeat is final.

The extremely close relationship of the two plays has been obscured by the rewriting which Massinger was forced to undertake.
His original play was about the Portuguese pretender who at the end
of the sixteenth century was claiming to be the Portuguese King
Sebastian, presumed killed at the battle of Alcacer-el-Kebir in
Morocco in 1578. (It was after this that Philip II of Spain annexed
Portugal.) The myth that Sebastian had not died and would return to
his kingdom became very strong in Portugal, and the story of one
particular claimant, active at the turn of the century, aroused great
interest in England as in the rest of Europe. On the accounts of this
pretender's adventures Massinger based his original play. But in
November 1630 Charles completed the Treaty of Madrid with Spain,
and in January Sir Henry Herbert refused a licence for Massinger's
play, 'because it did contain dangerous matter, as the deposing of
Sebastian king of Portugal by Philip the [Second], and there being a
peace sworn twixt the kings of England and Spain'.[3]

Massinger refused to abandon his project and rewrote the play. He
pushed its setting back a safe eighteen hundred years and substituted
Antiochus for Sebastian, Carthage for Venice, Bithynia for Florence,
Flaminius for the Spanish ambassador. Although Massinger used
historical material relating to the real Antiochus and to Hannibal, the
'classical' play as we have it is a fiction; Believe As You List is a play on
recent European history gone over with a paint-brush to make it look
like ancient history.[4]

In the rewritten story, the indispensable element of dubiety is lost. Antiochus is no longer a mysterious pretender; he is the true king returning. The earlier hero, the Portuguese pretender, was, like Warbeck, an enigma who puzzled and divided his contemporaries, a famous real pretender of modern history.

If, therefore, we compare the play that Massinger originally wrote with Ford's, we see that both men took the true story of a pretender to a European throne, a pretender whom events and history had discredited, and invested that pretender with dignity and credibility in his conflict with the established ruler. Although in considering Massinger's play we can talk only of what we have and not what we might have had, it is essential to keep his original purpose in mind.

Ford's prologue to *Perkin Warbeck* shows how conscious he was that he was reviving the outmoded genre of the history play. 'Studies have, of this Nature, been of late/So out of fashion, so unfollowed . . .'. Anachronisms though they may be, both *Perkin Warbeck* and *Believe As You List* genuinely belong to the tradition of the royal histories of the English stage and continue the metaphoric use of kingship examined in Chapters 3, 4 and 5. In particular they bring to new life that altercation of kings which, deriving from the paradox and antinomy in the Tudor exploitation of sacred monarchy, images the warfare of past and future for the soul of England; and they give an unexpected concreteness to the myth of the hidden king, showing him disowned and reviled on his second coming. Once again the fox sinks his teeth in the lion's throat.

In an essay which is by far the best study of *Perkin Warbeck*, Jonas Barish has argued that the play carries on 'the continuing dialectic between two modes of sovereignty', between 'the manipulator' and 'the one who plays the king beautifully', 'who dwells in an imaginative element distinct from mundane reality, and who fires our imaginations in response'. No doubt, if Warbeck had been king, he would have lost his sceptre like Richard II or Edward II. We should like kings to be like Perkin, argues Barish, but the 'politics of pragmatism' make it impossible. To achieve polarity, Barish suggests, Ford provoked a conflict with history. By making Henry VII unattractive, and by omitting Warbeck's confession of his deception, Ford forces us 'to re-experience events in something like their original disturbing density and ambiguity'.[5]

Barish has done a great service in insisting on the basic challenge in Ford's play. It is almost impossible for an Englishman to keep it as an open question between Henry VII and Perkin Warbeck: Henry VII was so 'obviously' the true king and Warbeck an impostor. But the openness is there and it is fundamental.[6] The critical argument about *Perkin Warbeck* has usually been about the mental state of the impostor, the man who had come to believe in the truth of the rôle he had adopted.[7] These discussions make assumptions about the hero's origins which the play refuses to make. If we stay inside the play, we recognise that the argument is about two styles of life, each calling itself kingly: only one can be the true one, and Ford insists that 'legitimacy' is a red herring in the competition to discern the counter-feit.

Anyone who reads Bacon's life of Henry VII, a main source for Ford, is struck not only by the King's unattractiveness, but by the uncertainty of his title. In the first part of his narrative, Bacon shows the victor of Bosworth, *de facto* king, debating how best to lay claim to legitimacy. There was his own right, as of the House of Lancaster, but that had been 'a title condemned by Parliament' and it opened up the equally legal claims of the scions of York. There were the rights of his future wife, Elizabeth, whom 'the party that brought him in' had arranged for him to marry; these gave him but a courtesy right to the throne. Finally, there were the sheer rights of conquest. This hesita-tion and self-debate are worth remembering in the opening scene of *Perkin Warbeck*, in which Henry is addressed with all the worship which we have learned to associate with the Tudor view of the sacredness of its own house. Durham gives us the second speech of the play:

> *Mercy* did gently sheathe the sword of *Justice*
> In lending to this blood-shrunk Commonwealth
> A new soul, new birth in your *Sacred person*.   (I.i.24–6)[8]

Since one voice in the chorus of obsequious attendants is that of Stanley, who is actually supporting Warbeck, we may wonder whether these adulations are not presented with some irony. If we look closely at the third speech in the play, it is fairly clear that Ford is proposing something more than a conventional view of the providen-tial role of Henry VII. The speech is Daubeney's, and it is of critical importance.

> Edward the Fourth after a doubtful fortune
> Yielded to nature; leaving to his sons,

> Edward and Richard, the inheritance
> Of a most bloody purchase; these young Princes
> Richard the Tyrant, their unnatural Uncle,
> Forced to a violent grave, so just is Heaven.
> Him hath your Majesty by your own arm,
> Divinely strengthened, pulled from his *Boar's sty*
> And struck the black Usurper to a Carcase.   (I.i.27–35)

Peter Ure could not believe that 'so just is Heaven' (in the sixth line) referred to the violent death of the princes in the Tower, and he altered the punctuation to make it belong to the succeeding sentence! But the sycophant Daubeney has less difficulty in seeing the hand of heaven in their death. Their father took the throne following the murder of Henry VI. Their death was a punishment for the crimes of their fathers. Richard III's violent death at the hands of Henry Richmond was *his* divine punishment. It is very difficult indeed to take seriously any theory of divine intervention after this barbarous speech. And the position of Henry as a violent usurper himself is made embarrassingly clear. That Henry was an adventurer is the burden of Warbeck's charge to his face:

> . . . Bosworth field:
> Where at an instant, to the world's amazement,
> A morn to Richmond and a night to Richard
> Appeared at once. The tale is soon applied:
> Fate which crowned these attempts when least assured
> Might have befriended *others*, like resolved.   (V.ii.69–74)

Daubeney's speech contains a further startling implication. Even if Warbeck *is* the man he claims to be, Richard of York, his claim is no more rightful than Henry's, being claimed by blood spilt rather than blood in his veins. At best, Henry the usurper faces Richard the son of the usurper.

The unimportance of 'blood in the veins' is further underlined in the exchange between Huntley and Dalyell on pedigrees. Huntley had married a princess, so his daughter Katherine has royal blood: for this reason, the non-royal Dalyell is not to be allowed to marry her. But Dalyell says he's a descendant of Adam Mure,

> whose daughter was the mother
> *To him* who first begot the race of Jameses
> That sway the Sceptre to this very day.   (I.ii.31–3)

The implication is that if we're to take our stand on descent, then royal blood is, like an Irish grandmother in America, owned by everyone. The oblique compliment to Charles I begins to look left-handed.

The first point to be established, then, is that by keeping the descent of Warbeck open during the play, and by questioning the divine and historical *right* of Henry VII to the throne, Ford manages to balance his great opposites, and leaves his audience to decide who is truly royal. Henry has a bad time of it, and we should be clear how markedly Ford places him in the machiavellian camp. His strength and ruthlessness are clear even in the compliments to him, as we see in Daubeney's speech – 'struck the black Usurper to a Carcase'. He is a statesman of great ability and foresight; he has a very good intelligence-network, and he knows the value of the appearance of clemency. The second scene of Act II is classic. Stanley's plot has been discovered: Henry piously hopes that the traitor may find mercy, but allows himself to be persuaded by the Bishop of Durham that mercy would be dangerous. As Stanley enters, Henry quickly exits, for 'If a' speak to me, / I could deny him nothing.'

Henry's masterpiece, of course, is detaching King James of Scotland from Warbeck. It is done by Pedro Hialas, envoy of Spain, who is well bribed by Henry. Hialas persuades James of the beauty of a Christian peace in Europe (IV.iii.1–16). James regretfully acknowledges that 'a general peace' is a greater good than the one thing which stands in its way, his protection of Warbeck. All the high talk is undercut within the scene by the references to the real motives of self-interest in each of the three parties, Spain, Scotland and England. James delightedly rehearses what he's got, 'and all / For Warbeck not delivered, but dismissed? / We could not wish it better.' He tells Warbeck that 'the dignity of State directs our wisdom' (it is interesting to observe how the words 'wise' and 'wisdom' are used throughout the play with connotations of cunning and policy). Henry has lured James (IV.iv.24–31) into casting off Warbeck, and it has all been done in the most high-minded way. That James has given preference to a lower human value, statecraft, over the higher one of trust and friendship is made absolutely clear (IV.iii.35–49).

Against the powerful figure of the resourceful and successful politician, surrounded by flatterers telling him he can do no wrong, stands the saintly Warbeck, who spontaneously wins the admiration of those who can gain nothing from him. King James speaks of his reaction to Warbeck as 'instinct of sovereignty' (II.iii.42) and contrasts 'kingly York' with 'Welsh Harry' (II.iii.60–4). There is no need to emphasise the dignity of Warbeck's bearing, his sincerity and attractiveness, since these are so obvious. Katherine's love for him is the seal on his integrity and worth, and her fidelity a denial of those who accuse him of deception.

> Harry Richmond!
> A woman's faith hath robbed thy fame of triumph.   (V.iii.101–2)

True love and royalty stand as mutually enforcing metaphors. The love is a symbol of majesty: majesty is a way of describing love. This exchange of realities and metaphors may clearly be seen in the two major scenes between Warbeck and Katherine, in Act III, Scene ii, and Act V, Scene iii. In strong contrast, Henry appears alone (Bacon had spoken of his coldness to his wife Elizabeth; *Works*, 1826, v, p. 19); and his thinly veiled offer to make Katherine his mistress (V.ii.152–7) further distinguishes his concept of personal relationships from Warbeck's.

For modern readers, there is a certain effeminacy in Ford's picture of the 'new king': his delicacy and frailty could not be further removed from the strength of an earlier picture of a new king, Tamburlaine. Perhaps Ford meant to qualify a too-extreme contrast. Henry's ability to rule, his firmness and control, are not the parts of a villain, and Warbeck's sensitivity occasionally meets some justified Scottish rebukes. But in the main, the play's contrast between the ruler and the claimant is, in personal terms, entirely on the side of the claimant.

In Massinger's play,[9] the contrast between policy and personal worth is even more marked. 'Rome's encroaching empire' (I.i.105) is one of materialism and self-interest on the widest scale. Flaminius is an enthusiastic and dedicated servant of the *idea* of the Roman Empire:

> In the brass-leaved book of fate it was set down
> The earth should know no sovereign but Rome.   (I.ii.135–6)

His rôle dictates its own scale of values:

> By my birth
> I am bound to serve thee, Rome, and what I do
> Necessity of state compels me to.   (II.i.124–6)

In the 'labyrinth/Of politic windings' in which this necessity of state involves him, he has to become 'a Protean actor' (III.i.14–16). He warns Marcellus that anyone in power must remember 'your faculties are the state's, and not your own' (V.i.168).

The maintenance of Rome's hegemony demands that the returned

Antiochus gets no credence, or, if he gets credence, no support. It proves all too easy for the agent of an all-powerful state to persuade subject people where their interest lies, however reluctant they may be to deny what they know to be true; and where persuasion fails, intimidation works. Prusias, King of Bithynia, receives Antiochus with open arms. When Flaminius asks him to renounce his guest, he indignantly repudiates him: 'Shall I for your ends/Infringe my princely word? ... I will not buy your amity at such loss' (III.iii.105–6). But when Flaminius offers him the choice of giving up Antiochus, or war, Prusias yields. Then Antiochus enters:

> Prusias.   I am sorry.
> Antiochus. Sorry? For what? That you had an intent
>   To be a good and just prince? Are compassion
>   And charity grown crimes?
> Prusias.   The gods can witness
>   How much I would do for you. And but that
>   Necessity of state–
> Antiochus.   Make not the gods
>   Guilty of your breach of faith; from them you find not
>   Treachery commanded.   (III.iii.190–7)

The contest between Antiochus and Flaminius, as the former seeks the recognition and support which the latter must prevent, is extremely well presented, because the struggle is one-sided only in the outcome, and not in moral terms.[10] Either Rome or Antiochus is a lie or a fiction: there is no room for both, and one must displace the other (II.ii.190–4). Antiochus has returned from the life of contemplation to serve his country, to rescue it from vassalage.

> The Genius of my country, made a slave,
> Like a weeping mother seems to kneel before me,
> Wringing her manacled hands.   (I.i.50–2)

His kingly bearing wins an immediate response: true majesty cannot be concealed (II.ii.138; IV.iv.33–4). Everywhere he wins moral victory, but practical defeat. Flaminius hounds and pursues him. When finally he has him in his power, his business is to uncreate him, to get him to unsay himself and declare himself counterfeit. Temptations have no effect, and Flaminius turns to duress: he humiliates and degrades him before the people and then sends him to the galleys.

> Is it not sufficient
> That the locks of this once royal head are shaved off,
> My glorious robes changed to this slavish habit,

> This hand that grasped a sceptre manacled,
> Or that I have been as a spectacle
> Exposed to public scorn . . . ?
>
> . . .   .
>
>   Do what you please.
> I am in your power, but still Antiochus,
> King of the lower Asia, no impostor.   (IV.iv.50–5; 65–7)[11]

Massinger was much more of a political dramatist than Ford.
During his whole career, he was dealing with political themes in his
plays, many of them directly or indirectly topical, and he was several
times in trouble with the authorities for coming too close to reality for
comfort, as in *Believe As You List*. The early collaboration with
Fletcher, *Sir John van Olden Barnavelt*, dealing with contemporary
events in the Netherlands, was banned outright by the Bishop of
London. Charles I himself refused to allow a licence for *The King and
the Subject* (not extant) in 1638 because a speech in it, referring to a
forced loan, was 'too insolent'.[12] Some speeches in *The Bondman*
became a kind of national inheritance, to be brought out in critical
times like those when there was fear of a Napoleonic invasion.[13] Even
a comedy like *The Great Duke of Florence* (1627) is throughout preoccupied with the problem of absolutism. A Byzantine tragicomedy,
The Emperor of the East (1631) contains a strange satiric interlude on
the way projectors and informers (so indispensable a feature of the
English court) were corrupting the empire. It is scarcely possible to
think that the highly developed concern for national honourableness
so prominent in *The Bondman* and *The Maid of Honour*, and the accompanying contempt for the moral failings of the mighty, had nothing to
do with Massinger's opinion of English society.

S. R. Gardiner rather innocently supposed that many of Massinger's plays could be read as allegories in which James, Charles,
Buckingham and the Elector Frederick play prominent parts.[14] He
argued that Massinger's connection with the Pembroke family would
have led him to support, as Pembroke did, the anti-Spanish and
anti-Buckingham party at court which wanted more positive
assistance for the Elector Palatine. Gardiner's identifications are
absurd on two grounds. First, if Massinger *had* in such thin disguise
criticised James and Buckingham he would never have survived;
secondly, the proposed allegories can involve total misreadings of the
plays.[15] Yet Gardiner's essay is important: that the historian who
knew more about this period than any previous or subsequent

scholar should have had, as he read Massinger's plays, the constant feeling of echoes of real situations is something which cannot be overlooked. Gardiner made the mistake of pushing too hard: had he been content with topicality at a deeper level, his essay would have told us more about the political reference of Massinger's plays than it does.

What was there, then, in the spirit of the times which might have influenced Massinger, and by implication Ford, in fashioning his pretender play?

The years preceding the signing of the Treaty of Madrid in 1630 were years in which growing anger at Charles's autocratic attempts to raise money without the help of Parliament was coupled with humiliation and shame at the disgraceful failures of English arms at Cadiz, the Ile de Rhé, and La Rochelle. In those years also, the Palatinate remained unfreed, and the Protestant forces in Europe under Mansfeld were defeated. A great many Englishmen, faced with the continued failure by James, Charles, and Buckingham to assist Frederick with whole-hearted assistance at the right time and in the right place, had the growing conviction that the causes both of Protestantism and of English national honour were being betrayed. The sense of affront in the attempts to raise the forced loan and in the shaming incompetence of English naval and military adventures made the mood of the newly assembled Third Parliament in the spring of 1628 one of the gravest concern for the preservation of England, of her national honour, and of the ancient rights of her people. It was the need to restore the past which was the burden of the speeches by Coke, Wentworth, and Selden. 'The violated rights of the subject must first be vindicated. The very being of the commonwealth, they declared, was at stake.' So wrote Gardiner.[16] 'It is conceived,' said Sir Walter Erle, 'that the subject had suffered more in the violation of the ancient liberties within these few years than in the three hundred years before.'[17] Eliot's speech of 3 June made a strong contrast between England in the days of Elizabeth and England under Charles and Buckingham.

What perfect English heart is not almost dissolved into sorrow for the truth? For the oppression of the subject . . . the whole kingdom is a proof. And for the exhausting of our treasures, that oppression speaks it. What waste of our provisions, what consumption of our ships, what destruction of our men have been! . . . We were never so much weakened, nor had less hope now to be restored.[18]

It must not be thought that the resentment was entirely a matter of principle: it was, for the merchants, a matter of money. The valiant merchant Richard Chambers exclaimed, 'Merchants are in no part of the world so screwed and wrung as they are in England. In Turkey they have more encouragement.'[19] For this, he was arrested and brought before the Star Chamber.

Charles eventually gave his assent to the Petition of Right, and in August 1628 Buckingham was assassinated. But confrontation could not be avoided. By January and February 1629, it had become clear that the issue was one of sovereignty: who was to govern England? 'Actum est de imperio.'[20] In March 1629, Parliament was dissolved and Eliot and the eight members were imprisoned. Charles entered on the eleven-year-long career of his personal rule.

It is of the utmost importance to stress that nostalgia and reaction were basic elements in the opposition to Charles at the time that *Perkin Warbeck* and *Believe As You List* were written. The appeal voiced by Eliot, Wentworth, and Selden was to the 'ancient rights' of the people. The complaint was not that Charles was a feudal incubus, hampering progress and the advancement of freedom, but that, in his autocracy and would-be absolutism, he was a dangerous innovator. Lawrence Stone's book, *The Causes of the English Revolution 1529–1642*, clearly illustrates the basic conservatism of the early period of the English revolution and relates it to the profound and wide-spread reactionary element in revolutionary movements as a whole. (When the split came ten years later those M.P.s who took Parliament's side were on average ten years *older* than those who sided with the king.)[21] Those who opposed Charles wished not to advance but to return, and the reign of Queen Elizabeth took on a quite extraordinary sentimental lustre as the golden image of all that life under the Stuarts failed to be.[22]

In a situation of national humiliation, coupled with fear of the encroachment of a new kind of absolutism, and a tendency to look to the past for an image of what ought to be, it seems very natural to me that one of the strongest myths of mankind should be revived by Ford and Massinger, the myth of the hero who returns from the dead to succour his oppressed people.[23] The myth has attached itself to Arthur, to Harold, to James IV of Scotland, to Parnell. The Sebastian cult, interestingly, has been one of the most long-lived versions of the myth of the 'sleeping hero': it manifested itself until the end of the nineteenth century.

> The plot in which the vine takes root
> Begins to dry from head to foot:
> The stock soon withering, want of sap
> Doth cause to quail the budding grape:
> But from the neighbouring elm, a dew
> Shall drop, and feed the plot anew.

So runs the oracle's riddle in Ford's *The Broken Heart*.

My main proposition, therefore, is that both Perkin Warbeck and Antiochus represent a luminous figure appearing from the mists announcing that he is the dead past, newly come alive in order to bring succour to an ailing nation. He has a kind of beauty of being, he is the guardian of the idealised, authentic, undivided life, when truth and government were not separated. It is a notable blend of romance and reality that in Massinger's play it is the merchants who are most obviously suffering under the Roman yoke, and long for the old régime (I.ii.63–88; 158–89); it was the merchants who had the most to complain about over Charles's attempts to exact subsidies.

A charismatic figure of lost royalty would have had a great emotional appeal at a period when many of Charles's subjects looked on the occupant of the throne as the dried husk of a king. But we must renounce two things completely if we are to make sense of the conflict of the two 'competitors for kingdoms' (Ford's phrase) in each play. The first is the temptation to read the plays allegorically, and the second is the nineteenth-century view of Charles I as the pale figure of an obsolete Divine Right theorist holding up the cause of economic liberty. For if we don't renounce these things, it will appear ludicrously 'unhistorical' that the returning king-hero should suffer defeat at the hands of mercilessly efficient machiavellian statecraft, incarnate in Charles I of all people. As Henry VII or Philip II (as it was in the original version) began to take shape in the dramatist's mind, he was not a mask for the incompetent Charles I, but a metaphor for a kind of modernism which, however odd it seems, might have been thought to include the objects of Charles's policies.

Trevor-Roper's theory of the general crisis of the seventeenth century recognises as a fundamental element in the unease of Europe an alarm at the growth of the impersonal power of the Renaissance state.[24] Absolutism belonged to the future in Europe,[25] and the fact that Charles was incompetent was no bar to feeling in his policies the merciless wind of change.

The machiavel, as the representative of unwanted progress and modernism, had haunted the imagination of English dramatists for fifty years. As he appears in these pretender plays, he seems bound for a highly successful future as he completes his task of eroding and replacing traditional human and social values. Both *Perkin Warbeck* and *Believe As You List* are very pessimistic plays, and they by no means share the confidence of Ralegh as expressed in the epigraph to this chapter. We are invited to see in each play a spiritual hollowness in the established government, and to share a conviction that the ethics of success on which it builds are bound to suppress the qualities of truth represented by the saintly king beckoned up from the past. It will seem to us that it is with an irony of remarkable tartness and an historical sense of remarkable acuteness that Ford chose for his modernist king Henry VII, first of the Tudors, whose son and grand-daughter worked so hard to produce that alibi of mystical kingship which, I have argued, provided for the dramatists their recurrent regal image for the values of the past. In *Perkin Warbeck* the Tudors are opposed by their own shadows.

In associating Massinger and Ford with a deep current of hostility to Charles, I have made it quite clear that their position is not anti-monarchical. Everyone was a monarchist in 1630 and dramatists were utterly dependent on the monarchy for the continuance of their profession. The force behind the pretender figure is the feeling that Charles was betraying the monarchy. But the time was rapidly pas-sing when it was possible to represent the conflict as a competition between two kings. It seems to me a strangely prophetic stroke that in the enforced revision of his play Massinger had to exchange the kingdom of Spain for the republic of Rome, so that the ethos of modern expediency and progress became associated with republican-ism. The year 1630 was about the time when many thoughtful people who had opposed Charles began to question their loyalties and ask whether their belief in what monarchy ought to stand for did not demand their support of the King in spite of their dislike of his actions. As Wentworth joined the King's service, he made his great speech at York, expressing his belief in 'those mutual intelligences of love and protection descending and loyalty ascending which should pass and be the entertainments between a king and his people'.[26] A close friend of Massinger's, the notable lawyer Henry Parker, made a different decision. He was the first person to propound a theory of the sovereignty of Parliament, and he wrote, 'Reason of state is something

more sublime and imperial than Law . . . When war has silenced Law
. . . Policy is to be observed as the only true Law.'[27] This is the
language of Massinger's Flaminius, also agent of a republic. Twenty
years after Massinger and Ford wrote their plays, the king had
become the natural symbol of traditional relationships and 'ancient
rights'. As the contention moved from drama into history, Charles
switched rôles and as sacred martyr wore the robes of Perkin Warbeck
and Antiochus. The vehicle for modernism and progress was the
Commonwealth. In 1630, the simplicity of these divisions had not
established themselves; in the theatre, the warfare in the soul of
England could be best expressed as it had been for forty years, as a
contention between rival kings.

The exact circumstances in which Massinger and Ford came to
write their pretender plays cannot be discerned. Though they were
friends, the appearance of the two plays may be a coincidence. But the
fact that the two plays exist side by side helps us considerably to see
the force of each as a political play exploiting the meaning of the terms
'counterfeit' and 'natural' in the period of perturbed and perplexed
relationships between monarch and people about the year 1630.[28]

PART TWO: YEATS'S IRELAND

8

OUR IRISH THEATRE

Cultural nationalism and the European theatre

At the end of the eighteenth century, Shakespeare's English history plays, which had contributed powerfully to England's national awareness at the end of the sixteenth century, began a new life, profoundly important and long-lasting, in developing the sense of national awareness in other countries. The founding of the Irish Literary Theatre in 1899 (the predecessor of the Irish National Theatre, 1902, and the Abbey Theatre, 1904) is perhaps the most prominent event in a European story in which the self-realisation of nations is held to require a theatre to create and broadcast the spiritual values of the nation's past – a theatre for which Shakespeare's was the admired model. The uniting of the three strands – Shakespeare, values of the past, national self-discovery – began with Herder. His reading of Shakespeare (1763) and Ossian (1769) were vital to the development of his ideas about culture, which became standard in the nineteenth century. For a man to know himself he must know his nation, and for a nation to know itself it must know its past, particularly the richness of its primitive imagination stored up in its folk-lore and legends. In the spiritual rejuvenation which depended on the recognition of *place* and the *past*, the poet was to have a task of first importance, for there was magic in poetry, able to move a people into action. 'A poet is a creator of a people; he gives it a world to contemplate, he holds its soul in his hands.'[1] Herder's belief that Shakespeare's plays were steeped in folk-lore and race memory was based on misunderstandings but proved in numerous ways an idea of extraordinary fertility (informing for example the work of C. L. Barber on the Comedies in recent years). Archaic and folk material remained as a primary support of cultural nationalism and was able to do without the help of Shakespeare, whose English history plays became the focus of attention.

Schiller had said in 1783, 'Had we but a national theatre, we would become a nation.'[2] He lamented the lack of German historical subjects for drama,[3] and after reading Shakespeare's Histories in 1798 wrote enthusiastically to Goethe, 'It would truly be worth the trouble to adapt this whole series of eight plays for the German stage. It might introduce a new epoch. We must really talk this subject over.'[4] The idea of a Shakespearian historical drama for Germany made a resounding conclusion for A. W. Schlegel's *Lectures on Dramatic Art and Literature*, delivered at Vienna in 1808. In the field of dramatic literature, he said,

the most glorious laurels may yet be reaped by dramatic poets who are willing to emulate Goethe and Schiller. Only let our historical drama be in reality and thoroughly national ... Let it, at the same time, be truly historical, drawn from a profound knowledge, and transporting us back to the great olden time. In this mirror let the poet enable us to see, while we take deep shame to ourselves for what we are, what the Germans were in former times, and what they must again be ... What a glorious picture is furnished by our history, from the most remote times ... What a field for a poet who, like Shakespeare, could discern the poetical aspect of the great events of the world![5]

The great Polish patriot, Adam Mickiewicz, banished from a dismembered Poland by the Czar, wrote in 1828 to A. E. Odyniec about the latter's play.

If you read Shakespeare, you will yourself recognise better and understand the faults in your own poem. Just concentrate on each of Shakespeare's plays ... I repeat once more that the only kind of drama answering the needs of our age is historical drama ... There are no new dramatic poets to be found in our own country ... We may imitate Shakespeare, Schiller and Goethe, at any rate, adapting their forms to our national requirements. I should like you to begin by adapting some of the plays of these great masters, but Shakespeare in particular.

In a later letter, he wrote that he was 'a dedicated admirer of Shakespeare'. 'I repeat a million times, that our age needs historical dramas.'[6] The Polish nation had ceased to exist as a political entity after the third partition of 1795. Censorship of the theatre was rigorous, and was even more severe after the unsuccessful rebellion against the Russians in 1830–1. But at this very time 'the histories of Shakespeare came to make a definite appeal in the theatre ... They were extolled by patriots as being those plays which, by their example, might arouse an enthusiasm in the Polish youth for the history of their own fatherland.'[7] Julius Stowacki had seen Kean act *Richard III* in England in 1831 and in the seclusion of the Swiss Alps began writing plays heavily influenced by Shakespeare. 'The creation of a national drama for Poland with its own heroes figuring in it, all moulded in the spirit of Shakespeare, was his aim.'[8]

The creator of cultural nationalism in Ireland was Thomas Davis, whose achievements before his death at the age of thirty-one in 1845 were quite extraordinary. His father was English; he was a Protestant and a graduate of Trinity College, Dublin. It was to a T.C.D. audience that Davis made his famous pronouncement, 'Gentlemen, you have a country!' He was closely in touch with European movements and ideas, and his movement, Young Ireland, reflects La Giovine Italia of Mazzini. His journal, however, which began publication in 1842, was called *The Nation*. 'We desired to make Ireland a nation' – and in the spirit of Wolfe Tone the nation included all who loved and served Ireland wherever they came from: 'Irish must no longer mean Celtic.'[9] The aim of those founding the journal, the prospectus said, was

to direct the popular mind and the sympathies of educated men of all parties to the great end of Nationality . . . Nationality is their first great object – a Nationality which will not only raise our people from their poverty . . . but inflame and purify them with a lofty and heroic love of country – a Nationality of the spirit as well as the letter – a Nationality which may come to be stamped upon our manners, our literature, and our deeds.[10]

Quite unlike Yeats, Davis was an active politician and was eager to advance Ireland's technology and industrial self-sufficiency. He had a keen eye for the potential of national resources, and even foresaw the mechanical winning and industrial use of peat which Bord na Móna put into operation a hundred years later.[11] All the more remarkable, therefore, is his devotion to Ireland's past – her art, music, and legends – and to the creation of an Irish literature.

National poetry is the very flowering of the soul – the greatest evidence of its health, the greatest excellence of its beauty . . . It shows us magnified, and ennobles our hearts, our intellects, our country and our countrymen – binds us to the land by its condensed and gem-like history, to the future by examples and aspirations.[12]

Davis encouraged Ireland's painters to paint Irish scenes and her writers to write of Irish subjects. The poetry of Young Ireland, including Davis's own, was republished as *Spirit of the Nation*, and was immensely influential in succeeding generations. There is little about Shakespeare in Davis's writings, but he did think about drama. To his friend D. O. Madden, Davis wrote:

Have you ever tried dramatic writing? Do you know Taylor's 'Philip Van Artevelde', and Griffin's 'Gisippus'? I think them the two best serious dramas written in English since Shakespeare's time. A drama equal to either of them on an Irish subject would be useful and popular to an extent you can hardly suppose.

This letter is quoted in Sir Charles Gavan Duffy's history of the Young Ireland movement, which of course Yeats knew, and he quoted it disparagingly in an article on Young Ireland in *The Bookman* in 1897, as evidence of the belief that any man could become a writer if he gave his mind to it.[13] Yeats never paid proper tribute to the achievements of Thomas Davis, whose work he was continuing and extending. There is no knowing how the literature and drama of Ireland might have improved in quality and extended in range if it had not been for Davis's tragically early death and the wider tragedy of the Famine which followed so soon afterwards.

Towards the national theatre in Norway Yeats always showed the greatest respect: it was the nearest thing recent history had to show to the kind of theatre he wished to establish in Ireland. The political situation of Norway in 1850 was very different from that of Poland or Ireland. Norway had at last won her independence from Denmark in 1814, and the anomalies and injustices of the constitutional union with Sweden which was then forced on her were in process of being eased. So when in 1849 Olé Bull founded his national theatre in the little town of Bergen, the patriotic drive was not for freedom from foreign rule but to establish the spiritual and cultural entity of the Norwegians, rid at last of the imposed Danish culture. J. W. McFarlane writes, 'By mid-nineteenth century, constitutional independence in Norway was still a comparatively recent thing; the people craved reassurance that despite the political youthfulness of the nation they nevertheless belonged to an ancient kingdom; they wanted to be reminded of their long history and their great traditions.'[14] This reassurance the young Ibsen was willing to provide, as resident dramatist for the Bergen theatre. In 1851 he wrote a rhyming Prologue for a festival in Christiana to raise funds for the new theatre. In olden times, he said, poetry was regarded as an honourable activity, and the poet won approval from king and people. 'The bold skald took his seat by the king's side, high in the banquet hall.' But when times changed and the spirit of the people was cowed, the poet fell silent. Even when they emerged from their winter sleep and broke the chains which bound them the people were not receptive to poetry again. But now art 'like a harp's sounding board, amplifying the strings of the people's soul' is presenting beautiful images from valley and mountain, and from the distant past. But the theatre was not yet established – 'that art which everywhere found native soil, and sent out its deep roots among the people. For by it life is most truly interpreted, and presented sharply and most clearly to our gaze.' Now the theatre asks the people to provide it with a home. It will tell about the vanished glory and splendour of the past, and about the rich activity of present-day life.[15]

In 1859, now at the national theatre at Christiana, Ibsen still saw the rôle of the artist as a nation's 'spiritual eyes', revealing the essence of the nation by showing its continuity in time. In a petition to Parliament on behalf of the theatre he wrote:

This fight in the service of a higher freedom is fought here, as elsewhere, mainly by our artists and authors, the spiritual eyes of the people . . . Our writers have, by their words, taught the people to love the past with all its vicissitudes; they have presented to our gaze an image of the life of the people in forms both true and noble.[16]

Ibsen was sent abroad by the committee of the Bergen theatre in 1852, and in Copenhagen he saw several plays of Shakespeare's – his first – including *Hamlet* and *Lear*. In Dresden he saw *Hamlet* again and possibly *Richard III*. There are superficial echoes of *Hamlet* and *Lear* in *Olaf Liljekrans* (1857); Alfhild strongly echoes the mad Ophelia, and Olaf speaks to her with the rude accent of Hamlet; the bard owes much to Lear's Fool; and the climax of the play is heralded by the outbreak of a thunderstorm. *The Pretenders* (1863) is more essentially Shakespearian. Going back to medieval Norway, its subject is the feud between rival contenders for the throne; questions of fitness to be a king, the curse of a divided country, and the tragedy of civil war are all fundamental Shakespearian themes, and the sacredness surrounding the idea of the kingdom's unity is strongly reminiscent of Shakespeare.

In three ways, Ibsen's early plays for the Norwegian theatres interest us as anticipations of the later Irish theatre. First, the use of national history as subject, as in *The Pretenders*; secondly, the use of national legends, as in *The Vikings at Helgeland* (1858), a conflation of material from several sagas; and thirdly, in the use of folk-lore, as in

Olaf Liljekrans (and in *Peer Gynt*). Yeats knew that excellent play *The Vikings at Helgeland*, which William Archer had translated in 1890, and he referred to it more than once. It is extremely successful in presenting the heroic age without absurdity or sentimentality, conveying the foreignness of its values while convincing us of their vitality and importance. Yeats would not have known *Olaf Liljekrans*, and is unlikely ever to have heard of the early fragment, one and a half acts, which Ibsen wrote while he was a student in 1850 and in modified form incorporated into the later play. This uncompleted play was entitled *Rypen i Justedal*. (McFarlane translates as 'The Grouse in Justedal'; Meyer prefers 'the ptarmigan' for *rypen*.) The subtitle was 'National Play in Four Acts'. This is surely the most Yeatsian thing Ibsen wrote. It seems strange that *The Land of Heart's Desire* could have been written in ignorance of it.

The play is set in medieval times after the Black Death. There is a part of the mountains, Justedal, where no one dare go – the Black Death killed off all who lived there. The hero Bjørn has been there and is strangely disturbed by music which pulls him away. He meets first a mysterious minstrel, and then the elf-child Alfhild, singing. The second act moves right away from this restless world of mountain, music, dream, and faery to the bourgeois reality of Bjørn's home. His father, a grasping man, has planned a marriage for him which neither he nor the intended bride wants. Years before this the father managed to get his own elder brother Alf dispossessed and turned out over a love-marriage. An aged and mysterious wandering minstrel enters the house, and, bringing up the unsavoury matter of that wickedness of years before, is turned out. Bjørn goes back to the mountains, meets the dream-child Alfhild and vows his love for her. It turns out that her protector is the mysterious minstrel. The fragment ends with music from the elfin world with which Alfhild is so closely in touch.

The new play *Olaf Liljekrans* destroys most of the charm of this fragment in spinning it out into a well-plotted play, though in its different way it presents powerfully enough the Yeatsian conflict of the world of every day and the tormenting world of spirit in the soul of the hero. But since this conflict is not easily solvable by theatrical resolution, the sheer absence of any conclusion in the earlier piece makes it much more satisfactory. (In *The Land of Heart's Desire*, Yeats made *his* 'troll-struck' heroine simply collapse and die at the climax of the play, and that is a false enough ending.) It is not difficult to see, with the little help which *Olaf Liljekrans* is able to give us, what is the meaning of *Rypen i Justedal* and why Ibsen called it 'a national play' (apart from the fact that he got the story from a book called *Norwegian Tales*). Alfhild is clearly the orphan of Alf who was driven out of society by his greedy and corrupt brother. She has survived the searing Black Death, and lives alone in the hills in the company of the spirit world, protected by a poet. She preserves the values of the old world when mankind was spiritually alive, and she draws towards her – without design – the heir of the materialistic world – and the poet, like Prospero, blesses their conjunction.

It is all in the true spirit of the age. National rejuvenation is to be won under the guidance of the poet who keeps alive the knowledge of the world of spirit which earlier ages more instinctively knew and enshrined in folk literature. Bjørn breaks out of the sordid and loveless materialism of modern society, presided over by the Christian minister Mogens (compare Father Hart in Yeats's play) and, seeing a vision of the world before the Black Death, embraces it, and . . .?

Ibsen moved away from folk-beliefs, sagas, and medieval history as he moved away from Norway itself. Yeats defiantly said in 1897 that he thought the earlier Ibsen was the greater Ibsen. In the same sentence (in 'The Celtic Element in Literature') he was on safer ground in his praise of Wagner for bringing home the excitement of the romance of legend to the modern world. It is an oddity, however, that the man who unlike Yeats really knew and loved Wagner, Edward Martyn, modelled his first contribution to the Irish Literary Theatre, *The Heather Field*, on the later Ibsen. The controversy in Ireland as to whether Wagner, his theatre at Bayreuth, and the subjects of his music dramas were fit models for an Irish national drama is very important and I shall turn to it shortly. But now, with this briefest of sketches of what lay behind Yeats in the amalgamation of nation, poet, theatre, and the past, we can turn to Yeats's own ideas about a theatre for Ireland.

The founding of an Irish theatre

There had been several attempts over the centuries to found an Irish theatre. When Thomas Wentworth came to Dublin in 1633 as Lord Deputy with his policy of Thorough, it seemed to him that his new court in Dublin Castle required that *sine qua non* of the court in Whitehall – an active theatre. He therefore established the first professional playhouse outside London in these islands. John Ogilby was brought over to run it, and players and musicians were recruited from London. In 1637 the theatre was built in Werburgh Street, near the Castle. Ogilby imported James Shirley as resident playwright.[17] Shirley had trouble in gauging the taste of his new audience and in 1639 in something like desperation wrote his preposterous play *St Patrick for Ireland* (extermination of snakes and all). In the Prologue he wrote:

> We know not what will take; your palates are
> Various, and many of them sick, I fear.
> . . .   .
> We should be very happy if, at last,
> We could find out the humour of your taste
> That we might fit, and feast it.[18]

The theatre collapsed of course in the turmoil of events, and, as in England, revived wonderfully at the Restoration. But however brilliant the theatrical life of Smock Alley, the Dublin theatre remained a subsidiary of the London theatre throughout the whole of the eighteenth century. Since it was basically a provincial theatre, talent naturally migrated to the metropolis, London. Ireland bred nearly all the great comic dramatists of the English language after Jonson – Congreve, Farquhar, Goldsmith, Sheridan, Wilde, and Shaw – and they all wrote for the London theatre. Charles Shadwell, however, resident dramatist at Smock Alley from about 1715 to 1720 (and like Shirley an Englishman), tried to create a drama with Irish subjects, and experimented in both comedy and tragedy. The prologue to his awful *Irish Hospitality, or Virtue Rewarded* says firmly, 'Each Nation should support a theatre.'[19] His most ambitious play was a tragedy on the subject later to be used by both Yeats and Lady Gregory, Dermot MacMurrough's fatal bringing of Strongbow and the Normans into Ireland to help him in his feud with the High King Rory O'Connor. *Rotherick O'Connor King of Connaught, or, The Distressed Princess* is a third-rate work but it was a pioneer play in using Irish history to reflect upon present times, and, as the historian of the Irish stage W. S. Clark says, 'it was the climax of [Shadwell's] endeavour to relate the Dublin drama and theatre to the nationalistic sentiments among Protestant as well as Catholic Irish'.[20] Shadwell is pretty careful not to upset Dublin Castle, but poor Eva, daughter of MacMurrough, can never forgive her father for bringing the Normans over, and she prophesies that Strongbow will 'in time make slaves of all this island'.

There were isolated attempts to follow Shadwell's example in Irish historical tragedy,[21] but it was the stage-Irishman, whom Yeats so abominated, who became established in the later eighteenth century, through the work of dramatists like Charles Macklin and Thomas Sheridan. The latter's famous reign at Smock Alley, however, was challenged in 1749 by Paul Hiffernan and a group of gentlemen who planned to reopen the Capel Street theatre to encourage new plays by Irish writers.[22] Sheridan was forced into emulation, and tried to meet the patriotic demand, but the plays and masques he put on were not successful, and Henry Brooke's allegorical ballad-opera *Jack the Giant-Queller* fell foul of the censor.

The aridity of the London commercial theatre in late-nineteenth-century London, extending of course to its satellite theatre in Dublin, was to Yeats a sign both of the materialist values of the Saxons and of the waning of their cultural greatness. He wished as much to bring poetry and literary value into the drama as to create a theatre for Ireland. It was the Irish Literary Theatre that was established in 1899, and each of the three words in that title is of the same importance.

In 1933, writing a Preface to an edition by Horace Reynolds of his early writings for American newspapers, *Letters to the New Island*, Yeats said, 'I had forgotten my early preoccupation with the theatre, with an attempt to free it from commercialism with a handsome little stage in a Bedford Park Clubhouse.' He is talking of the reviews he wrote from London of Todhunter's verse plays around 1890–1. Yeats was very optimistic that 'we shall yet have a genuine public, however small, for poetic drama',[23] and wished that Todhunter (an Irishman and a founding member of the Irish Literary Society a year later) would eschew Greek themes and turn away from cosmopolitanism.

We are not content to dig our own potato patch in peace. We peer over the wall at our neighbour's instead of making our own garden green and beautiful. And yet it is a good garden and there have been great transactions within it, from the death of Cuchulain down to the flight of Michael Dwyer from the burning cabin. Dr Todhunter could easily have found some pastoral incident among its stories newer and not less beautiful than anything in Tempe's fabled vales.[24]

This was 1890. Reviewing Todhunter elsewhere in 1891, he wrote, 'When our political passions have died out in the fulfilment of their aim [Home Rule!], shall we, I wonder, have a fine native drama of our own? It is very likely.'[25] Yeats had for some time been at work on *The*

Countess Cathleen and had written to Katharine Tynan in 1889 about his hopes to have it acted in Dublin.[26] Looking back on these times in 1922, Yeats said:

> I had definite plans; I wanted to create an Irish Theatre; I was finishing my *Countess Cathleen* in its first meagre version, and thought of a travelling company to visit our country branches; but before that there must be a popular imaginative literature.[27]

The 'country branches' were of the National Literary Society, founded in Dublin following the formation of the Irish Literary Society in London. There is no need to go over Yeats's efforts to create that 'popular imaginative literature' during the last ten years or so of the century. His own *Wanderings of Oisin* was published in 1889, and in such widely differing works as his successive volumes of verse, the prose books *Fairy and Folk Tales of the Irish Peasantry*, *The Celtic Twilight*, and *The Secret Rose*, he strove to set the example of the use of an Irish mythology for poetry and to indicate the richness of Irish legend, folk material and fairy story. In all those strenuous years of writing, debating, defining, organising, polemicising, feuding, from the late eighties throughout the nineties, during which the creating of a national literature was nearly Yeats's all-in-all, the theatre took a back place, and it was not until 1897 that out of the famous meetings with Lady Gregory and Edward Martyn recorded in Lady Gregory's *Our Irish Theatre* (she gives the year as 1898), when 'things seemed to grow possible as we talked', the Irish Literary Theatre began to take shape. With Yeats, Martyn, and George Moore as the first directors, its first season was in May 1899, with Yeats's *The Countess Cathleen* and Martyn's *The Heather Field*. It began as it continued in controversy and tumult. *The Countess Cathleen* had been in print for years. Before the production it was attacked as heretical and blasphemous in the pamphlet *Souls for Gold*. Cardinal Logue opposed it, and thirty-three members of the Royal University, including the important future radical nationalists Sheehy Skeffington and Kettle, signed a letter objecting to the play.[28] Martyn was deeply distressed, and uncertain about continuing the venture. The first performance, in the Ancient Concert Rooms in Dublin, was given under police protection.

The Catholic opposition to the new theatre I want to leave until the next chapter, when I discuss George Moore. Another controversy had been carried on in the columns of *The Daily Express*, and the articles were published in May 1899 in book form as *Literary Ideals in Ireland*. It began with a trenchant and intelligent article by John Eglinton (the pseudonym of W. K. Magee, librarian at the National Library), 'What Should be the Subjects of a National Drama?' Recognising that Ireland was now possibly ripe for a new literary movement, he questioned that the ancient Irish legendary material should be used in a new drama. There was no doubt that the legends provided situations and characters as suitable as those used in Greek tragedy, but 'the mere fact of Ireland having been the scene of these stories' didn't seem to make them especially important for a modern Irish writer, and he doubted 'whether anything but belles lettres, as distinguished from a national literature, is likely to spring from a determined preoccupation with them'. He recognised that the source of the interest in Irish folk-lore and antiquities was in Herder and the Germans, and recognised its attraction for those who were looking for 'the forgotten mythopoeic secret'. But 'these subjects . . . obstinately refuse to be taken up out of their old environment and be transplanted into the world of modern sympathies'. He concluded with the challenge that 'Ireland must exchange the patriotism which looks back for the patriotism which looks forward.' 'A national drama or literature must spring from a native interest in life and its problems and a strong capacity for life among the people.'

Yeats's reply, 'A Note on National Drama', was a brief piece edited out of another article. As evidence that ancient legends *can* be transplanted into the world of modern sympathies he cited Wagner, Ibsen's *Peer Gynt* and *The Vikings at Helgeland*, and William Morris. 'All great poets – Dante not less than Homer and Shakespeare – speak to us of the hopes and destinies of mankind in their fulness; *because* they have wrought their poetry out of the dreams that were dreamed before men became so crowded upon one another.' (The italics are mine.) As for Eglinton's contention that Irish legends had no special relationship with Irish writers, he insisted that we should be 'haunted by places'. The new movement should make Ireland 'a holy land to her own people'.

Eglinton's next article clarified the issue as not being merely ancient versus modern in subject-matter. It was a question of turning away from life. Wagner's Bayreuth theatre seemed to him totally unlike the democratic city-theatre of Athens. He distinguished the Wordsworthian type of poet 'able to confer on even common things the radiance of the imagination' and another type who 'looks too much away from himself and from his age, does not feel the facts of life enough, but seeks in art an escape from them'.

Yeats was now angry, and his reply was contentious, splenetic, and woolly. In his anger he revealed the basic paradox of his position as the doyen of a national drama. He accused Eglinton of believing in 'popular literature', a poetry which 'like all the lusts of the market-place' was an expression of its age. Even if it were true that Wagner's art were esoteric, it would not matter, because art can appeal only to the elect few, and it flows down to the masses 'as if through orders and hierarchies'. Poetry, he asserted, was not a criticism of life but 'a revelation of a hidden life' and the poet is a man removed from the hubbub of existence. It seems incredible that Yeats should speak of Shakespeare as one of his idols in an essay which contemptuously rejected popularity in favour of élitism (and Eglinton remarked on the absurdity of this in his reply), but it is even more striking that anyone with so fastidious and protective a view of art should be planning a national theatre. That he could also be proud, however, of the popularity of the art which had been filtered through to the masses is clear from an essay of this same year, written in May just after the first performances of the Irish Literary Theatre.

Certain plays, which are an expression of the most characteristic ideals of what is sometimes called the 'Celtic movement', have been acted in Dublin before audiences drawn from all classes and all political sections, and described at great length in every Nationalist newspaper . . . The 'Celtic movement', which has hitherto interested but a few cultivated people, is about to become a part of the thought of Ireland.[29]

To return to *Literary Ideals*, the controversy simmered down immediately as A. E. and William Larminie came in to part the contestants. Yeats's next contribution was his essay 'The Autumn of the Flesh', a much more carefully considered piece (reprinted as 'The Autumn of the Body' in *Ideas of Good and Evil*) which brought in questions of cultural renewals which we shall be looking at in a minute. There was an interesting final note from A. E. reminding us of the Renaissance view of the poet's rôle in creating heroes. Those who a generation ago had provided the bardic history of Ireland had shown Ireland Cuchulain, Fionn, Ossian, and Oscar, 'and so from iteration and persistent dwelling on a few heroes their imaginative images found echoes in life, and other heroes arose continuing their tradition of chivalry'. There was need now for new heroic figures 'whether legendary or taken from history' to succeed those, and inspire new generations.

Eglinton's questioning of Yeats's position is extremely perceptive and, of course, it is a questioning of the whole ethos of cultural nationalism, with its dedication to individual locality and the primitive imagination, as well as of the suitability of an esoteric concern with the past as the nutriment of a national drama. Yeats's great essay on 'The Theatre', which appeared in the first number of *Beltaine: The Organ of the Irish Literary Theatre* in May 1899 (reprinted, it says, from *The Dome*), shows him aware that the paradoxes of his position are not intellectual inconsistencies but are the necessary constituents of a perilous circumstance. He argues that his art *is* of the people. It is a recovery of the spiritual life of the people now lost except for a faint continuance in old legends and the folk-tales of peasant communities. The people 'that now is', the materialistic middle classes of our commercial cities, have got to be led back to the old life. This will not be done by plays about modern middle class life in big popular theatres. One must begin in a small way.

So, he says, 'We must make a theatre for ourselves and our friends . . . We hope to act a play or two in the spring of every year.' 'Our plays will be for the most part remote, spiritual, and ideal.'[30] Yeats's view of the *essential* 'popularity' of his esoteric theatre involves his whole cyclic and organic view of national literatures. The Renaissance had gathered up and disseminated a culture of the people that was dying in the face of oncoming material development (see above, Chapter 2).

All culture is . . . a labour to bring again the simplicity of the first ages, with knowledge of good and evil added to it. The drama has need of cities that it may find men in sufficient numbers, and cities destroy the emotions to which it appeals, and therefore the days of the drama are brief and come but seldom.

Now that English literature was dying of old age, Irish literature was preparing itself to replace it – but with a difference. Drama is of two kinds. The first is the Shakespearian. 'It has one day when the emotions of cities still remember the emotions of sailors and husbandmen and shepherds and users of the spear and the bow.' The second is the latter-day drama, when 'thought and scholarship' rediscover those ancient emotions.

In the first day, it is the art of the people; and in the second day, like the dramas acted of old times in the hidden places of temples, it is the preparation of a priesthood. It may be, though the world is not old enough to show us any example, that this priesthood will spread their religion everywhere, and make their Art the Art of the people.

There is a telling lack of confidence in the last sentence of this whether the new priestly theatre will ever popularise its religion. I find similar hesitations everywhere. In a lecture of some years earlier, 'Nationality and Literature' in 1893, Yeats introduced into the peroration a strange note of self-questioning (which I italicise):

I wished merely to show you that the older literatures of Europe are in their golden sunset, their wise old age, that I might the better prove to you, in the closing parts of my lecture, that we here in Ireland who, like the Scandinavian people, are at the outset [of] a literary epoch, must learn from them but not imitate them, and by so doing we will bring new life and fresh impulse not only to ourselves but to those old literatures themselves. *But are we really at the outset of a literary epoch? or are we not, perhaps, merely a little eddy cast up by the advancing tide of English literature and are we not doomed, perhaps, to its old age and coming decline?* On the contrary, I affirm that we are a young nation with unexhausted material lying within us in our still unexpressed national character, about us in our scenery . . . and behind us in our multitude of legends.[31]

In that first number of *Beltaine* which we have been talking about, published in the very month the Irish Literary Theatre opened, Yeats chose to republish an excellent article on 'The Scandinavian Dramatists' by the learned C. H. Herford (then Professor of English at Aberystwyth; he translated some of Ibsen's plays). He gave an account of the national movement in Norway, 1840–60, and described Ibsen's work in the national theatres at Bergen and Christiana. He went on, talking of the time when the Norwegian stage had successfully emancipated itself from Danish influence:

Ibsen was too solitary and self-centred a nature to comply submissively with the Nationalist formula when it had ceased to be a battle-cry. The battle won, it was inevitable that he who held that 'no one is so strong as the man who stands alone', should go his own way and work out his own ideal.

An artist of the first rank can, indeed, rarely take any other course. Nationalism in art is a cry of inspiring power in the early stages of artistic growth; it rallies the scattered forces of imagination, disciplines vagrant and chaotic enthusiasms, brings the neglected ore of tradition under an eager scrutiny which detects and disengages its hidden gold. But when all this is done, the artist who has an individual message will impress his own meaning and his own *cachet* upon the instruments of expression which the fire of national enthusiasm has forged ready to his hand. The Shakespeare of *Richard III* and *Henry V* passed into the Shakespeare of *Hamlet* and *Lear*.

In 1899, with the new Irish theatre scarcely born, Yeats had before him years of enormous effort, rewarded as few other men's have been, but even at the very outset the precariousness of his own relationship with a theatre that could be called 'national', and the likely brevity of any success he might achieve, seem to have been very much present to him. In a dithyrambic coda which he added in 1900 to his essay 'The Theatre', he wrote:

New races understand instinctively, because the future cries in their ears, that the old revelations are insufficient, and that all life is revelation beginning in miracle and enthusiasm, and dying out as it unfolds itself in what we have mistaken for progress.

It is a question of how quick the 'dying out' is going to be.

Yeats and Shakespeare

In April 1901, Yeats wrote to Lady Gregory from Stratford-upon-Avon.

This is a beautiful place. I am working very hard, reading all the chief criticisms of the plays and I think my essay will be one of the best things I have done. The more I read the worse does the Shakespeare criticism become and Dowden is about the climax of it. I[t] came out [of] the middle class movement and I feel it my legitimate enemy.[32]

Yeats was seeing the whole run of Shakespeare's Histories which were then being put on by F. R. Benson, a different play each night, in the historical order. The essay which he wrote, 'At Stratford-upon-Avon', is certainly one of the best things he wrote, and it has itself provoked some excellent criticism, notably in Peter Ure's essay, 'W. B. Yeats and the Shakespearian Moment'.[33] Yeats saw in the plays a fundamental contest between 'a wise man who was blind from very wisdom, and an empty man who thrust him from his place, and saw all that could be seen from very emptiness'. It is the contest between Richard II and the Bolingbroke who ousts him from the throne, between Hamlet and the Claudius who dispossesses him and the Fortinbras who follows him. The archetypes of the two opposed figures are 'the vessel of porcelain, Richard II' and 'the vessel of clay, Henry V'. Yeats is contemptuous of the qualities which Shakespeare gave to the successful dispossessors and contemptuous of the critics who supposed that these successful men won Shakespeare's admiration. 'To suppose that Shakespeare preferred the men who deposed his king is to suppose that Shakespeare judged men with the eyes of a Municipal Councillor weighing the merits of a Town Clerk.' Shakespeare, said Yeats, gave to Henry V 'the gross vices, the coarse nerves,

of one who is to rule among violent people', and he viewed the failure
of Richard II with sympathetic understanding:

> He saw indeed, as I think, in Richard II the defeat that awaits all, whether
> they be artist or saint, who find themselves where men ask of them a rough
> energy and have nothing to give but some contemplative virtue, whether
> lyrical fantasy, or sweetness of temper, or dreamy dignity, or love of God, or
> love of His creatures.[34]

It is very clear that this view of the Shakespearian binary system is an
Irish view. The rather sentimental nostalgia which suffused the ideology of cultural nationalism was strongest of all in Ireland. It was a
common idea that the values of the primitive past, which must inspire
the new nation, were qualities of imagination and impulse and
instinct and emotion and spontaneity which had got lost in a modern
world of materialism and hesitation and ratiocination and so on. The
notion that the Irish were in a special and privileged way guardians of
the much-needed values of the past, and were keeping alive the soul of
the ancient world amidst an alien and hostile modernism, received
tremendous impetus from Matthew Arnold's famous essay of 1867,
'On the Study of Celtic Literature'. Arnold, emphasising the Celtic
qualities of melancholy, other-worldliness, indifference to fact,
bravery in defeat, sensitivity to verbal and musical magic, gave his
great authority to the idea that Celtic ineffectualness and failure were
spiritually greater than the successfulness of Saxon materialism and
'drive'. John V. Kelleher's brilliant essay on the extraordinary
influence in Ireland of Arnold's study pointed out how very mistaken
Arnold was about the true spirit of Celtic literature, and how much he
owed to Ossian, whose melancholy defeatism itself owed much to the
disaster of the '45.[35] Mistaken or not, the gospel flourished in Ireland.
It is often argued that the philosophy of the spiritual superiority of
worldly failure grew strong after the collapse of Parnell and his death
in 1891. Be that as it may, it was accepted that the Celtic spirit was
utterly different from the Saxon spirit, and that the mark of the Celtic
spirit was a simple, dreamy heroism of olden times doomed to defeat
by its worldly, prosperous, practical modern foe. This gospel dominated the poetry of Yeats and the actions of Padraic Pearse.[36]

  To Yeats, the reason why critics of Shakespeare had misunderstood his history plays so far as to think that Henry V was Shakespeare's ideal king and that Richard II was despicable because he was
a poet and incapable of action, was quite simple. The critics were
Englishmen, incapable of understanding anything but the Saxon

values. 'Shakespearian criticism became a vulgar worshipper of success.' But the most important of these critics for Yeats was not English but a fellow Irishman, Edward Dowden, Professor of English Literature at Trinity College, Dublin. (Peter Ure has rightly emphasised the significance of Yeats's battle with Dowden.) Yeats, speaking of what he thought was the *wrong* attitude to the history plays, wrote:

Professor Dowden, whose book I once read carefully, first made these emotions eloquent and plausible. He lived in Ireland, where everything has failed, and he meditated frequently upon the perfection of character which had, he thought, made England successful.[37]

Dowden was a determined Unionist, and his cultural views were as firmly cemented to *his* political views as Yeats's were to his. Dowden detested Irish cultural nationalism, and expressed his gratitude that he had grown up acquainted with the poets of England 'and not on anything that Ireland ever produced'.[38] Yeats was not going too far in suggesting that Dowden's interpretation of Shakespeare was connected with his view of the proper relations between Ireland and England. For Yeats, therefore, the Shakespearian battle between the claimants for the crown of England becomes the battle between sensitivity and imagination on the one hand and calculating materialism on the other. The first is the Celtic virtue, the second the Saxon. The Celtic hero is doomed to failure and defeat; the Saxon, the empty man, rules over the human spirit which he has destroyed.

Yeats's Shakespeare is an honorary Celt. Beginning a new literary movement and inspiring a new theatre in the burgeoning new life of an old nation, Yeats was replacing the Shakespeare who initiated the cultural greatness of England. And in the sense that Shakespeare's England stood for Britain, union, empire, and shared culture, Yeats was bound to undo his work. But the idea of superseding was only a small part of Yeats's relationship with Shakespeare. To replace Shakespeare was to re-enact his rôle in the new epoch, and it is in Yeats's identification of his own position as regards Ireland at the end of the nineteenth century with Shakespeare's as regards England at the end of the sixteenth century that all the interest lies.

We have to write or find plays that will make the theatre a place of intellectual excitement – a place where the mind goes to be liberated as it was liberated by the theatres of Greece and England and France at certain great moments of their history.[39]

When Yeats looked back to Shakespeare as a liberator of England's imagination in the way he hoped to be a liberator of Ireland's imagination, it was, I suppose, inevitable that he should colour Shakespeare with the ideas of the nineteenth-century cultural nationalist, and see him deriving his artistic strength from the simpler and truer values of the past, and it was inevitable that these values should assume the distinct Irish qualities of worship of heroic failure. 'The popular poetry of England celebrates her victories, but the popular poetry of Ireland remembers only defeats and defeated persons.' So wrote Yeats in May 1899.[40] Two years later he had made Shakespeare an exception.

In going to Shakespeare to learn his own rôle, Yeats had found a Celtic Shakespeare. But this Shakespeare, created in the image of Yeats's own views, was still sufficiently Shakespeare to radiate back an intense light to illuminate Yeats's own ideas and his future path. Time and again Yeats says, echoing the fundamental tenet of nineteenth-century cultural nationalism, that Shakespeare's greatness lay in the tenaciousness of his hold on the old undivided human spirit, in his contact with the past and his contact with the people.

Every national dramatic movement or theatre in countries like Bohemia and Hungary, as in Elizabethan England, has arisen out of a study of the common people, who preserve national characteristics more than any other class, and out of an imaginative re-creation of natural history or legend.[41]

But time and again Yeats also shows that Shakespeare like other great Renaissance artists was able to gather together and disseminate those values only at the moment of their dissolution and replacement. Nowhere was this brief blaze more visible than in the Elizabethan drama, extinguished as Yeats explained (see above, Chapter 2, p. 17) at full height by the Puritanism which was as much a product of the Renaissance as the drama was. In his interpretation of the Histories, he described how Shakespeare reflected in his plays his deep consciousness of the warfare of past and future, and rightly gauged the measure of Shakespeare's sympathy with those imperious tragic figures, Richard, and Lear, and Antony, who fall to pieces because of their own inner contradictions and leave us feeling that the world has lost what is irreplaceable. With a partisan view of Shakespeare and a melodramatic idea of the movement of historical epochs,

Yeats somehow made fine imaginative discoveries about Shakespeare. And, even more important, the mythical contest which he thought to be fundamental in Shakespeare, between doomed sensitivity and masterful emptiness, became the 'interlocking device' which Peter Ure suggested was 'perhaps the basic module for all his thought'.[42] From Stratford, he went back to Coole Park and began *On Baile's Strand* which in the contest between the Fool and the Blind Man, Cuchulain and Conchubar, so marvellously recreates the Shakespearian tension.

But is it not the case that Shakespeare, the nationalist exemplar, for a hundred years the hero of intellectuals all over the world who longed to see their country morally armed for an independent future, has turned into a prophet of spiritual loss? The values which Yeats saw as being retrieved from the past in order to energise the future are now fighting a rearguard action, the forlorn hope against advancing modernism. Yeats, as we saw, had had his own answer in 1899 to the disturbing analogy of the transience of the English drama of Shakespeare's time. There were two 'days' for the drama inspired by primitive imagination, a 'day' when the old values are sliding into oblivion, and a 'day' when they are consciously being recovered. But the identification with Shakespeare in 1901 removes I think that never-confident optimism about the second 'day'.

Eglinton was basically right. It is impossible to found a *national* drama – a drama closely in touch with the people and going forward with their aspirations – with an esoteric drama looking always to Ireland's past. Thomas McAlindon ably argued that Yeats found his idealisation of aristocracy as against the coarse values of the middle classes justified in his contact with the English Renaissance poets and dramatists.[43] And it may be added that for some of these middle-class Elizabethans the aristocratic culture they invoked had as little *real* existence as it had for the middle-class Irishman.

Both Shakespeare and Yeats, it seems to me, take refuge against the values of modernity in a fiction of feudalism. For neither of them, in England in 1600 or in Ireland in 1900, were the mutual interdependencies and respect of lord and peasant realities. But they were magnificent metaphors for values which each felt were being lost. In *King Lear*, when the blinded Earl of Gloucester meets Edgar, he is being led by a nameless 'Old Man', who does not appear elsewhere in the play. Gloucester is impatient of his ministrations, but the Old Man insists. 'O my good lord, I have been your tenant, and your father's tenant, these fourscore years.' When Yeats revised *The Countess Cathleen* in 1912, he made the old peasant woman Mary say to the homecoming Countess:

> But first sit down and rest yourself awhile,
> For my old fathers served your fathers, lady,
> Longer than books can tell.   (ll. 93–5)

It is easy to be annoyed at Yeats's romantic ideas of the unity of poet, aristocrat, and peasant, and his disdain for hucksters and the modern 'common people' of the cities, but it is worth while remembering that in part it has to do with his identification with another poet who like him was in reality a bourgeois with a romantic nostalgia for feudalism.

Yeats had still to write his most 'nationalist' play, *Cathleen ni Houlihan* (see Plate 4), which was staged in 1902 with Maud Gonne in the title rôle, and the Abbey Theatre did not open its doors until Christmas 1904. But in those all-important writings on an Irish theatre year by year from 1901 onwards in *Samhain*, the underlying question is what a *national* theatre really means and how far it is compatible with the kind of national subject Yeats is interested in, and with the good art which he all his life insisted was the indispensable core of any national literature he was to be associated with. In 1902 Edward Martyn has brought up again the question of Yeats's fixation on the heroic material instead of 'the modern drama of society', and Yeats again rejects modernity. 'The drama of society would but magnify a condition of life which the countryman and the artisan could but copy to their hurt.'[44] In 1903, it is Padraic Colum's play against enlisting which makes him write:

I have no doubt that we shall see a good many of these political plays during the next two or three years, and it may be even the rise of a more or less permanent company of political players, for the revolutionary clubs will begin to think plays as necessary as the Gaelic League is already thinking them.

. . .   .

Though one welcomes every kind of vigorous life, I am, myself, most interested in 'The Irish National Theatre Society', which has no propaganda but that of good art.[45]

In 1904, the strain of argument is more intense, and the sense of enemies closing in more strong. What *is* a national literature?

Our friends have already told us, writers for the Theatre in Abbey Street, that we have no right to the name, some because we do not write in Irish, and others because we do not plead the National cause in our plays, as if we were writers for the newspapers. I have not asked my fellow-workers what they mean by the words National literature, but though I have no great love for definitions, I would define it in some such way as this: It is the work of writers who are moulded by influences that are moulding their country, and who write out of so deep a life that they are accepted there in the end.[46]

In 1908, a year after the riots attending the production of the greatest play Yeats's theatre produced, *The Playboy of the Western World*, Yeats's contribution to *Samhain* shows a man caught between the upper and nether millstones of political forces – 'the Nationalist attacks' and 'the Unionist hostility'.[47] The piece which follows this in the collection of writings on the theatre which Yeats put together as 'The Irish Dramatic Movement: 1901–1919' in *Plays and Controversies* (1923) was the 'Letter to Lady Gregory' of 1919, in which he wrote, 'I want to create for myself an unpopular theatre and an audience like a secret society where admission is by favour and never to many.'[48]

Yeats is a consequence of Shakespeare. His work to create an Irish national spirit, and a national literature and drama, could not have come into existence except as a counter to the results of the earlier English nationalism. Working at either end of a long historical epoch, these two national opponents have a strange similarity. Each of them draws artistic strength from the idea of a new nation which in truth he helps to bring into existence, and each of them recoils from everything which, in practical terms, the creation of the new nation involved. For each of them, the past of the nation is of intense importance, but, while that recovery of the past is meant to strengthen the nation in its future development, the past becomes a myth of foreboding, not so much a path to the future as an indignant repudiator of the future. And, for each of them, history becomes a continuous circling of self-destruction.

> We had fed the heart on fantasies,
> The heart's grown brutal from the fare.

Yeats's gloom about the future of Ireland intensified as independence became a reality. The mystic leader whom his writings summoned from the past to inspire the new nation, the *rex absconditus* of Ireland, never comes into his own. In *The Death of Cuchulain* (1939) the dying hero is finished off by the Blind Man, an Irishman, who has been promised twelve pennies for his head.

9

A PLAY-HOUSE IN THE WASTE: GEORGE MOORE AND THE IRISH THEATRE

George Moore's contribution to the drama of the Irish Literary Revival was not large; he reworked Edward Martyn's intractable *Tale of a Town* into *The Bending of the Bough*, and he collaborated with Yeats in *Diarmuid and Grania*. But his intervention in the Revival seems to me of striking significance in a study of theatre and nation.

As Synge was Yeats's triumph in his campaign to urge the scattered Irish writers to return to their homeland and write on Irish subjects, so Moore was his great failure. The two men bickered from the beginning. Moore followed Martyn in withdrawing from the Irish Literary Theatre in 1901 and took no part in the later history of the Irish National Theatre Society and the Abbey Theatre. Moore was already in his late forties when Martyn and Yeats brought him in – in London – to help with the production of the first offerings of the Irish Literary Theatre, *The Countess Cathleen* and *The Heather Field*, and made him a co-director of the whole enterprise. Synge was only twenty-five when Yeats met him in Paris and told him to go to the Aran Islands. But Lady Gregory was exactly the same age as Moore and age was no barrier to that extraordinary transformation which made her the keystone of the arch of the Revival. It wasn't lack of youthfulness that made Moore's commitment to Ireland fail to stick.

Yeats and Martyn seem to have thought that Moore was more of a professional in the theatre than he really was, though he was more intimate with it than they were. He had travelled for some weeks with a touring company in the Potteries in order to give authenticity to *A Mummer's Wife*. He had written his play *A Strike at Arlingford* in 1890, but the great actor-managers John Hare and Beerbohm Tree refused it. In 1891, J. T. Grein founded the Independent Theatre Society in London, in imitation of André Antoine's Théâtre Libre in Paris and in opposition to the commercial theatres and society drama. Moore became closely associated with the management of it and described its vain efforts to persuade a London audience to appreciate Ibsen, Shaw, and *avant-garde* 'intellectual theatre' in the introduction to Martyn's *The Heather Field* (1899). His own play, *The Strike at Arlingford*, was produced by the society in 1893. He was a novelist and story-teller, not a dramatist, and in *A Modern Lover* (1883), *A Mummer's Wife* (1885), *A Drama in Muslin* (1886), and *Esther Waters* (1894) had achieved four novels of considerable originality and power. As for his connections with Ireland before the founding of the Irish Literary Theatre, he had more or less formally renounced his country in *Confessions of a Young Man* (1886). 'All the aspects of my native country are violently disagreeable to me, and I cannot think of the place I was born in without a sensation akin to nausea ... I am instinctively averse from my own countrymen.'[1] The heir of 'the big house', Moore Hall on Lough Carra in County Mayo, he had cut adrift from Ireland as soon as he was twenty-one (his father having died three years previously) and spent six years in Paris failing to become an artist. The Land War and the failure of his rents in Ireland brought him to England to earn a living in 1880, and he turned to writing. Ireland became the subject of two of his books, *A Drama in Muslin* and *Parnell and his Island* (1887). *A Drama in Muslin* was later rewritten as *Muslin*. It ranks with Somerville and Ross's *The Real Charlotte* as one of the best Irish novels of the later nineteenth century. This story of the marriage-mart in the big houses in the west of Ireland, and in Dublin during the season, gets its force from the juxtaposition of the frivolous lives and social ambitions of the upper-class women with the real economic conditions of the Land War, with a poverty-stricken tenantry refusing to pay their rents, militancy and terrorism growing, and the landlords nervous about their income and their future. The novel ends with Alice, the plain sensible daughter, breaking with her family, marrying a socially conscious doctor – and emigrating to England. The last thing they see in Ireland is an eviction.

The Moores, like their neighbours the Martyns, were Catholics, and while it would be absurd to say that this enabled them to share the lives of the poor (Moore spoke no Irish), their intimacy with the religious life of the country gave Moore's writings about the people of Ireland an accent which is missing from the writings of the Anglo-Irish generally – and this must include even Synge. The first of the many brilliant sketches of country priests which he was to draw appears in *Parnell and his Island*, a book little read and much underestimated.

It understandably gave great offence in Ireland (and still does) and, as Moore recognised, it contributed greatly to the difficulty of his acceptance in Ireland at the turn of the century. It is a grim, sardonic, vituperative book, looking round Ireland and finding only desolation and doom. It is also a book of great vigour, with arresting portraits and vignettes, sparing no class. The Anglo-Irish sit in the Kildare Street Club 'gifted with an oyster-like capacity for understanding this one thing: that they should continue to get fat in the bed in which they were born'. The son of the big house is sent to London to find an heiress but only gets into debt. He eventually returns and takes in a peasant girl as 'housekeeper', has many children by her, and by marrying her in the end legitimises the last of these children as his heir. Irish girls allow themselves to be seduced in order to trap a husband – but the trap is not always well sprung. He looks at the ruined hovels where the land has been cleared. 'Family after family were dug out with crowbar and pick, as if they were rabbits, and were driven forth to die or to find their way to America.' Those who remain are a race 'that has been forgotten and left behind in a bog hole' in 'a country of failure and ruin' where nothing succeeds but patriotism. Militancy increases and brutality spreads out from its political origins to infect the whole tissue of Irish country life. James the patriot has a sharper intelligence than his cousins in the bog lands of the west, though 'he is cunning, selfish, cruel, even as they; his blood is thin with centuries of poverty, damp hovels, potatoes, servility'. He has become a Parnellite M.P. and sits in the Commons under the tyranny of Parnell's eye as he 'mumbles along with his rattletrap sentences'.

The study of an eviction is like Goya – macabre, beastly, frightening, but deeply human. The evicting landowner is a woman, a ruined alcoholic. She watches with deep satisfaction the scene of the woman peasant trying to resist the manhandling, her petticoats riding above her waist. Here man, or woman, is brutish on both sides. But Moore shows the humanity in the dehumanised. He says of the pitiless scene, 'It is infinitely pitiful and infinitely grotesque.'

The deep sense of doom and ruin which informs *Parnell and his Island* is accompanied by the ominous note of a coming retribution, of the forces that 'will win back to the Celt the land that was taken from the Celt' (p. 112). There is absolutely nothing here of the revolutionary fervour that at this time was infecting many Anglo-Irishmen. Quite the reverse. Moore speaks as a member of a class which must expect dispossession and ruin when the retribution comes. He sees the sons of the survivors of the Famine, now wealthy in America, supplying Parnell with funds – not for Home Rule, or independence, or freedom, but 'to prosecute to exile and ruin the war against landlordism'. Race hatred, he says is fundamental and inexpugnable. The Irish Americans are waiting to repossess their country. After Home Rule, they will seize on the first international jam which Britain gets into and then they 'will declare the independence of their island'.

I have dwelt on *Parnell and his Island* because like so much of Moore's writing it is impossibly unfair and immensely shrewd. It reveals that his commitment to nationalism and optimism in 1900 was a temporary intermission, but, more important, it shows the tenacity of an idea in his mind which comes clearly into our view only if we take his earlier with his later writings: that the coming independence of Ireland was not going to be the union of men of all creeds and backgrounds in the creation of a new liberated nation, but a repossession by the Catholic Irish of the land that had been stolen from them by the Protestant English, however many centuries ago the theft might have been.

The 'choice of life' was fundamental to Moore as it was fundamental to most Irish writers – certainly to the greater writers of this period: Shaw, Wilde, Yeats, Synge, Joyce, O'Casey. Where they should live was more than a matter of convenience, or beauty, or cheapness. For each of these men the problem put itself in quite a different way. Shaw needed the freer intellectual air of England, and the greater opportunities. Joyce needed exile from Ireland in order to re-create Ireland in a book. For Yeats and Moore the problem seems even deeper than for the others. The Joycean withdrawal was simply not a possibility for them, because it denied what was for them a fundamental dependence of the art that is created on the place in which it is created and the life that is lived therein. Crossing the St George's Channel – either way – was more than a gesture, or an escape; it was a commitment, and a declaration about the purpose of their life and the nature of their art. You cannot say for either of them that his life was at the service of his art, or that his art was at the service of his life. Yeats took the old ruined tower of Thoor Ballylee, rebuilt it and for a period made it and his life there the chief symbol of his poetry and an image of his country and his times. In a kind of anti-heroic anticipation of this gesture, Moore (years earlier) rented the quiet little house in Ely Place, Dublin, which A.E. found for him.

He had come back to Ireland in order to work in some way for a new Irish culture, and a new art would grow out of a new life.

In *Hail and Farewell*,[2] Moore keeps asking people, especially A.E., why they think he has come to Ireland. A disappointing answer is always given. For example, A.E. says (*Salve*, p. 158) he thinks of him as the Voltaire of Ireland, ridiculing stupidity. Moore is vague about the answer he would have liked. 'I came to give back to Ireland her language,' he makes himself say, but that is rhetoric. Earlier in the same volume (*Salve*, pp. 20–1) during another interrogation of A.E. on this same point, he remembers a cruelty of Whistler's which hurt him deeply years before. '"Nothing," he said, "I suppose, matters to you except your writing." And his words went to the very bottom of my soul, frightening me.' Moore indicates that the remark devastated him because he recognised how near he was to the state where 'nothing really matters but one's work' – a state which is 'near madness'. Was he 'capable of sacrificing brother, sister, mother, fortune, friend, for a work of art'? Moore clears himself of the charge, in that by coming to Ireland he was leaving a safe literary career behind him for the uncertainties of what, as a writer, he might be able to do in Ireland. It is important for him to clear himself of the charge, because he knows its validity, he knows how far his life *is* at the service of his art; he has always had before him (and he has put before us) the hope that a very successful book, or series of books, might come out of a return to Ireland. But his commitment to Ireland, he hoped, was not in order to help himself as a writer, but to help Ireland in his profession of writer. The essence of the matter is belief in the Yeatsian chiasmus: no fine nationality without literature, no fine literature without nationality. Moore hoped that Ireland would benefit from his writing, and that his writing would benefit from Ireland. This is the answer which we assume he would like A.E. to have given. That the return to Ireland would give a new meaning to his existence, which would create a new richness in his art, which would help the new Ireland to know herself and advance herself.

Piecing out Moore's real views from *Hail and Farewell* is a hazardous business, and later in this chapter I shall try to suggest at which level of seriousness that garrulous, opinionated, and subtle work ought to be read. In the meantime I blend it with other evidence, particularly the plays. The date at which in *Hail and Farewell* Moore heard the famous voice in Chelsea summoning him to Ireland is somewhere at the end of 1900, after Moore had been engaged for some time, in and out of Ireland, with the Irish Literary Theatre. All that work was only the prelude to the 'choice of life', when, disgusted with all things English because of the Boer War, he took up Dublin as his permanent residence. It was at this time (at the end of *Ave*) that the perplexing comedy of Ireland's new messiah began. In *The Bending of the Bough*, which was performed in Dublin in February 1900, we can see Moore rehearsing the question – abstractly as much as with any personal reference – how far the outsider may be a leader. Yeats called it 'the first dramatisation of an Irish problem'.[3]

With some help from Yeats and Lady Gregory, Moore worked up *The Bending of the Bough* from the manuscript of *The Tale of a Town* which Martyn surrendered to him when his co-directors' efforts to knock his play into shape became too painful for him. Yeats was excited by the transformation and wrote to A.E., 'Moore has written a tremendous scene in the third act and I have worked at it here and there throughout. If Martyn will only consent, it will make an immense sensation and our theatre a national power.'[4] But Moore was never happy with what he had done. 'I recast the play,' he wrote to his brother, 'but not enough. I should have written a new play on the subject.'[5] He greatly strengthened and deepened the play as a whole but to gain a greater range he seriously weakened the original in one respect. Martyn's plot was a straightforward story of the commercial competition of two seaports, one Irish and one English, for the steamship traffic to America. The competition is weighted against the Irish port by the whole burden of the Anglo-Irish relationship; the English town has deprived the Irish town of its living by sharp practice and doesn't care and won't pay the moneys it owes. The question of the play was, what could the municipal corporation do to get justice and recompense from its rival in the prevailing political climate? Moore chose to turn Martyn's municipal feud into an allegory of national politics. The particularity of Martyn's two ports is rubbed out into the vagueness of Northhaven, a decayed and anonymous town with a Celtic seascape, and Southhaven, a prosperous and bustling neighbour in the lowlands which can be reached either by sea or by train. (One commentator thought that Moore had translated the play from Ireland to Scotland.) The allegory becomes so thin at times that municipal councillors talk of 'the spiritual destiny of the Celtic race'. Since the play is no longer the tale of a town but the tale of two nations, the remnants of Martyn's subject of feuding corporations become a positive nuisance, and the matter of the steamships a perplexing confusion. The play is not, like Martyn's, a naturalistic fiction *within* the Irish situation but a creaking fantasy *about* that situation. Moore should have removed the municipal plot altogether and let the new play stand clear as a study of national politics.

The issue is of a hopelessly divided Council, longing for a leader to unite them. Their life is dominated by 'Southhaven' across the water. Alderman Kirwan has some strong ideas, but he has no charisma. He talks (well enough, we think) about 'our empty crumbling harbour'. 'At the foot of beautiful mountains, at the edge of a bright, windy sea, the death-rate is higher than in any town within a hundred miles.' One alderman, who hopes for a plum job in the Southhaven corporation, maintains that their prosperity depends on keeping in with the big city, whence, after all, all real culture flows. To which Kirwan replies, 'We have exchanged our arts, our language, and our native aristocracy for shoddy imitation.'

Kirwan fortunately has a most enthusiastic disciple, Jasper Dean, who has just been made an alderman. He has all the qualities of leadership that Kirwan lacks. After a few speeches from him about sinking differences, the good of the people as a whole etc., the Council to its great surprise finds itself united in a firm policy of intransigence towards Southhaven. Dean has been brought up in Southhaven, and in the second act describes his conversion by Kirwan to the mystique of his native land. Meaning was suddenly given to his life, and 'all that had seemed right was suddenly changed to wrong'. And now – 'It is a necessity of my being to believe in the sacredness of the land underfoot; to see in it the birthplace of noble thought, heroism, and beauty, and divine ecstasies.' The lonely hills 'sit there brooding over our misfortunes, waiting for us to become united with them and with each other once more'.

Some of the best 'theatre' in the play is the disquiet of Dean's Anglo-Irish aunts, who have brought him up so carefully, at this disreputable turn to a low, radical, anti-English cause. They worry him little. His Achilles heel is his intended wife, Millicent, very much of the Southhaven establishment, who enjoys the picturesque landscapes of Northhaven, but is not prepared to have only a small share in her husband's life. Kirwan is not sure how Dean will emerge in the contest between his new political ideals and Millicent. Kirwan is a very interesting and well-drawn character, like the aunts and Millicent deriving from hints in Martyn's original but developed out of all recognition. One of his most interesting moments is when Macnee, the truculent man of the people, promises Dean the support of 'the clubs'. Dean protests to Kirwan that such people understand nothing of *their* ideals. But Kirwan gently tells him that he has been taken up by the people because he is not of the people: it is the very difference that is the reason for his political success. Dean is 'the romantic element outside them, the delight they follow always'. As for Kirwan, he unexpectedly says that for his part, he feels with the people. Their 'mysterious subconscious life' is 'the only real life'. To be with them is to be united with the essential.

It now becomes clear to us – and it is this which *might* make the play worth reviving – that Dean's rhetoric, whether urging resolution to the Council or explaining the mystique of homeland, which has not been very convincing to us, doesn't interest Kirwan at all. Dean asks him point-blank whether he thinks he'll last. After a pause, Kirwan replies:

If the moment has arrived, you will suffice. Your speech which carried the Corporation with you and your speeches to the people do not convince me so much of your individual capacity as that the moment has come, and that you really are part and parcel of the movement of a nation. Your ideas are merely personal, it is Macnee's ideas that are universal and valid. You are their voice for the moment. (1900 edn, revised version, pp. 59–60)

But Dean doesn't stick, because in the end he can't bear to be thrown over by Millicent. He hates himself, of course. 'The shallow and the light-souled are always the chosen of the people, and the shallow and the light-souled betray the people, because they are as God made them.' He doesn't go to the next meeting, his policies are reversed, and the mob chases the aldermen up the street. Dean asks Kirwan if there is nothing he can do. Kirwan says, 'There is an antiquarian society. You might join it, and advocate the preservation of our antiquities.'

The brain-child of Edward Martyn, but indefeasibly the finished product of George Moore, *The Bending of the Bough* is an extraordinary offering as the third production of the Irish Literary Theatre, both in the irony with which the new leader is presented, and the underlying philosophy (which we have already glimpsed) that the real force that is going to move Ireland is a deep inarticulate force of the people, which will take up from time to time a 'voice for the moment' from someone outside themselves. There is no questioning the irony with which the new leader's rhetoric is presented, nor that this rhetoric is the solid bedrock of the movement for whom Moore is writing. In his own home, Dean is asked to say what exactly happened that the Council should pass a unanimous vote. Dean replies:

The people here have decided suddenly that this town shall not crumble into ruin, that its people shall not be driven into exile, that its language shall not pass away. (*Turning to* Kirwan.) And the destiny of the race, tell them what that is.   (1900 edn, revised version, p. 47)

Kirwan is embarrassed, and evades the question. He may have given Dean his ideas, but he does not talk in this way. Aunt Caroline, told that a man in the street has said, 'The hills are on fire', remarks, 'Jasper said only what Kirwan has been saying for years and such words do not set the hills on fire.' To which Alderman Leech replies, 'Ah, there it is, you see. One can't explain these things.'

The keenness of Moore's ear for platitudes is shown in his account in *Ave* of the time he spent in Dublin working with the Irish Literary Theatre, particularly in his account of the dinner which T. P. Gill gave in honour of the new theatre, and Gill's own speech on that occasion (*Ave*, pp. 147–9). Language is one of the major themes in *Hail and Farewell*: language suitable for a new Irish culture – and language unsuitable. Moore's determination to settle in Ireland and identify himself with her striving to make a new culture for herself, a determination arising from a feeling that he had been summoned to serve if not to lead, was taken after the writing of his two plays. His baffling claim, in *Hail and Farewell*, never clear of comic presentation and self-mockery, that 'no Messiah had been found by me at the dinner at the Shelbourne Hotel because the Messiah Ireland was waiting for was in me and not in another' (*Ave*, p. 366), derives from his sense of the shallowness of the Jasper Deans of the nationalist movement, and the falsity of the language which was being used, which revealed the shallowness.

When Moore, perhaps it was ten years afterwards, came to describe in *Ave* the planning and collaborative writing of *Diarmuid and Grania*, he turned the whole episode into farce. The farcical treatment is Moore's valedictory comment on the venture, which was the first attempt of the new theatre to realise the ideal of Irish cultural nationalism and turn a great Irish legendary love-tragedy into a modern drama to inspire a nationalist movement. But Moore's satire does not arise from the essential inappropriateness of the legendary material (Eglinton's view), but from his sense of the paralysing uncertainty about what the language of the new culture was to be. As the story is so famous the impossibility of retelling briefly the arguments about the kind of language needed will not worry us. Yeats's bitter words against Moore in *Dramatis Personae*, written thirty-five years after the event, confirm the bitterness of the struggle over the language. Moore's account of Yeats's eventual brainwave may not be wholly fictional. Moore was to write the play in French, Lady Gregory was to translate this into English, Taidgh O'Donoghue was to translate the English into Irish, Lady Gregory would then translate the Irish text into English, and Yeats would then 'put style upon it'. A main issue was the question of dialect (*Ave*, pp. 346–9). Moore says that Yeats wanted to try an Irish dialect, and that he objected because 'a peasant Grania' would be unsuitable in 'an heroic play', and because he thought any dialect which they could achieve would be false.

I don't think that one can acquire the dialect by going out to walk with Lady Gregory. She goes into the cottage and listens to the story, takes it down while you wait outside, sitting on a bit of wall, Yeats, like an old jackdaw, and then filching her manuscript to put style upon it, just as you want to put style on me.
(pp. 348–9)

Moore returned in his final volume, *Vale* (1914), to this question of dialect in a prolonged critique of the famous Kiltartan English fashioned by Lady Gregory herself. He takes as text Yeats's praise of her style in his preface to *Cuchulain of Muirthemne* in 1902:

Lady Gregory has discovered a speech as beautiful as that of Morris, and a living speech into the bargain. As she moved about among her people she learned to love the beautiful speech of those who think in Irish, and to understand that it is as true a dialect of English as the dialect that Burns wrote in.

Moore asserts that basically Lady Gregory's style consisted 'of no more than a dozen turns of speech' dropped into very ordinary English. Moore strongly supports the idea that English English was tired out compared with the colloquial English spoken in the Irish countryside, but he denies that Lady Gregory has got that language. He quotes a passage and says, 'To my ear – and I come from the same country as Lady Gregory – this is not living speech.' There is no real effort made, he claims, 'to fashion a language out of the idiom of the Galway peasant' (pp. 182–3).

Eventually, incredible though it seems, Moore and Yeats achieved a *modus vivendi* for writing *Diarmuid and Grania*. Yeats put it this way in *Dramatis Personae*:

Our worst quarrels, however, were when he tried to be poetical, to write in what he considered my style. He made the dying Diarmuid say to Finn: 'I will kick you down the stairway of the stars.' My letters to Lady Gregory show that we made peace at last, Moore accepting my judgement upon words, I his upon construction.[6]

The play which resulted, however, was a dead thing. When it was staged in 1901, Joseph Holloway noted: 'General verdict favourable if not enthusiastic.' He thought the ceremonial side, and the Funeral March provided by Elgar, very impressive. On the whole, he said, the play is 'a beautiful piece full of weird suggestiveness, but lacking here and there in dramatic action'.[7] Neither Yeats nor Moore saw fit to publish it – it was first printed in 1951.[8] Its lifelessness comes about from many sources. It lacks a dominating dramatic idea and the lack is well shown by the fact that the foretold death of Diarmuid, the climax of the play, by the black boar, has no essential connection with his relation with Finn and Grania, which is the subject of the play. None of the three main characters is sufficiently interesting to make the situation which develops from their interaction interesting. Above all, the heroic world and its values lie there inert and uncommunicative. The play's lack of success is very sad, but it is the kind of casualty unavoidable in a thought-up national theatre.

When Moore settled in Ireland he had all this behind him, but his efforts did not then look to him as they did in the days of disenchantment when he wrote *Hail and Farewell*, nor as they do to us. He was full of enthusiasm for the creation of a new Irish literature, convinced that the future was with small countries and new languages. He had long felt that the new Irish literature ought properly to be in the Irish language. He has written tellingly in *Ave* of his realisation of what he had lost in boyhood through the superiority of his class to the language of tenants and servants. Irish was never spoken by ladies and gentlemen –

Men had merely cudgelled each other, yelling strange oaths the while in Irish, and I remembered it in the mouths of the old fellows dressed in breeches and worsted stockings, swallow-tail coats and tall hats full of dirty bank-notes which they used to give to my father.   (p. 155)

His brother, Colonel Maurice Moore, had nevertheless learned Irish and was an enthusiastic Gaelic Leaguer notwithstanding his profession as an officer in the British Army. Moore wrote blackmailing letters to his brother and bullying letters to his sister-in-law to insist that his nephews should take the opportunity he had lost and learn the native speech of their country or he would disinherit them. Less vicariously, he began to write stories to be read in the new/old language. These, written in English of course, were translated into Irish and published in *The New Ireland Review*. Moore then published them in England as *The Untilled Field* in 1903 – a collection he added to later. The stories are excellent: some of the best things Moore ever did. Although there are some kindly portraits of priests – simple, devoted men seeking to achieve something in a country exhausted by poverty and emigration – the book has a single burden, one of foreboding so far as Moore's future in Ireland went, and that is of the constraint imposed on the human spirit in Ireland by the domination of all aspects of life by the Catholic Church in the person of the parish priest. Art, politics, but above all sex are the regions of frustration. The best that those who defy the priests can manage is to leave the country. If emigration is a chief theme, so is the return of the exile. One long story, 'The Wild Goose', deals with the return of a wanderer, who falls in love with the beauty of the country and the beauty of a devout woman whom he marries. He goes in for politics, becomes a leader, finds the church opposing him – and his wife siding with the church – so he becomes a wanderer again. *The Lake*, a novel which Moore published in 1905 (and revised in 1921), was originally intended as a short story for *The Untilled Field* but outgrew its bounds. Here the man who eventually has to break out from the shackles of the church is the priest himself, Father Gogarty. The priest finds himself entirely taken up by thoughts of the emancipated woman whom he has banished from the parish because of her free living. As he writes to her, she begins to sow doubts in his mind. He has a long struggle with his love of his homeland, his care for his parishioners, his duty to God. But finally he leaves his clothes by the lake and secretly emigrates to freedom. The ending jars, because Moore has so lovingly and tenderly described the beauty of his own home scenery and the devotion of the unhappy priest to his calling that the appeal to us of the Emancipated Life is precisely nil. This is not the only time when one feels that the intensity of Moore's realisation of the sombre beauty of a decaying land is a good deal more important than his opinions about its restrictiveness. But there is no doubt about the strength of those opinions.

The most powerful story in *The Untilled Field* for me is 'A Playhouse in the Waste'. Its hero is Father McTurnan, whom we have met in a previous story, when, obsessed with the decline in Catholicism

through the continuing drain of emigration, he was planning to write
to the Pope to suggest that priests should marry in order to bring more
Catholics into the world. Moore tells that story, 'A Letter to Rome',
tenderly and amusingly. 'A Play-house in the Waste' is altogether
starker. If one of Moore's strengths in his Irish writings is the evoca-
tion of the haunting beauty of the landscape, another is his ability to
convey its dreariness and desolation.

That day I had seen a woman digging in a patch of bog under the grey sky.
She wore a red petticoat, a handkerchief was tied round her head, and the
moment she caught sight of us she flung down the spade and ran to the hovel,
and a man appeared with a horn, and he blew his horn, running to the brow of
the hill. I asked the driver the reason of their alarm, and he told me that we
had been mistaken for the bailiff. This was true, for I saw two little sheep
hardly bigger than geese driven away. There was a pool of green water about
this hovel, and all the hovels in the district were the same – one-roomed
hovels, full of peat smoke, and on the hearth a black iron pot, with traces of
some yellow meal stirabout in it. The dying man or woman would be lying in
a corner on some straw, and the priest would speak a little Irish to these
outcast Celts, 'to those dim people who wander like animals through the
waste', I said.
   The grey sky has blown over these people for so many generations that it
has left them bare as the hills.   (1903 edn, p. 229)

The teller of the tale finds Father McTurnan knitting. He seems to
have a fine library, but he has given up reading, and knits for his
indigent parishioners, and meditates on further relief works. (Already
the scene shows 'bits of roads' leading nowhere.) His most grandiose
scheme, about which he was unwilling to speak, was a playhouse, and
this had actually been built. The priest had found some medieval
Latin Morality plays and had translated them into Irish. His vision
was of a sort of Oberammergau in this desolate part of the Irish coast,
with people coming from all over to the festival.

A grey, shallow sea had slowly eaten away the rotten land, and the embay was
formed by two low headlands hardly showing above the water at high tide.
   'I thought once,' said the priest, 'that if the play were a great success a line
of flat-bottomed steamers might be built.'   (pp. 231–2)

The narrator sees the playhouse. One wall has fallen down, and
though it would not take much to rebuild it, the project has clearly
been abandoned. Gradually, the narrator pieces out the story. The
girl who had been chosen to play the part of Good Deeds 'had been led
astray one evening returning from rehearsal – in the words of my

car-driver, "She had been 'wake' going home one evening."' When her pregnancy showed,

her mother took the halter off the cow and tied the girl to the wall and kept her there until the child was born. And Mrs Sheridan put a bit of string round its throat and buried it one night near the playhouse. And it was three nights after that the storm arose and the child was seen pulling the thatch out of the roof.

As the priest put it, the people looked upon the wind as a manifestation of God's disapproval. He thought that the playhouse had been seen by them as a levity, and it had disturbed the course of their piety. So he gave it up – and took to knitting and appealing to the government for further relief works. The story is not intended as an allegory, but it is impossible not to see it as symbolic of Moore's growing pessimism about establishing the arts in Ireland.

The Untilled Field was originally intended to provide good reading-matter for those learning their language. But Moore was gradually becoming convinced that the Irish-language cause was irretrievably linked to Celtic Catholicism, and that Catholicism was irretrievably anti-art. Early on, Moore said, he had argued that Ireland needed 'not a Catholic, but a Gaelic University'. Edward Martyn agreed with him, 'adding, however, that Gaelic and Catholicism went hand in hand – a remark which I did not understand at the time, but I learnt to appreciate it afterwards' (*Ave*, p. 328). In *Salve*, T. P. Gill is reported as saying, 'Plunkett is a Protestant, and a Protestant can never know Ireland.' Moore expostulated, 'A Protestant that has always lived in Ireland?', and Gill replied, 'Even so. Ireland is Catholic if she is anything' (*Salve*, p. 91). Even before the turn of the century, the man whom F. S. L. Lyons calls 'the apostle of Irish Irelandism', D. P. Moran, had been insisting on the primacy of the Gael in Ireland, and rejecting the quality of Irish nationalism preached by the Protestants from Grattan to Parnell as irrelevant and subversive of 'Irish civilisation'. 'The Celtic note' of the predominantly Anglo-Irish revival he called 'one of the most glaring frauds that the credulous Irish people ever swallowed'.[9] The decision of Edward Martyn to side with his co-religionists instead of his fellow Anglo-Irishmen and withdraw from the Irish Literary Theatre was an important indication of the way the lines of battle were being drawn, and, with the arrival of Synge and the attacks on his work by writers like Arthur Griffith and James Connolly (not the Labour-leader) as libellous of Irish morality and destructive of national pride and the nationalist cause, there is pretty open warfare between a predominantly Catholic nationalism and a predominantly Protestant literary movement.

Perhaps the most zany section of *Hail and Farewell* is the prolonged patter of Moore proving to all his friends that no great art has ever been produced by Catholicism (Newman, for example, doesn't count because he was bred a Protestant). Convinced that cultural progress was impossible under Catholicism, Moore felt first that he must publicly renounce his own Catholicism and become a Protestant, and then devote himself to his new mission, the liberation of his country from priestcraft (*Vale*, p. 291). Cut off on the one side from Yeats and his circle, and now cut off the from Gaelic League, he had a lonely field to till. The great difficulty in appreciating and assessing this third mission of Moore's in Ireland is the perplexing tone of the book he wrote in order to achieve his mission – *Hail and Farewell*. How can we take anything seriously in this bumptious, loquacious, egotistic, malicious work? How can we take his account of his feelings seriously and how can we take the book itself as a serious contribution to anything? We can be greatly helped by Herbert Howarth's two excellent essays on Moore,[10] particularly the later one, which is an excellent study of the way in which 'Moore's comic picture of himself as the martyr-prophet' can have status as a 'sacred book'. 'He is the hero of his book, but a comic hero, one of the first of the "anti-heroes".'

Critics may urge that *Hail and Farewell* is mock-heroic. In fact, it encompasses a mock-heroic technique, in which Wagner is Moore's panel of reference as Homer is Fielding's or Joyce's: but like *Ulysses* it goes far beyond mock-heroic and its figures are the more heroic for being foolish.   (p. 91)

This is very well said. *Hail and Farewell* is full of phrasings suggesting messianic and apostolic summonings, and they are always undercut by Moore's irony. Yet they *do* have status, as Joyce's ironic and mocking comparisons of Bloom with Elijah and Christ have status. Those who laugh at him for saying that he heard a voice in Chelsea saying 'Go to Ireland' fail to see that he laughed at himself first, and those who see that he laughed at himself may fail to see how – as another Irishman showed in *The Importance of Being Earnest* – one may make deeply serious uses of triviality.

'So the summons has come,' I said – 'the summons has come;' and I walked, greatly shaken in my mind, feeling that it would be impossible for me to keep my appointment with the lady who had asked me to tea that evening.
                                                                (*Ave*, p. 366)

So at the end of *Vale* he writes that from the time he had discovered that since the Reformation no Catholic had written a book worth reading, his belief had not faltered that he was 'an instrument in the hands of the Gods, and that their mighty purpose was the liberation of my country from priestcraft' (p. 291). And suddenly, he says, it was revealed to him what spear and buckler the gods were going to give him. '"But an autobiography," I said, "is an unusual form for a sacred book."'

It may not always work, but to write a comic book is the traditional Irish way of trying to influence the world, and once the validity of its irony is accepted, its effectiveness grows enormously. This is particularly so in what I consider in some ways the most important part of the book, the account of his estrangement from his brother over his renunciation of Catholicism and the religious education of his nephews. It is cast in the usual bantering and cocky way, and Moore comes out very badly indeed. The comedy is black, and Moore's account so angered his brother that eventually there was a total and final breach between them. Moore felt, rightly or wrongly, that it was necessary for him to give a fictionalised and facetious version of his arguments and transactions with his brother to illustrate the depth and the pain of the cleavage from home and family which was the result of the recognitions which he had come to, and their absolute primacy. In the end he *was* 'capable of sacrificing brother, sister, mother', but not to a work of art.

The most loyal of Moore's friends in Ireland was John Eglinton, the man who had opposed Yeats over the Celtic primitivism of the projected Irish national drama in 1899. In 1923, Eglinton chose to leave Ireland and he settled in Flintshire. Moore welcomed him and told him that with their shared views on 'the Irish character and papistry' Eglinton would never be at home in the new nation, 'and since the burning of my house I don't think I shall ever be able to bring myself to set foot in Ireland again'. (Moore Hall had been burned down by the Republicans during the Civil War, in 1923.) After Moore's death, Eglinton published an essay, 'Recollections of George Moore', published in *Irish Literary Portraits* (1935). It strongly emphasised the fundamental seriousness of Moore, though he 'sacrificed everything to audacity'. He spoke of Moore's 'caustic insight' and his 'disposition to recognise in himself a comic figure'. Of *Hail and Farewell*, he said:

Into Moore's mouth were put the words of judgement on the Ireland that was passing away, the Ireland of the old ideals in which people had ceased to believe and of new ones which had no relation to fact. His voice is the voice of common sense, just as the voice of Cervantes is the voice of common sense.

(p. 102)

Years earlier, in 1917, Eglinton republished some of his essays, and pointedly called them *Anglo-Irish Essays*. The Preface is a quite remarkable piece of writing. It is an uncompromising view of the madness of the Anglo-Irish who, betrayed by England at the Union in 1800, fatuously surrendered themselves to the racist ambitions of Irish Ireland. In considering the responsibility of the Anglo-Irish for the 1916 rising ('Did that play of mine send out/Certain men the English shot?') he says that for a quarter of a century, the Anglo-Irish took over the terms and traditions of the 'mere Irish' and by so doing stultified the real traditions of their own past, and advanced the religious and race antipathies of Catholic Ireland. It is a powerful and bitter essay by a man who believed in cultural union when most people were preaching cultural separatism, and a man who was never taken in by the idea that nationalism could result in anything but Catholic repossession.

Moore's notion in 1887 that the Irish Americans, descendants of those sent out on the death-ships by the Anglo-Irish landlords during the Famine, would return to repossess the land was off the mark. But his constant sense of a deep force within the people which would resume what it had lost centuries before was absolutely justified. This sense, apparent in *Parnell and his Island*, is strong also in *The Bending of the Bough*, his own contribution to the national drama of Ireland, in which he saw with quite remarkable foresight the need of that subterranean or chthonic force to acquire an articulate leader from outside with romantic views, 'a voice for the moment'. While Yeats and his theatre diverged more and more widely from the nationalist movement they had come to serve, that movement, inspired by Yeats's Cuchulain, went forward to perform its deeds for which, if we may take Sean O'Casey's plays as a true record, the phrase 'terrible beauty' is something of a euphemism.

10

NOTHING IS CONCLUDED

Sean O'Casey, Denis Johnston, Brendan Behan

Ten years ago in Strangeways Prison I stopped trying to find political solutions and began seriously to write.

Brendan Behan[1]

Theatre and nation seem to live each other's life; tragic hero and ruler die each other's death. Kings and princes were put to death weekly in the English theatre in Tudor and Stuart times, and when Charles I was executed Marvell called him a royal actor on a tragic scaffold. Padraic Pearse in his play *The Singer* rehearsed the rôle of sacrificial victim which he acted in earnest in the Post Office in 1916. The closeness of the play to the life of the nation is particularly striking in the story of the Irish drama since the Troubles. The determination over so many years to find a theatrical image for the confusion and distress of a country seems unique. The determination is all the more interesting because as Behan's words indicate the last thing the dramatists have been trying to do is to indicate solutions. Their burden is that there is no solution and no end to Ireland's difficulties. It is as though there is something special about drama and something special about Ireland that has made writer after writer explore and exploit the resources of the theatre with the hope of getting the formless turbulence of Ireland into recognisable shape. The endeavour has at least produced some wonderful plays. In this chapter I touch briefly on just a few of the best known, by Sean O'Casey, Denis Johnston, and Brendan Behan – a slum Protestant, an Anglo-Irishman educated at Cambridge, and a Catholic republican imprisoned for I.R.A. activities: *The Shadow of a Gunman* and *The Plough and the Stars*, *The Old Lady Says 'No!'* and *The Moon in the Yellow River*, and *The Hostage*.

Colaiste Mhuire Luimneach

Denis Johnston's expressionist play *The Old Lady Says 'No!'*, written in 1926 but first produced at the Gate Theatre, Dublin, in 1929, bears for its title what was scribbled on the manuscript when it came back from the Abbey Theatre. And it is not surprising that Lady Gregory, whose arresting dramatic sketches of Ireland's history take such a straightforward view of who's to blame for Ireland's troubles, should be unsympathetic to a play which is so coy about responsibility. Like all the plays I am discussing, it has as its centre an accidental or contingent death. It is a dream-play in which an actor taking part in a sentimental play about the life of Robert Emmet is knocked out and has a nightmare about being the real Emmet wandering through the Irish Free State. At one point the crowd becomes menacing, questioning his identity and threatening him (there are overtones of the rejection of Parnell), and 'Emmet', excited, gets hold of a revolver: 'I warn you I won't be interfered with, I am going on at all costs' (p. 50).[2] The gun goes off and a man in the crowd is fatally injured. The other death in the play is historical: the gratuitous murder of Lord Kilwarden by Emmet's followers, 'the justest judge in Ireland . . . dragged from his coach by the mob and slaughtered in the road' (p. 34). 'I did my best to save him,' pleads Emmet. 'What more could I do? . . . It was horrible. But it was war.'

It is an accidental death that is the climax of *The Plough and the Stars*, first produced in the year Johnston's play was written. Bessie Burgess, the slum Protestant whose son is at the front and who is wholly pro-British, is succouring Nora, the demented widow of the Irish Citizen Army officer who has been killed in action against the British in 1916. She tries to push Nora away from the dangerous window and as she does so she is shot by British soldiers trying to nail a sniper. The soldiers break into the house:

– Oh Gawd, we've plugged one of the women of the 'ouse.
– Whoy the 'ell did she gow to the window? Is she dead?
– Oh, dead as bedamned. Well, we couldn't afford to toike any chawnces.
                                                        (vol. 1, p. 260)[3]

No one knows who shot Minnie Powell at the end of *The Shadow of a Gunman*. Minnie had taken the suitcase full of Mills bombs which the horrified Davoren and Seumas had discovered in their room, and the Black and Tans arrested her and took her away. Their lorry is ambushed by the guerrillas; Minnie is shot as she jumps off the lorry in the confusion.

Davoren. . . . Do you realise that she has been shot to save us?

Seumas. Is it my fault; am I to blame?

Davoren. It is your fault and mine, both; oh we're a pair of dastardly cowards to have let her do what she did.   (I, p. 156)

The English soldier's death at the end of *The Hostage* is similar. Leslie, the hostage, is due to die in revenge for the hanging of an I.R.A. youth. But the house in Dublin where he is being kept is raided by the police, and in the pandemonium he is shot. Probably by the I.R.A., as Minnie was probably shot by the Auxiliaries, but it might in both cases have been by the other side, and the dramatists leave it as unclear as it would have been in reality.

Pat. Don't cry, Teresa. It's no one's fault. Nobody meant to kill him.

Teresa. But he's dead.   (p. 108)[4]

The death in *The Moon in the Yellow River* is different; it is a deliberate killing. But the tangled knot of responsibility for the death leads Dobelle to this reminiscence of his uncle.

A most peculiar thing! I had quite forgotten the incident, it's so many years ago. I was driving with my uncle in one of those old-fashioned high dog-carts. We were coming back from duck-shooting and a rabbit ran across the road directly in front of us. I remember it distinctly now. My uncle rose from his seat, took a careful aim, and shot the horse through the head. It was a most surprising incident at the time.   (p. 72)

It was in 1975 that the Peace Movement was started in Belfast by Mairead Corrigan and Betty Williams. Mairead Corrigan was the aunt of three children who were killed by a car that went out of control when the I.R.A. gunman who was driving it was shot by the security forces. The death of these children was precisely the cross-fire death with an infinite web of responsibility which has seemed to dramatists the most poignant and stark reality of the continuing Irish conflict. 'I draw the line,' said Seumas, 'when I hear the gunmen blowin' about dyin' for the people, when it's the people that are dyin' for the gunmen!' (I, p. 132). O'Casey's plays, like Johnston's and Behan's, are about victims. Sometimes it seems that not only Minnie and Bessie but everyone in the play is a victim: ordinary unimportant people caught up by the impersonal forces of international hatred and destroyed. But one soon sees that everyone contributes – by pettiness, vanity, self-delusion, carelessness, sentimentality, selfishness, cowardice – to the embroilment. The international hatred feeds on and grows by the weakness of the little inoffensive people whom it crushes. In speaking of *The Hostage* in *Brendan Behan's Island* (1962), Behan said he had had at the back of his mind the story of the ambush of some young British soldiers by a Flying Column of the I.R.A. in Kerry during the War of Independence.

> At the time I heard this story, I thought it was tragic and I still think so. I mean, the fellows who shot them had nothing against them and they had nothing in particular against the people that were shooting them. But that's war. It's only the generals and the politicians that are actively interested in it.
>
> (p. 16)

That is easily said. Trust the tale and not the teller. *The Hostage* gives us a much more profound idea of the stretch of responsibility for violence. The only acquittal is Lear's 'None does offend, none, I say none'; because everyone is in the business.

The main factor contributing to disaster in all the plays I am discussing is the intoxicating power of the language of romantic nationalism, a *damnosa hereditas* that cannot be shaken off. If modern Irish drama is a drama of victims, they are chiefly victims of language.

There is a sentimentality about the past, a sentimentality about the present, and a sentimentality about the future. It is the dramatist's task to show the fatal interconnection of these sentimentalities, and to expose the sentimentality by the brutal juxtaposition of word with event. *The Old Lady Says 'No!'* begins as a sentimental re-creation of Ireland's heroic past – Robert Emmet's unsuccessful rising in 1803 and his love for Sarah Curran. This playlet was 'made up almost entirely', said Johnston in the preface, 'from lines by Mangan, Moore, Ferguson, Kickham, Todhunter, and the romantic school of nineteenth-century Irish poets'. It opens with the revolutionary song of the 1790s, 'The Shan Van Vocht' (the poor old woman, Ireland: the other Old Lady of the play) which echoes throughout the play as it echoes through *The Hostage* (see p. 3).

> Yes! Ireland shall be free
> From the centre to the sea:
> Then hurrah for Liberty!
> Says the Shan Van Vocht.

The other song which echoes through these plays is T. D. Sullivan's commemoration of the Manchester Martyrs of 1867, 'God Save Ireland'.

> 'God save Ireland,' said the heroes; 'God save Ireland,' said they all:
> 'Whether on the scaffold high, or the battle-field we die,
> 'O what matter, when for Erin dear we fall!'

This is sung falteringly by Emmet ('I . . . can't . . . remember . . . my lines'), and by little Tommy Owens in *The Shadow of a Gunman*, the enthusiastic patriot whose loose talk about the gunman he proudly but wrongly supposes to be in their midst brings the Black and Tans to the tenement.

It is not Johnston's purpose in the opening playlet to ridicule Robert Emmet. The playlet is meant to be an historical play as put on at the time (the twenties) in the Free State. The use of the flowery and sugary language of the nineteenth-century poets and their patriotic hymns, and the resounding language of Emmet himself in the dock, is meant to show the newly independent Ireland's image of its past, an image which in Johnston's view, as we see later in the play, radically and fatally moulds its image of itself. The important Syngian blind man who taps about the stage in the latter part of the play has this to say:

In every dusty corner lurks the living word of some dead poet, and it waiting for to trap and to snare them. This is no City of the Living: but of the Dark and the Dead!

(p. 70)

It is the old cause, corrupted in the first place by the falsetto of the language in which it was expressed, and seemingly never able to die, which dominates both *The Moon in the Yellow River* of 1931 and *The Hostage* of the late fifties. In the former play both the German engineer Tausch, drawn to Ireland by the romance of a new, free, uncorrupted society, and also the man who opposes him, the boyish Robin Hood figure Darrell Blake, deeply saturated in the ideas of nineteenth-century nationalism, political and cultural, deny the existence of a divided Ireland, and are able to conceive the new Ireland only in the Yeats and Hyde terms of a rural country free from the stain of commerce and technology. In *The Hostage*, the brilliant conception of Monsewer caricatures Erskine Childers and, further back, the half-English Thomas Davis with his cry, 'Gentlemen, you have a country!' 'He was born an Englishman,' says Pat, 'remained one for years . . . He had every class of comfort until one day he discovered he was an Irishman.' (pp. 14, 15) He learned Irish and when the Rising took place he fought for Ireland. Now his mind has more or less gone, and he lives in the brothel (relying on his allowance from England), 'making plans for battles fought long ago against enemies long since dead' (p. 6). The new I.R.A. campaign is seen as part of his lunacy. He is active in the scheme to get hold of a British hostage, and he is proud of the death of the I.R.A. boy in Belfast.

It makes me proud; proud to know that the old cause is not dead yet, and that there are still young men willing and ready to go out and die for Ireland.

(pp. 39–40)

To which Teresa says, 'He is mad to say that the death of a young man will make him happy.'

The sentimentality about the future is strongest of course before the Rising has taken place. Words lure young men to their doom, and the accused in the dramatists' dock is Padraic Pearse. The most famous passage in *The Shadow of a Gunman* is Seumas's speech beginning 'I wish to God it was all over. The country is gone mad' (1, p. 131). It ends with this exchange.

Seumas. . . . an' their creed is, I believe in the gun almighty, maker of heaven
        an' earth – an' it's all for 'the glory o' God an' the honour o' Ireland'.
Davoren. I remember the time when you yourself believed in nothing but the
        gun.
Seumas. Ay, when there wasn't a gun in the country; I've a different opinion
        now when there's nothin' but guns in the country.

The movement from rhetoric to action is the centre of each of our plays. In his own play, *The Singer*, Pearse made Sighle express a voluptuous vision of the dead bodies of the fallen patriots.

They will go out laughing . . . And then they will lie very still on the hillside, –
so still and white, with no red in their cheeks, but maybe a red wound in their
white breasts, or on their white foreheads.
        . . .   .
I am proud other times to think of so many young men, young men with
straight, strong limbs, and smooth, white flesh, going out into great peril
because a voice has called to them to right the wrong of the people. Oh, I
would like to see the man that has set their hearts on fire with the breath of his
voice![5]

In the second act of *The Plough and the Stars*, the voice of the man who is silhouetted outside the window of the public house preaching the sanctity of hate and the redemption of bloodshed is that of Pearse. The words are culled from a number of his writings, the most powerful from 'The Coming Revolution' and 'Peace and the Gael'.

Bloodshed is a cleansing and sanctifying thing, and the nation that regards it
as the final horror has lost its manhood.

The old heart of the earth needed to be warmed with the red wine of the
battlefields.

Heroism has come back to the earth . . . When war comes to Ireland she must welcome it as she would welcome the Angel of God!

(I, pp. 193; 196; 202–3)

We witness the fervour which these words create in the hearers from Fluther to Captain Brennan. And in his heroic declaration, 'Ireland is greater than a wife!', Clitheroe echoes the bridegroom in Yeats's play *Cathleen ni Houlihan* who leaves his bride to follow the old woman to join the rising.

In *The Old Lady Says 'No!'*, the voice of Emmet suddenly changes to that of Pearse and the oration at the graveside of O'Donovan Rossa is quoted again.

Life springs from death, and from the graves of patriot men and women spring living nations.

(pp. 44–5)

Johnston's image of the patriot-hero, Emmet/Pearse, whose words draw men forth to die, is that of somnambulist and actor. It was a brilliant idea that a man acting the part of Emmet should become in his confused dream the real Emmet in the newly independent Dublin. Emmet thus becomes the dreamer, the man living in the Irish dream which Synge's plays define, and which Bernard Shaw so brilliantly described in Doyle's speech in the first act of *John Bull's Other Island*. And this dreamer is also an actor. So the bitter figure of Grattan sees him. 'Go out', he says, '. . . before you crucify yourself in the blind folly of your eternal play-acting'.

So, as Emmet passes through Dublin, a de-glorified patriot-hero faces the de-glorified society which has been achieved with so much human blood. The prime movers delude themselves as well as others. They are the first victims of the histrionic eloquence which mesmerises others, and the republic which is initiated with death and suffering is totally unlike anything they promised. Johnston admitted in his Preface that the play was written when 'several years of intermittent and unromantic civil war had soured us all a little towards the woes of Cathleen ni Houlihan'. But his play is important not only as expressing the mood of a moment of history but also as a view of the national life that could not be presented except through the theatrical forms it so brilliantly exploits.

The classic theatrical exhibition of the distance between the emotive rhetoric of nationalism and what that rhetoric leads to is the contrast in *The Plough and the Stars* between the rhapsody of the Voice in Act II about the redeeming power of blood shed for Ireland, and

Lieutenant Langon's horrified realisation in Act III that the wetness in his clothes is his own blood.

> D'ye think I'm really badly wounded, Bill? Me clothes seem to be all soakin' wet . . . It's blood . . . My God, it must be me own blood!   (I, p. 234)

There is Bessie Burgess too; her blood is poured out and she had *no* wish to offer it for Ireland. 'I'm bleedin' to death, an' no one's here to stop th' flowin' blood.' Blood poured out for Ireland is different in reality from what it is in a public speech. So we say that in the theatre O'Casey starkly points out the gap between the rhetoric of fanatics and the reality of the death and bloodshed which they are responsible for. But of course these real deaths of Langon and Bessie are not real at all. They are only play-acting, and this real blood which is contrasted with the fantasy-blood of psychotic speeches is only stage-blood. It is an understanding of this which gives a special grim effectiveness to the deaths in *The Old Lady Says 'No!'* and *The Hostage*. The death of Joe, the man in the crowd accidentally shot in the lung by Emmet, is very moving. But the murderer at the end of the play lies down on the stage and becomes again the concussed actor just where he was when he was knocked out at the beginning of the play. It was all a dream, and a dream within a play: an actor acting an actor dreaming he'd shot someone. No one's really dead; no one's really knocked out.

The ending of *The Hostage* is less subtle but more powerful. It shattered one spectator at least. I never saw Joan Littlewood's London production, but the 1960 Dublin production was closely modelled on it. The raid at the end is very funny indeed and it is while we are still weak with laughter that our attention gradually focuses on the body of the dead soldier.

> *Teresa kneels by the body. The others bare their heads.*
> *Teresa.* Leslie, my love. A thousand blessings go with you.
> *Pat.* Don't cry, Teresa. It's no one's fault. Nobody meant to kill him.
> *Teresa.* But he's dead.
> *Pat.* So is the boy in Belfast Jail.
> *Teresa.* It wasn't the Belfast Jail or the Six Counties that was troubling you, but your lost youth and your crippled leg. He died in a strange land, and at home he had no one. I'll never forget you, Leslie, till the end of time.
>   (p. 108)

I have rarely been so moved in the theatre. Up to this point, the whole play, so funny, so intelligent, so well written, moving along as a riotous musical farce, never serious and never silly, had justified its tone to the full. But a death is a death, and the derisory note had vanished.

> Thus march we playing to our latest rest;
> Only we die in earnest, that's no jest.

The natural relationship of the English boy and the Irish girl standing out against the anti-life dedications of those assenting to the old cause had reached its apogee in death, as it does in *Romeo and Juliet*. And then, when the 'ghostly green light' came over the stage and the corpse of Leslie began to stir and rise and he began to sing the envoi, eventually joined by the whole cast, I was shocked to the core.

> The bells of hell,
> Go ting-a-ling-a-ling,
> For you but not for me,
> Oh death, where is thy sting-a-ling-a-ling?
> Or grave thy victory?   (p. 109)

I simply could not attune myself to this return to flippant song and dance. I was had, of course; superbly trapped by the power of theatrical illusion. But I don't regret my innocent involvement in Leslie's death and Teresa's response. The strength of my initial response *against* the ending helped me to understand its great value. Behan, or rather Behan and Joan Littlewood, insist that the play is only a play and that the dead man is only an actor. Of course he's going to get up again; he would be taking a bow in a minute anyway. The return to 'irresponsibility' is a sharp reminder that it's a theatre we're in. The words of the final song are important.

> The bells of hell
> Go ting-a-ling-a-ling
> For you but not for me.

No, it's not in the play-world that people are dying, but out there in the real life of the audience and the distressful country beyond. 'For you but not for me.' Not for him as he is Leslie, but for him as he is a citizen of the country as he puts on his overcoat and goes home.

    To be deeply moved by Leslie's death is to acknowledge the power of the fake that O'Casey contrived in contrasting the rhetorical shedding of blood with the 'real' deaths of Langon and Bessie. To destroy that emotion is not only to make the sharp Brechtian comment that we should not mistake the place where the action is really happening, as I have just argued. It makes as well what I think is a more important point. What we have witnessed is only acting; but it was a true image of death. Leslie's death mirrors real deaths, as do the deaths of Minnie, Langon, Bessie, Blake. Our emotions proclaim it is true; the playwright proclaims it is a fiction. Its status then is a true fiction – like the whole of the wild farce which precedes it. By not claiming more for the stage-death than it warrants, the play authenticates the rest of the drama as having a status equal to that death. *The Hostage* is not a boisterous farce coming to its moment of truth. It is truth all along: such truth as the theatre provides. If we in the audience are told in the final chorus that it is among us that the real deaths take place, we are also told by implication that it is among us that the mad farce is really operating. And the same implication is made in Johnston's play by the 'theatricality' of Joe's death: our own condition is mirrored by the tragi-comic nightmare of the rest of the play. Sean O'Casey forged the magnificent weapon of fused comedy and tragedy for the stage representation of the grotesqueness of Ireland's troubles (though the Irish predilection for using the comic mode for serious matters is of long standing). If his humour now seems ponderous and his dialogue clumsy we reflect how much is owed to him by his successors. In *Borstal Boy* Behan tells us with what glad recognition he found *Juno and the Paycock* and *The Plough and the Stars* in the borstal library.

To return to Johnston, the evaluation which *The Old Lady Says 'No!'* makes of the national situation of Ireland is made purely in theatrical terms. Expressionism and much older conventions of the theatre allowed him to make complex 'statements' about heroism, unreality, self-deception, unwitting cruelty, hypocrisy, shallowness, sentimentality, and so on. It is the theatre which enables him to tell us what he sees, and perhaps also it is the means by which he sees. I cannot help thinking, however, that although it may be a little too subtle for wholly successful communication on the stage, the comic tone of the first half of *The Moon in the Yellow River* is Johnston's more remarkable achievement, perhaps the most interesting of all attempts to create a theatrical mode which will declare the national situation. There is Tausch with his romantic fervour to serve the new Ireland, utterly bewildered by the seeming lunacy of everything. There is the aunt who keeps her bicycle in the bedroom and hands out militant leaflets. There is the famous Irish engineer who has given it all up and returned to Ireland to play with model trains. There is the gunman who crumples into ignominious obedience when the housekeeper recognises him as her own son. There is the discovery that the

terrorists' explosives have been allowed to get wet in the rain. There is
the home-made piece of artillery which refuses to work. The leader of
the Diehards is a gentlemanly and courteous figure. We have an
amusing and disarming sort of comic-opera tone, with an under-
ground movement of desperadoes, led by a Byronic hero, who are as
likeable as they are impractical. We recognise the comfortable convention and we laugh at its familiar outsider figure – the serious
Teuton baffled by the irrationality of it all. It is all very jolly and cosy.
Even when Tausch has managed to summon government troops, and
Blake knows they are coming, the tone is maintained. Blake, slightly
drunk, holds a plebiscite on whether they should go ahead and blow
up the powerhouse. He is clearly a stage version of a very long line of
ineffectual Irish insurgent-idealists. When Lanigan arrives with the
troops, the talking still goes on. Blake sings Ezra Pound's little poem,
accompanying himself on the piano, about Li-Po who died drunk
while trying to embrace the moon in the Yellow River. Then Lanigan
shoots him dead. Una Ellis Fermor wrote (incredibly) that 'the
transition is a little ill-prepared'.[6] It is not prepared at all, and that is
the point. There is perfect consonance in total disjunction. The rather
chummy, rather arch attitude which the play strikes towards these
loveable rebels, inefficient, innocent, idealistic, is suddenly and completely banished. We in the audience have all been indulgent watch-
ers of a game in which the final move is death. The mood of the play is
impossible to think of except as a theatrical mood – an easily recognised and accepted mood. Yet it translates, perfectly, to an accusation
of criminal irresponsibility, or rather criminal responsibility, in those
who participate and those who observe. We in the audience are
accused by the levity of our own enjoyment and our assent to the
'typically Irish' humour of the whole enterprise, which beneath the
indulgent surface is wretched, rotten, evil.

The play has a whole act still to go. Eventually, the last of the dud
shells is heaved over on to the slag heap. And it explodes, and blows
up the power house. 'There's no end and there's no solution', says
Dobelle wearily. He comes to better terms with his daughter, and on
the personal level there is quite a hopeful ending to the play, though
politically it is as despairing as the rest.

One might say that since the early twenties the Irish dramatists, even
if they offer no solutions, have been trying to exorcise the devil in Irish
political life by naming it and displaying it in the theatre. But the

unending repetitiveness of the Irish crisis decade after decade shows how slight is the power of the theatre in the political arena. As I began to write this chapter in the autumn of 1977, there were three murders by the I.R.A. in Ulster within a week. A young mother was murdered by machine-gun fire as she slept. The life of her three-year-old child was saved by the teddy-bear she was clutching. (The mother was a part-time helper in the official Ulster Defence Regiment.) A prison officer was shot down in his car. The driver of a school bus was murdered by machine-gun fire and a child in the bus was injured; the driver was not the I.R.A.'s intended victim but a relief driver just taking over for the day. The wind in Ireland is always changing, and always reverting to the same direction.

In these closing chapters I have hardly mentioned the greatest Irish dramatist, Synge. In two plays he gave the most vivid theatrical expression possible of two Irish conditions. In *The Playboy of the Western World* he described for all time the irresistible attraction of the Irish towards the man who has killed his father, a second nature deeply implanted by centuries of enforced subservience. The hero always turns out to be a fake, and the father is not in fact killed, but the hero is always being re-created, since the temptation to accept the accolade is too great to hold out against, as Davoren in *The Shadow of a Gunman* as well as Christy Mahon found. The second condition, found more often among the writers than among the activists, is when the ever-present dream, obscuring and falsifying the true nature of things, evaporates, and it appears that there is no Messiah and nothing to be hoped for. This is the condition imaged in the blind beggar Martin in Act II of *The Well of the Saints* when he has lost the comfort of the illusions of his blindness and is enduring the terror of the miracle of being able to see, and to see as sighted men cannot see.

Grand day, is it? . . . Or a bad black day when I was roused up and found I was the like of the little children do be listening to the stories of an old woman, and do be dreaming in the dark night that it's in grand houses of gold they are, with speckled horses to ride, and do be waking again, in a short while, and they destroyed with the cold, and the thatch dripping, maybe, and the starved ass braying in the yard?

'The starved ass braying in the yard'. If to some extent the writers of Ireland were responsible for creating the dreams that have acted like drugs on the people of Ireland they have more than made up for it by the bleakness with which some of them have imaged the life that needs the drug of dreams. Both Synge and Beckett are specialists in figuring the deceptions we furnish ourselves with to avert knowledge of the nothingness underfoot. Their characters are often vagrants and dispossessed people in a barren land, sometimes blind, and they talk continuously in order to keep going. Perhaps the most electrifying image of despair in the modern Irish theatre however comes from Yeats himself, in that great play *Purgatory*, which he wrote at the end of his life. Ireland is now a burnt-out house where the dead parents re-enact their ruinous copulation. The Old Man, their heir, who has killed his own father, now before our eyes stabs with the same knife his own son, 'who would have passed pollution on'. As he moves away, thinking he has 'finished all that consequence', he is horrified to hear yet again the returning hoof-beats of his father coming back.

> Her mind cannot hold up that dream.
> Twice a murderer and all for nothing,
> And she must animate that dead night
> Not once but many times!
>   O God,
> Release my mother's soul from its dream!
> Mankind can do no more. Appease
> The misery of the living and the remorse of the dead.

Retrospect

It was not the purpose of this book to establish a thesis about theatre and nation or to make, though they have not been avoided, large historical generalisations. I have tried to illuminate the relationship between two theatres and the communities which they served, communities separated by a sea and by three hundred years of history, but communities united by the twisted thread of that history. I have worked within certain assumptions rather than hypotheses about the two reciprocals – theatre and nation, England and Ireland – and I have tried in each of the individual studies to investigate a different aspect or level of interaction. How tendentious these investigations look I cannot say, but I have tried to be empirical, and I discovered many things in the writing which I did not expect to find. I had no wish to demonstrate a thesis and I had no particular wish to write a history: I have been more concerned with a means of deepening the perspective whereby one views individual plays. So a conclusion, in the sense of a final idea or theory, *quod erat demonstrandum*, is not what this book works towards. I should like, however, as an ending, to look back in the light of all that stands between to O'Leary's challenge,

quoted at the beginning of the Introduction, that there is no fine
nationality without literature, and no fine literature without nationality.

With whatever sacrifice of 'fineness', it is clear that nationality gets
on much better without literature than with it once it moves from the
realm of ideas into the world of action. The theatre is more a thorn in
the flesh than a flower in the buttonhole. It constantly upset the city
authorities in Elizabethan London and offended the patriotism of
twentieth-century Dublin. The nation does not *need* literature in the
way in which Ben Jonson and Yeats thought it did. It uses what it
wants; it needs slogans and marching-songs; it needs above all a
camouflage of ideals and dreams to bewitch its followers. So it takes
what it wants, corrupting the literature in the process and perhaps
corrupting the writer too.

As for the writer, C. H. Herford was right to remark (see above,
p. 204) that the enthusiasm for incipient nationhood may start the
writer off, but in so far as he has anything worth while to offer, his path
must be one of divergence. The values which any credible writer holds
and wishes to see incarnate in his nation are invariably at odds with
the attainment, maintenance, and extension of power. The stone's in
the midst of all. The theatre itself can't be institutionalised or
nationalised. In Queen Elizabeth's day various compromises, expe-
dients, and improvisations provided a lucky blend of freedom and
control and enabled the theatre to live in an uniquely fruitful *modus
vivendi* with the national government. It could not possibly last and
the greater movement towards institutionalisation under James I
weakened the theatre and hastened its suppression. It will be clear
(Chapter 6) that I do not regard the splendours of the Jacobean and
Caroline court masque as one of the glories of English drama.

In part, therefore, this book is a set of studies of disillusionment
and growing bitterness among those who have responded enthusiastically to the idea of providing by means of the theatre a spiritual core
to a nation's progress. All in their different ways John Lyly, Ben
Jonson, W. B. Yeats, and George Moore retraced their steps and
altered their ideas. Shakespeare and Synge show less disenchantment
because they show less expectation.

At the same time, however, theatre and nation, mutually disenchanted partners, constantly nourish each other and to some extent
support each other. The Elizabethan historical drama, rough
diamond as it is, was seen in its own time in England and throughout

the world in the nineteenth century as a unique expression of a people's spirit, even if a close examination of Shakespeare's Histories shows a conservatism and indeed a pessimism which is hardly flattering to those who were urging the nation on. The drama of kingship, from Marlowe to Ford, takes its images from the symbols by which *realpolitik* works and in a play which may seem far away from topicality mimes a past, present, and future which *realpolitik* would not recognise, nor accept. I hope that in the first half of this book I have not seemed to be seeking to turn some of the best English plays into political allegories. I don't think *Tamburlaine*, *Sejanus*, *The Tempest*, *Cymbeline*, *Perkin Warbeck* are directly or indirectly strictly topical plays like *A Game at Chess* or for that matter *Gorboduc*. I have tried to show that the plays I discuss deepen their significance when their themes and conflicts are seen to extend beyond themselves to reflect the fundamental concerns and tensions of their age. The least likely of plays throws up on the cyclorama behind it a shadow play in which higher destinies are worked out. Irish plays hardly need this anagogic approach: they deal so directly with the confusions of their times. This directness is partly an index of the different origin of the Irish theatre, which was built up quickly and deliberately as a national theatre, whereas the Elizabethan theatre, though quick to flower, grew up slowly and organically.

It is impossible for me to conceive of serious drama, comedy or tragedy, which is not, consciously or unconsciously, a hieroglyph of the pressures and tensions within the community outside it. To accept that, however, is only the beginning, because most identifications of the *Zeitgeist*, marxist or non-marxist, offer the identification as a substitute for literary criticism rather than as a position from which literary criticism may begin. At any rate, I accept this much of the converse in O'Leary's statement, that the conflicts in plays subsist on and are nourished by a nation's conflicts whether the relationship is overt or subliminal. Criticism has to take the relationship into account, though, heaven knows, the perils of producing para-criticism are increased a hundredfold. What I have written on Ben Jonson is an attempt to sail between Scylla and Charybdis; to try to keep a clear eye on the individual work of art while keeping within a focused field of vision companion works, and what we know of the man and the movements of the times he lived in. Scylla is the distortion which comes from excluding what lies beyond the work one is concentrating on; Charybdis is the distortion which comes from substituting for criticism mere recognitions and identifications of the outside world in the work of art.

Such argument as this book maintains relates to a parallelism between Shakespeare and Yeats, at either end of a single historical process leading from the institution of the United Kingdom and the British Empire to their dissolution in our time. Shakespeare created Yeats, for Yeats without the idea of the Irish nation is meaningless, and the Irish nation limped into being because Elizabeth and James subjugated and colonised Ireland. Yeats sought mentors to instruct him as prophet to the new Ireland and found them in the men whose culture he wanted to replace: Jonson and Shakespeare, but particularly Shakespeare. I have tried to describe the extremely strange way in which Yeats's rapid move from herald of the new age to *laudator temporis acti* and prophet of doom was influenced by what he saw in Shakespeare.

The theatre of Ireland in the last fifty years or so has set out to objectify into stage images the violence and strife which were in the womb in Shakespeare's day. Brilliant though many of the plays are, they have had no effect on the national situation. Shakespeare's *Cymbeline* had absolutely no effect on the English policy of his day towards Ireland, either. Shakespeare's vision of imperial peace in that play depended on the recognition by a colony that achieved its independence by armed struggle that its future lay not in fighting or self-assertion but in co-operation within a shared culture. There is yet a third political entity which some time has got to be created from England, Scotland, Wales, and the two Irelands, and it *will* emerge when the visions and the warnings of the dramatists I have been discussing move into the centre of people's consciousness. If this new 'nation' has the good luck to inspire a great theatre, I hope their relations will be more amicable than their predecessors' but not less vital. The less 'nationality' is preached, the better both theatre and nation are likely to fare.

NOTES

Chapter 1

1 *Letters to the New Island*, ed. H. Reynolds, 1934, reprinted 1970, p. 174.
2 *Ibid.* pp. 75–6.
3 Reprinted in W. B. Yeats, *Essays and Introductions*, 1961, pp. 356–83.
4 *Variorum Plays of W. B. Yeats*, ed. R. K. Alspach, 1966, p. 316.
5 *Yeats the Playwright*, 1963, pp. 37–8.
6 *PMLA*, LXXXII (1967), 157–69.
7 *Letters*, ed. A. Wade, 1954, pp. 478–9.
8 It is worth noting that the Oldest Pupil's speech, lines 158–65 of *The King's Threshold*, contains a close paraphrase of Jonson's dedication to *Cynthia's Revels* in the words 'the Courtly life/Is the world's model'.
9 *Letters*, p. 426.
10 *Journal of the Ivernian Society*, v (1913), 153–66, 203–19; reprinted in *Irish Bardic Poetry*, ed. D. Greene and F. Kelly, Dublin Institute for Advanced Studies, 1970. There is an immortal account of Osborn Bergin in the second volume of Frank O'Connor's autobiography, *My Father's Son*, 1968, Ch. 11.
11 'The Professional Poets', *Seven Centuries of Irish Learning*, Radio Éireann Thomas Davis Lectures, ed. Brian O Cuív, 1958, p. 50.
12 Taken from E. C. Quiggin, 'Prolegomena to the Study of the Later Irish Bards 1200–1500', *Proceedings of the British Academy*, v (1911–12), p. 114.
13 'The Professional Poets' (see note 11), p. 57.
14 Bergin (see note 10), pp. 206–7.
15 *Ibid.* pp. 212–13 (slightly edited).
16 Smyth's report (1561) was not published, but it shows the information available in London. See *Ulster Journal of Archaeology*, 1st series, VI (1858), 165–7.
17 'A Note on Irish Poets and the Sidneys', *English Studies*, XLIX (1968), 424–5.
18 D2v. The reference was found in D. B. Quinn's *The Elizabethans and the Irish*, 1966, p. 126.
19 Thomas Smyth (see note 16). (Text from David Greene, in 'The Professional Poets' (see note 11), pp. 45–6 (slightly edited).)
20 *A View of the Present State of Ireland*, ed. W. L. Renwick, 1970, pp. 72–4 (punctuation changed).
21 From a poem by Cian Ó Heachaidhén. See Bergin (note 10), p. 215.

Chapter 2

1 Cf. E. Engelberg, *The Vast Design*, 1964, pp. 13–19, and Peter Ure, *Yeats and Anglo-Irish Literature*, 1974, p. 211.
2 Yeats, *Essays and Introductions*, 1961, pp. 109–10.
3 *Beltaine (The Organ of the Irish Literary Theatre)*; see *Essays and Introductions*, p. 167 (my italics).
4 *Essays and Introductions*, p. 110 (my italics).
5 E. K. Chambers, *The Elizabethan Stage* (4 vols., 1923, hereafter referred to in text and notes as *ES*), I, p. 236.
6 Jonson also quotes from the play in *Poetaster*, 1601, III.iv.168. The Herford and Simpson note (IX, p. 556: see note 42 to Ch. 4, below) wrongly gives the publication date of *Histriomastix* as 1600 instead of 1610, obscuring the fact that Jonson knew the play in MS or from performances.
7 A. Kernan, 'John Marston's Play, *Histriomastix*', *Modern Language Quarterly*, XIX (1958), 134–40; P. J. Finkelpearl, 'John Marston's *Histriomastix* as an Inns of Court Play: A Hypothesis', *Huntington Library Quarterly*, XXIX (1966), 223–34, and *John Marston of the Middle Temple*, 1969, pp. 119–24; G. L. Geckle, 'John Marston's *Histriomastix* and The Golden Age', *Comparative Drama*, VI (1972), 205–22.
8 *ES*, IV, p. 18; A. Caputi, *John Marston, Satirist*, 1961, pp. 82–8, 251–5; Finkelpearl (see note 7).
9 Cf. M. C. Bradbrook, *The Rise of the Common Player*, 1962, pp. 45–7.
10 See Caputi, *John Marston, Satirist*, pp. 82–3.
11 His lectures are ludicrous, and one sympathises with those who have supposed a primitive layer in a revised play, and those who like Kernan think the pedantry is satirical.
12 The references are to vol. III of H. Harvey Wood's edition of Marston's plays (1934–9).
13 *The Three Parnassus Plays*, ed. J. B. Leishman, 1949, p. 338.
14 To Chambers and Bentley may be added M. C. Bradbrook's *The Rise of The Common Player*, 1962, and *Enduring Monument*, 1976; Andrew Gurr, *The Shakespearean Stage 1574–1642*, 1970; and Glynne Wickham, *Early English Stages*, vol. II (Pt 1, 1963; Pt 2, 1972).
15 See the full account by Wickham, *Early English Stages*, II, Pt 2, pp. 9ff.
16 Cf. E. S. Morgan, 'Puritan Hostility to the Theatre', *Proceedings of the American Philosophical Society*, CX (1966), 340–7.
17 Cf. Jonas Barish, 'The Antitheatrical Prejudice', *Critical Quarterly*, VIII (1966), 329–48, and 'Exhibitionism and the Antitheatrical Prejudice', *English Literary History*, XXXVI (1969), 1–29.
18 E.g. Edmund Grindal, Bishop of London; see *ES*, IV, p. 266.
19 See F. S. Boas, *Queen Elizabeth in Drama*, 1950.
20 Wickham, *Early English Stages*, II, Pt 1, Ch. 3, 'State Control of British Drama, 1530–1642'.
21 Hazlitt's Dodsley, VI, p. 482.
22 *Ibid*. pp. 450–1.
23 *Ibid*. p. 478.

24 *Pierce Penniless his Supplication to the Devil*. In *Thomas Nashe*, ed. S. Wells, 1964, pp. 65–6.

25 J. P. Feil, in *Shakespeare Survey*, XI (1958), 109.

26 See L. G. Salingar, 'Les Comédiens et leur public en Angleterre de 1520 à 1640', *Dramaturgie et société... aux xvie et xviie siècles*, ed. J. Jacquot, 1968, pp. 525–76. Recent volumes of the *Collections* of the Malone Society (see note 27) will be supplemented by the publications of the projected *Records of Early English Drama*.

27 G. E. Dawson, Malone Society *Collections*, VII, 1965; W. Mepham, *Essex Review*, LVII (1948).

28 W. C. Hazlitt, *English Drama and Stage*, 1869, p. 256.

29 In the work cited in note 26.

Chapter 3

1 F. le Van Baumer, *The Early Tudor Theory of Kingship*, 1940, p. vii.

2 *Cambridge Modern History*, III, pp. 750, 752.

3 Baumer, *The Early Tudor Theory of Kingship*, p. viii.

4 *Ibid*. p. 32; G. R. Elton, *England Under the Tudors*, 2nd edn, 1974, pp. 162–4.

5 *Eikon Basilike*, quoted by Figgis, *The Divine Right of Kings* (1896), 1922 edn, p. 256.

6 L. Stone, *The Causes of the English Revolution 1529–1642*, 1972, pp. 88, 65.

7 Edmund Spenser, *The Shepherd's Calendar*, April eclogue.

8 *Elizabeth I and the Unity of England*, 1960, p. 181.

9 J. E. Neale, *Queen Elizabeth and her Parliaments 1584–1601*, II, 1937, p. 391.

10 James I, *Works*, 1616, p. 529.

11 J. P. Kenyon, *The Stuart Constitution 1603–1688: Documents and Commentary*, 1966, p. 8; F. D. Wormuth, *The Royal Prerogative 1603–1649*, 1939, p. 41.

12 Kenyon (see note 11), p. 9; Wormuth (see note 11), p. 105.

13 Stone (see note 6), p. 89.

14 The authorship is sometimes ascribed to R. Mocket. I owe the reference to D. Willson, *James VI and I*, 1956, pp. 294–5.

15 'An Epitaph to the Eternal Memory of Charles I', in *Poems*, ed. T. L. Pebworth and C. J. Summers, 1973.

16 Figgis, *The Divine Right of Kings*, p. 256.

17 *The Tudor Revolution in Government*, 1953, p. 20.

18 See Chambers, *ES*, vols. I and IV; G. E. Bentley, *The Jacobean and Caroline Stage*, esp. vol. VII; M. S. Steele, *Plays and Masques at Court*; Glynne Wickham, *Early English Stages*.

19 S. Anglo, *Spectacle, Pageantry, and Early Tudor Policy*, 1969, pp. 4–5.

20 *Ibid*. p. 266–7.

21 D. M. Bevington, *Tudor Drama and Politics*, 1968, p. 8. The incident is discussed (on p. 49) in an important book on the political basis of Elizabethan pageantry and drama, Marie Axton's *The Queen's Two Bodies: Drama and the Elizabethan Succession*, 1977, which appeared too late for me to make use of it.

22 Hunter, *John Lyly*, 1962, Ch. 3; Bradbrook, *The Rise of the Common Player*,

1962, Ch. 11; Bevington, *Tudor Drama and Politics*, Ch. 13. See also a valuable essay by Marion Jones, 'The Court and the Dramatist', in *Elizabethan Theatre*, ed. J. R. Brown and B. Harris, 1966, pp. 169–95.

23 F. S. Boas, *University Drama in the Tudor Age*, 1914, pp. 102–3.
24 See more fully Ch. 6, pp. 141–4.
25 'If this is your will, and I have deserved it, why are your thunderbolts idle, Virgin, Mother, Princess?' (Adapted from Ovid, *Metamorphoses*, II, 279.) The text of the petitions is from G. K. Hunter, *John Lyly*, pp. 85–6.
26 Hunter, *John Lyly*, pp. 29–30.
27 *Ibid*. p. 34.
28 Cf. G. L. Geckle, 'John Marston's *Histriomastix* and the Golden Age', *Comparative Drama*, VI (1972), 205–22.
29 See the Introduction to Bond's edition.
30 Line references for Marlowe's plays are to the Oxford edition, ed. Roma Gill, 1971.
31 See U. Ellis-Fermor's edition of *Tamburlaine*, 1930, p. 113, and her book *Christopher Marlowe*, 1927, p. 29.
32 *Shakespeare and the Homilies*, 1934, p. 25.
33 'Marlowe's *Edward II*; Power and Suffering', *Critical Quarterly*, I (1959), 194.
34 See Harry Levin, *The Overreacher*, 1952, p. 110: 'The court of Edward almost seems to anticipate the absolutism and favoritism of the Stuarts.'

Chapter 4

1 See C. M. Bowra, *From Virgil to Milton*, 1948, Ch. 3.
2 G. G. Smith, *Elizabethan Critical Essays*, 1904, I, p. 255.
3 *Ibid*. II, pp. 260–2.
4 Charles Whibley, *Cambridge History of English Literature*, 1908, III, Ch. 15. See also A. L. Rowse, *The England of Elizabeth*, 1950, Ch. 2.
5 *Marlowe and the Early Shakespeare*, 1953, pp. 105–8. Contrast Irving Ribner, *The English History Play in the Age of Shakespeare*, 1957, p. 95.
6 Bevington, *Tudor Drama and Politics*, 1968, Ch. 14; Sanders, *The Dramatist and the Received Idea*, 1968, pp. 30–5.
7 See pp. 74–86 below.
8 E. K. Chambers, *William Shakespeare*, 1930, II, pp. 323–7.
9 Thomas Nashe, *Works*, ed. R. B. McKerrow, II, p. 212.
10 *Apology for Actors*, 1612, B4r. There is a facsimile edited by R. H. Perkinson, 1941. Chambers gives extracts (from a reprint) in *ES*, IV, pp. 250–4.
11 *Apology for Actors*, F3r. Heywood completes his sentence with the claim that history plays also instruct subjects to be obedient etc.
12 See the Malone Society Reprint of the play.
13 *The Original Writings and Correspondence of the Two Richard Hakluyts*, ed. E. G. R. Taylor, 2 vols., 1935, I, p. 175 and II, p. 456.
14 'The Politics of Shakespeare's History Plays', *New Shakspere Society Transactions*, 1874, p. 417.
15 It is impossible to say precisely what Macmorris means by 'Ish a villain,

and a bastard, and a knave, and a rascal.' The subject of the sentence may be Ireland, Macmorris, or Fluellen. It makes no difference to the main point at issue.

16 *Shakespeare's Military World*, 1956, p. 79.

17 See the article in *Dictionary of National Biography*.

18 There are useful brief accounts of Essex's campaign in E. P. Cheyney's *A History of England from the Defeat of the Armada to the Death of Elizabeth*, 1926, and Cyril Falls, *Elizabeth's Irish Wars*, 1950.

19 A. Collins (ed.), *Letters and Memorials of State*, 1746, II, p. 133.

20 *Ibid.* p. 134.

21 *The Essential Shakespeare*, 1932, p. 96.

22 See A. C. Sprague, *Shakespeare's Histories: Plays for the Stage*, 1964, pp. 2. 92–6.

23 *King Henry the Fifth's Poet Historical*, 1925, p. 88.

24 Cheyney (see note 18), p. 479. No source given.

25 *A View of the Present State of Ireland*, ed. Renwick, 1970, p. 67.

26 *Ibid.* pp. 48 and 65.

27 *Ibid.* pp. 124 and 153.

28 *Ibid.* p. 108.

29 I owe the reference to N. P. Canny, in his important article, 'The Ideology of English Colonisation: From Ireland to America', *William and Mary Quarterly*, 3rd series, XXX (1973), 575–98.

30 Cf. Hall's Chronicle as quoted by E. M. W. Tillyard, *Shakespeare's History Plays* (1944), 1962 edn, pp. 44–5.

31 In the work cited in note 14, pp. 418–19.

32 W. Camden, *Britannia*, trans. by P. Holland, 1610, p. 63.

33 'The Tempest: Conventions of Art and Empire', in *Later Shakespeare*, ed. J. R. Brown and B. Harris (Stratford-upon-Avon Studies 8), 1966, p. 193.

34 F. A. Yates, *Astraea*, 1975, pp. 116, 87; see also Hans Kohn, 'The Genesis and Character of English Nationalism', *Journal of the History of Ideas*, I, (1940), 69–94.

35 James I, *Works*, 1616, pp. 487, 488, 489.

36 D. H. Willson, *James VI and I*, 1956, p. 13.

37 *Remains*, 1605, p. 3.

38 David Williams, *A History of Modern Wales*, 1950, pp. 35ff.

39 *A View of the Present State of Ireland*, pp. 67, 153.

40 James I, *Works*, p. 511.

41 See G. Wilson Knight, *The Crown of Life*, 1947; Northrop Frye, 'The Argument of Comedy', *English Institute Essays 1948*, 1949; J. P. Brockbank, 'History and Histrionics in *Cymbeline*', *Shakespeare Survey*, XI (1958); Emrys Jones, 'Stuart *Cymbeline*', *Essays in Criticism*, XI (1961); Bernard Harris, 'What's Past is Prologue: *Cymbeline* and *Henry VIII*', *Later Shakespeare* (see note 33).

42 C. H. Herford, P. and E. Simpson (eds.), *Ben Jonson* (11 vols., 1925–52; hereafter cited in text and notes as *HS*), VII, p. 84.

43 See Willson, *James VI and I*, pp. 320–30.

44 *History of England 1603–1642*, 1884, I, pp. 434, 441.

45 The first of these is reprinted in Alexander Brown, *Genesis of the United*

States, 1870, I, pp. 337–53; the second is in Peter Force, *Tracts*, Washington, 1844, III.

46 *The New Life of Virginia*, 1612, D4v, G2r.

47 The first two extracts are from the original publication in 1610: K2v, H4r. The third one is given by Chambers, *ES*, IV, p. 254.

48 The poem was printed in L. Keymis's *Relation of the Second Voyage to Guiana*, 1596. Text here from E. K. Chambers's *Oxford Book of Sixteenth-Century Verse*.

49 See the opening of my book, *Shakespeare and the Confines of Art*, 1968.

50 Morton Luce, in the Arden *Tempest*, 1901; C. M. Gayley, *Shakespeare and the Founders of Liberty in America*, 1917; A. W. Ward, *Shakespeare and the Makers of Virginia*, 1919; R. R. Cawley, 'Shakespeare's Use of the Voyagers in *The Tempest*', *PMLA*, XLI (1926), 688–726; Leslie Hotson, *I, William Shakespeare*, 1937; D. G. James, *The Dream of Prospero*, 1967. There is an excellent survey of the literature by Charles Frey in '*The Tempest* and the New World', *Shakespeare Quarterly*, XX (1979).

51 Cawley and James (see note 50).

52 See note 33.

53 The Folio gives this speech to Miranda, but the continuity of the dialogue makes it clearly Prospero's, as most editors give it.

54 'Two Unassimilable Men', in *Shakespearian Comedy*, ed. M. Bradbury and D. Palmer (Stratford-upon-Avon Studies 14), 1972, pp. 212, 239.

Chapter 5

1 There is an excellent chapter by A. R. Humphreys on twentieth-century criticism of the history plays in *Shakespeare: Select Bibliographical Guides*, ed. S. Wells, 1973. He does not however mention H. A. Kelly's astringent study of providential patterns in *Divine Providence in the England of Shakespeare's Histories*, 1970.

2 Of this speech Wilbur Sanders wrote: 'The kind of human/critical awareness which Shakespeare has set in motion in the course of the play makes short work of the platitude with which he tries to wind it up' (*The Dramatist and the Received Idea*, 1968, p. 73).

3 See for example J. E. Neale, *Elizabeth and her Parliaments 1584–1601*, on morale during the 1593 Parliament, and G. R. Elton, *England Under the Tudors*, 2nd edn, 1974, p. 456.

4 Kott, *Shakespeare Our Contemporary*, 1964, p. 4ff.

5 Cf. A. P. Rossiter, *Angel With Horns*, 1961, p. 43; see also his p. 37, with the strange rewriting of Yeats: 'Another Troy will rise and rot, another lineage feed the crow.'

6 Cf. my comment on this in *Shakespeare Survey*, XI (1958), 18.

7 The greatness of Elizabeth's reign so strikingly imaged in Cranmer's prophecy in the play *Henry VIII* is for me no evidence of Shakespeare's views about the course of history, since I am convinced that Fletcher wrote that part of the play. The prophecy seems to me evidence of the nostalgia of the young Jacobeans for the glories of the past reign. The fact that

Shakespeare left this bit to his youthful collaborator is interesting enough;
it is his final evasion in an evasive play.

8 See above, Ch. 3, and also Elton, *England Under the Tudors*, pp. 160–5, and
 E. F. Kantorowicz's indispensable *The King's Two Bodies*, 1957.

9 Cf. Hans Kohn, *The Idea of Nationalism*, 1945, p. 6.

10 *The Sovereign Flower*, 1958, p. 13.

11 See my *Person and Office in Shakespeare's Plays* (Annual Shakespeare Lecture
 of the British Academy, 1970), pp. 10–11.

12 See F. W. Brownlow, *Two Shakespearean Sequences*, 1977, pp. 46–52.

13 The New Arden edition of *King John*, 1954, p. xxvii.

14 G. Bullough, *Narrative and Dramatic Sources of Shakespeare*, IV, p. 25.

15 In l. 155 the Folio reads 'heaven' for 'God'; this must be a later change, to
 avoid offending the law against profanity.

16 See my discussion in *Person and Office in Shakespeare's Plays*, p. 14.

17 See, for example, Ch. 4 of Tillyard's *Shakespeare's History Plays*, and Alvin
 Kernan, 'The *Henriad*: Shakespeare's Major History Plays', *The Revels
 History of Drama in English*, III (1975), 269–99.

18 See *Person and Office in Shakespeare's Plays*, pp. 9–15. Brownlow's *Two Shakespearean Sequences* contains a very good study of sacred kingship in *Richard II*.

19 *The Lion and the Fox*, 1927; 1966 edn, p. 21.

Chapter 6

1 E.g. in the standard edition of Jonson's works, edited by Herford and
 Simpson (see note 42 to Ch. 4), I, p. 411–12; G. B. Jackson, *Vision and
 Judgement in Ben Jonson's Drama*, 1968, p. 48.

2 See, e.g., E. M. Waith, in *Modern Language Quarterly*, XII (1951), 13–19; D.
 M. Bevington, *Tudor Drama and Politics*, 1968, pp. 286–7.

3 See R. C. Jones, 'The Satirist's Retirement in Jonson's "Apologetical
 Dialogue"', *English Literary History*, XXXIV (1967), 447–67.

4 See, e.g., *HS*, X, p. 428; E. W. Talbert, 'The Interpretation of Jonson's
 Courtly Spectacles', *PMLA*, LXVI (1946), 454–73; S. Orgel, *The Jonsonian
 Masque*, 1965; D. B. J. Randall, *Jonson's Gypsies Unmasked*, 1975.

5 Cf. J. Barish, 'Jonson and the Loathed Stage', *A Celebration of Ben Jonson*,
 ed. W. Blissett, J. Patrick, R. W. Van Fossen, 1973, pp. 27–53.

6 E.g. the Induction to *Bartholomew Fair*, *HS*, VI, pp. 13–17, the interventions
 of 'Grex' in *Every Man out of his Humour*, especially at the end of III.vi (*HS*,
 III, p. 515), and the Induction to *Cynthia's Revels* (*HS*, IV, p. 36).

7 The enormous and growing volume of criticism of Jonson's works, chiefly
 in the United States, is a corpus of interpretation circulating among
 academics. The danger of this purely professional *conversazione* is illustrated by a remark by Stephen Orgel. Orgel has done as much as anyone to
 insist that Jonson's masques can only be spoken of in terms of the total
 occasion – not only the sight and sound as well as words, but the presence
 of the monarch, the mingling with the audience, etc. Yet in *The Jonsonian
 Masque*, p. 99, he writes, 'Among Jonson's masques, there seem to me few
 successes quite so brilliant as *Neptune's Triumph*.' *Neptune's Triumph* was
 never performed.

8 Cf. J. A. Bryant, Jr, *The Compassionate Satirist*, 1927, p. 2.
9 See note 6.
10 *Satiromastix*, I.ii.309–14.
11 Cf. J. Barish, *Jonson and the Language of Prose Comedy*, 1960, p. 8. Like everyone who writes on Jonson, I am continuously in debt to this outstanding work.
12 *Greene's Groatsworth of Wit*, ed. Harrison, 1923, p. 45.
13 *Henslowe's Diary*, ed. R. A. Foakes and R. T. Rickert, 1961, p. 73.
14 See G. E. Bentley, *The Profession of Dramatist in Shakespeare's Time*, 1971, p. 31.
15 See J. Aubrey, *Brief Lives*, ed. O. L. Dick, 1949, p. 269.
16 See G. E. Bentley, *Shakespeare and Jonson: Their Reputations in the Seventeenth Century Compared*, 1945.
17 *HS*, I, pp. 41, 202; B. N. de Luna, *Jonson's Romish Plot*, 1967, pp. 130–5.
18 *Boccaccio on Poetry*, ed. C. G. Osgood, 1930, p. 55.
19 *Arte of English Poesie*, ed. G. D. Willcock and A. Walker, 1936, p. 17.
20 Italics are mine. Cf. also Spenser's 'Ruins of Time', especially lines 421–7; and J. Burckhardt, *Civilisation of the Renaissance in Italy*, Pt II, 2nd section.
21 *HS*, VII, p. 313, 303. J. C. Meagher, in *Method and Meaning in Jonson's Masques*, 1966, Ch. 7, has a valuable discussion of Jonson's view of the poet's rôle in creating and preserving heroic virtue.
22 Cf. S. Orgel and R. Strong, *Inigo Jones: The Theatre of the Stuart Court*, 1973, I, p. 12.
23 Ed. W. L. Renwick, 1970, p. 73.
24 See O. B. Hardison, Jr, *The Enduring Monument: A Study of the Idea of Praise in Renaissance Theory and Practice*, 1962, p. 28.
25 Cf. Barish, *Jonson and the Language of Prose Comedy*, p. 88.
26 The three endings of the play – stage, quarto, and folio – are all available in *HS*, III, pp. 597–604. It is not very easy to perform the jig-saw puzzles necessary to make out the successive texts, however, and a facsimile of the Quarto (e.g. Malone Society, 1920) is recommended.
27 *ES*, III, p. 362; *HS*, IX, p. 186.
28 See the second Epilogue for *The New Inn*, *HS*, VI, p. 491.
29 See note 2.
30 Bevington, *Tudor Drama and Politics*, pp. 286–7.
31 This irony is discussed by Inga-Stina Ewbank in *A Book of Masques*, 1967, pp. 415–18, and M. C. Bradbrook in *The Living Monument*, 1976, pp. 65–6. A year or two later Beaumont wrote one of the masques to celebrate the marriage of Princess Elizabeth to the Elector Palatine.
32 *Every Man Out of his Humour*, III.vi.191–212 (*HS*, III, p. 515).
33 See *Memoirs of the Life of Colonel Hutchinson*, ed. C. H. Firth, 1906, p. 64.
34 Gilbert, *Philological Quarterly*, XXII (1943), 211–30; Gordon, *Journal of the Warburg and Courtauld Institutes*, VIII (1945), 107–45.
35 *The Jonsonian Masque*, and *Inigo Jones* (see note 22), with R. Strong.
36 *Jonson's Gypsies Unmasked*, p. 37.
37 *The Jonsonian Masque*, pp. 93–7.
38 *Ibid*. pp. 71–2.
39 See Orgel, *The Jonsonian Masque*, p. 190.

40 The whole history of the convention of Praise in poetry is documented in Hardison's *The Enduring Monument* (see note 24).
41 *Jonson and the Language of Prose Comedy*, p. 244. See also J. C. Meagher, *Method and Meaning in Jonson's Masques*, 1966, p. 161.
42 'Jonson's *Epigrammes*: The Named and the Nameless', in *Ben Jonson: Quadricentennial Essays*, a special number of *Studies in the Literary Imagination* (Georgia State University), VI (1973).
43 See *Journal of the Warburg and Courtauld Institutes*, VIII (1945), 129.
44 *Inigo Jones* (see note 22), I, p. 13.
45 *The Illusion of Power*, 1975, pp. 88–9.
46 E.g. Barish, *Jonson and the Language of Prose Comedy*, pp. 251, 259.
47 An interesting article by G. D. Hamilton in *Studies in English Literature*, XI (1971), 265–81, demonstrates that the extensive appeal by the characters of *Sejanus*, and especially Sejanus himself, to Fortune as the ultimate control of human life is ironically used by Jonson, and that Tiberius has the rôle which they attribute to Fortune. This corrects the emphasis in an article in the same number (pp. 250–64) by K. W. Evans, which nevertheless gives a good account of the simple (and politically irrelevant) idea which Jonson has of the all-wise paternalistic ruler.

Chapter 7

1 Ralegh, *Works*, 1751, II, p. 318.
2 Malone Society reprint of *Believe As You List*, ed. C. J. Sisson, 1927, p. v.
3 *The Dramatic Records of Sir Henry Herbert*, ed. J. Q. Adams, 1917, p. 19.
4 The original play sometimes shows up under the paint work; see the Malone Society Reprint, pp. xvii–xx.
5 J. Barish, '*Perkin Warbeck* as Anti-History', *Essays in Criticism*, XX (1970), 167–8, 157, 152.
6 Apparently Sir George Buc (died 1622) regarded Perkin's genuineness as an open question. See W. H. Phelps, 'John Ford's *Perkin Warbeck* and the Pretender Plays 1634–1746', unpublished Ph.D. dissertation, Princeton University, 1965
7 The most interesting discussions in this kind are by Ure, in his Revels Plays edition, 1968, p. lxxix, and by Clifford Leech in *John Ford and the Drama of his Time*, 1957, p. 93.
8 Quotations from *Perkin Warbeck* are modernised from the 1634 Quarto (facsimile in 'The English Experience' series). The Quarto's use of italics is preserved except in proper names, as also is the use of capital initial letters. Line numbering is from the Revels Plays edition.
9 Quotations from *Believe As You List* are modernised from the Clarendon Press edition, ed. Edwards and Gibson, 1976, of *The Plays and Poems of Philip Massinger*, vol. III.
10 Roma Gill, in '"Necessitie of State": Massinger's *Believe As You List*', *English Studies*, XLVI (1965), 407–16, argues that in Flaminius Massinger presents a serious and not unfavourable incarnation of Machiavelli's ideal ruler.

11 In the first line of these extracts I have taken the liberty of disagreeing with both the Malone Society and my co-editor in the Clarendon Press edition, who prefer Massinger's original 'It is . . .' to the book-keeper's correction 'Is it . . .?'

12 *The Dramatic Records of Sir Henry Herbert*, pp. 22–3.

13 See the Introduction to B. T. Spencer's edition of *The Bondman*, 1932.

14 S. R. Gardiner, 'The Political Element in Massinger', *Contemporary Review*, 1876, pp. 495–507.

15 Particularly in the case of *The Maid of Honour*, in which Massinger carefully points to the dishonourableness of the military adventure which Gardiner's thesis makes Massinger approve of. See my 'Massinger the Censor' in *Essays on Shakespeare and Elizabethan Drama*, ed. R. Hosley, 1962, pp. 344–5.

16 S. R. Gardiner, *History of England 1603–1642*, 1884, VI, p. 231.

17 *Ibid.* VI, p. 268.

18 *Ibid.* VI, p. 300.

19 *Ibid.* VII, pp. 4, 84.

20 *Ibid.* VII, p. 63.

21 Stone, *The Causes of the English Revolution 1529–1642*, 1972, p. 133.

22 See C. V. Wedgwood, *Oliver Cromwell and the Elizabethan Inheritance*, Neale Lectures in English History, 1939.

23 Cf. C. Hill, *Puritanism and Revolution*, 1965, p. 55.

24 H. R. Trevor-Roper, 'The General Crisis of the Seventeenth Century', in *Crisis in Europe 1560–1660*, ed. T. Aston, 1965, reprinted 1970, pp. 59–95.

25 Stone (see note 21), pp. 132–3.

26 Gardiner, *History of England*, VI, p. 26.

27 M. A Judson, 'Henry Parker and the Theory of Parliamentary Sovereignty', *Essays in History and Political Thought in Honor of C. H. McIlwain*, 1936, p. 156.

28 Since this essay first appeared in 1974, Anne Barton has provided a valuable background to the political questioning in Stuart history plays in her essay, 'He that plays the king: Ford's *Perkin Warbeck* and the Stuart history play', in *English Drama: Forms and Development*, ed. M. Axton and R. Williams, 1977, pp. 69–93. She adds Cokaine's *Trappolin Supposed a Prince* and Cartwright's *Royal Slave* (1633 and 1636) to the plays in which an idea of kingship is set against the bleak realities of Charles's reign.

Chapter 8

1 J. G. Herder, *Sämtliche Werke*, ed. Suphan (33 vols., 1877–1913), VIII, p. 33, quoted by Isaiah Berlin, *Vico and Herder*, 1976, p. 203. For Herder's views on literature and nationalism, see A. Gillies, *Herder*, 1945.

2 Quoted by J. W. McFarlane, *The Oxford Ibsen*, 1 (1970), p. 4.

3 H. Lindenberger, *Historical Drama*, 1975, p. 8.

4 *Correspondence with Goethe*, trans. by L. D. Schmitz, 2 vols., 1877, 1, p. 433.

5 Trans. by J. Black, 1846, p. 528.

6 Stanislaw Helsztynski, 'The Fortune of Shakespeare in Poland', *Poland's Homage to Shakespeare*, 1965, pp. 18–19.

7 Josephine Calina, *Shakespeare in Poland*, 1923, p. 17.

8 *Ibid.* p. 39.

9 Sir Charles Gavan Duffy, *Young Ireland: A Fragment of Irish History*, 1880, pp. 48, 155.

10 *Ibid.* p. 80.

11 T. Davis, *Essays Literary and Historical*, ed. D. J. O'Donoghue, 1914, p. 213.

12 *Ibid.* p. 368.

13 P. L. Marcus, *Yeats and the Beginning of the Irish Renaissance*, 1970, p. 10. The two plays which Davis mentions (by Sir Henry Taylor and Gerald Griffin), though they both reached the London stage by the kindness of Macready, have been justly forgotten. They are blank-verse historical plays.

14 *The Oxford Ibsen*, II (1962), p. 1.

15 Summarised from J. W. McFarlane's trans. in *The Oxford Ibsen*, I, pp. 608–10.

16 *The Oxford Ibsen*, II, p. 2.

17 All this information is from W. S. Clark's indispensable *The Early Irish Stage*, 1955, Ch. 2.

18 1640 quarto, A2r.

19 Charles Shadwell, *Works*, 2 vols., 1720.

20 *The Early Irish Stage*, p. 174.

21 See W. S. Clark, *The Irish Stage in the County Towns 1729–1800*, 1965, p. 289.

22 See Esther K. Sheldon, *Thomas Sheridan of Smock Alley*, 1967, p. 136.

23 *Letters to the New Island*, 1933; 1970 reprint, p. 217.

24 *Ibid.* pp. 106–7.

25 *Uncollected Prose*, ed. J. P. Frayne, I, 1970, p. 193.

26 *Letters*, ed. A. Wade, 1954, p. 114.

27 *Autobiographies*, 1955, p. 200.

28 Lennox Robinson, *Ireland's Abbey Theatre*, 1951, p. 8, and C. C. O'Brien, *States of Ireland*, 2nd edn, 1974, pp. 61, 63.

29 From 'The Literary Movement in Ireland', reprinted by Lady Gregory in *Ideals in Ireland*, 1901.

30 *Essays and Introductions*, 1961, p. 166. The following two extracts are from pp. 167 and 168.

31 *Uncollected Prose*, ed. Frayne, I, p. 273.

32 *Letters*, ed. Wade, p. 349.

33 *Yeats and Anglo-Irish Literature*, 1974, pp. 203–24.

34 *Essays and Introductions*, p. 106.

35 'Matthew Arnold and the Celtic Revival', in *Perspectives of Criticism*, ed. H. Levin, 1950, pp. 197–221.

36 Cf. W. I. Thompson, *The Imagination of an Insurrection*, 1967, and M. Brown, *The Politics of Irish Literature*, 1972.

37 *Essays and Introductions*, p. 104.

38 Dowden, *Letters*, 1914, p. 184.

39 Written in 1903. *Explorations*, 1962, p. 107.

40 From 'The Literary Movement in Ireland' (see note 29).

41 Written in 1906. *Explorations*, p. 222.

42 Ure (see note 33), p. 208. Cf. also L. E. Nathan, *The Tragic Drama of W. B. Yeats*, 1965, pp. 104–6.

43 'Yeats and the English Renaissance', *PMLA*, LXXXII (1967), 157–69.
44 *Explorations*, p. 96.
45 *Ibid*. p. 100.
46 *Ibid*. pp. 155-6.
47 *Ibid*. p. 239.
48 *Ibid*. p. 254.

Chapter 9

1 *Confessions of a Young Man*, Ch. 8; Penguin edn, 1939, p. 99.
2 All references to *Hail and Farewell* are to the first editions: *Ave*, 1911; *Salve*, 1912; *Vale*, 1914.
3 *Autobiographies*, 1955, p. 430.
4 *Letters*, ed. A. Wade, 1954, p. 327.
5 J. Hone, *The Life of George Moore*, 1936, p. 221. Moore discusses some of the problems of taking over the play in *Ave*, sections XI and XII, especially pp. 288–9. Moore was unwise enough to send the text of the play to Fisher Unwin before rehearsals had finished, and his latest (and radical) alterations could not be incorporated. Some extra copies were printed with the revisions, and as a result there are two quite distinct versions with the same 1900 imprint. See H. E. Gerber, *George Moore in Transition: Letters to T. Fisher Unwin and Lena Milman, 1894–1910*, 1968, pp. 184–95 and E. Gilcher, *A Bibliography of George Moore*, 1970, pp. 56–8. I have used the revised version. Martyn published his original text in 1902. There is a short comparison of the two plays by Una Ellis-Fermor in *The Irish Dramatic Movement* (1939), 2nd edn, 1954, pp. 124–32. Patrick McFate, in an article in *Eire–Ireland*, VIII (1973), 52–61, called '*The Bending of the Bough* and *The Heather Field*: Two Portraits of the Artists', suggests the presence of A.E.'s ideas in the Kirwan-Dean philosophy of the play, and notes the possibility of Moore's self-identification with Dean.
6 *Autobiographies*, p. 435.
7 R. Hogan and M. J. O'Neill (eds.), *Joseph Holloway's Abbey Theatre*, 1967, pp. 14–15.
8 By W. Becker in *The Dublin Magazine*. The text is reprinted in *The Variorum Plays of W. B. Yeats*, ed. R. K. Alspach, 1966.
9 F. S. L. Lyons, *Ireland Since the Famine*, 2nd edn, 1973, pp. 232, 238.
10 *The Irish Writers*, 1958, pp. 32–82, and *George Moore's Mind and Art*, compiled by Graham Owens, 1968, pp. 77–98.

Chapter 10

1 Rae Jeffs, *Brendan Behan, Man and Showman*, 1966, p. 35.
2 References for Denis Johnston are to *Collected Plays*, 2 vols., 1960. Curiously, each play is separately paginated.
3 References for Sean O'Casey are to *Collected Plays*, 4 vols., 1949–51.
4 References for *The Hostage* are to the 3rd edn, 1962.
5 *Collected works of Padraic H. Pearse: Plays, Stories, Poems*, 1917, pp. 9–10.
6 *The Irish Dramatic Movement*, 2nd edn, 1954, p. 203.

INDEX

WITHDRAWN FROM STOCK